The *Lifestyles* of The RICH and FAMOUS™ COOKBOOK

The Lifestyles of The RICH and FAMOUS™ COOKBOOK

RECIPES AND ENTERTAINING SECRETS FROM THE MOST EXTRAORDINARY PEOPLE IN THE WORLD

Robin Leach

Text and photographic styling by

Diane Rozas

VIKING
STUDIO
BOOKS

VIKING STUDIO BOOKS
Published by the Penguin Group
Viking Penguin, a division of Penguin Books USA Inc.,
375 Hudson Street, New York, New York 10014, U.S.A.
Penguin Books Ltd, 27 Wrights Lane,
London W8 5TZ, England
Penguin Books Australia Ltd, Ringwood,
Victoria, Australia
Penguin Books Canada Ltd, 10 Alcorn Avenue, Suite 300,
Toronto, Ontario, Canada M4V 3B2
Penguin Books (N.Z.) Ltd, 182–190 Wairau Road,
Auckland 10, New Zealand

Penguin Books Ltd, Registered Offices:
Harmondsworth, Middlesex, England

First published in the United States of America by Viking Penguin,
a division of Penguin Books USA Inc., 1992
This paperback edition published 1994

1 3 5 7 9 10 8 6 4 2

Lifestyles of the Rich and Famous™ and Champagne Wishes—
Caviar Dreams™ are trademarks of Television Program
Enterprises, Inc.

Grateful acknowledgment is made for permission to use the following copyrighted works:
Photographs by Marcel Loli on pages 2, 3, 14, 16–23, copyright Marcel Loli
Elizabeth Taylor and Larry Fortensky's wedding portrait by Visages on page 24, reproduced by permission.
Recipes from The Romance of Food by Barbara Cartland. Copyright © 1984 by Barbara Cartland. Published by Doubleday and
Company, Inc. By permission of the author.
Recipes from The Wolfgang Puck Cookbook by Wolfgang Puck. Copyright © 1986 by Wolfgang Puck. By permission of Random
House, Inc.
Photographs of Martha Stewart by Michael Geiger on pages 135, 137 and recipes from Martha Stewart's Quick Cook by Martha
Stewart. Photographs copyright © 1983 by Michael Geiger. Recipes copyright © 1983 by Martha Stewart. By permission of
Clarkson Potter, Inc., a division of Crown Publishers, Inc.
Photographs of Randy Travis by Jeff Katz (page 202), by Jackson Goff (pages 204–7), and recipes from Randy Travis' Favorite
Recipes by Randy Travis. Copyright © 1989 by
Hatcher Corporation. By permission of the author.
Photograph of Chris Evert by Mark Sennet on page 240, People Weekly/ © 1991 Mark Sennet.
Photograph of Regis Philbin on page 252, Steve Friedman/Buena Vista.

The Library of Congress has catalogued the hardcover edition as follows:
Leach, Robin.
The Lifestyles of the rich and famous cookbook: recipes and
entertaining secrets from the most extraordinary people in the
world /
Robin Leach with Diane Rozas.
p. cm.
ISBN 0-670-84245-1 (hc.)
ISBN 0 14 02.3800 X (pbk.)
1. Cookery, International. 2. Entertaining. 3. Celebrities—
Social life and customs. I. Rozas, Diane. II. Lifestyles of the
rich and famous (Television program). III. Title.
TX725.A1L33 1992
641.59—dc20   91-45173

Printed in the United States of America
Set in Bembo

Designed by Joseph Rutt

Dedication

To our loyal family of viewers around the world, and to all the "Lifestyles" staff and executives for their support and encouragement, especially our leader, Al Masini.

◆ ◆ ◆ ◆ ◆ ◆ ◆ ◆ ◆ ◆ ◆

Acknowledgments

We would like very much to thank the following for their contributions to *The Lifestyles of the Rich and Famous Cookbook*:

To Michael Fragnito, publisher of Viking Studio Books, for his enthusiasm and insight, from beginning to end.

To Martha Schueneman, our editor, who gave of her time and talents. To Joseph Rutt, who designed a beautiful book out of hundreds of recipes and thousands of photographs. To Roni Axelrod, who produced this book in record time. To Neil Stuart, for his contributions to the jacket design. And to all the staff at Viking Studio Books and Viking Penguin who participated in making this book.

To Charles Pierce, for the development of the recipes, both writing and testing.

A special thanks to Marianne Strong, literary agent, who helped to put this book in motion.

(*Acknowledgments are continued on page 268.*)

Contents

◆ ◆ ◆ ◆ ◆ ◆ ◆ ◆ ◆

A Note from Robin Leach

◆ ◆ ◆ ◆ ◆ ◆ ◆ ◆ ◆ ◆ ◆

Back in Harrow, England, where I spent the first twenty years of my life, I would never have imagined the incredible mealtime experiences the future would bring forth. I grew up on a basic English diet, which meant that once a week the food was good—roast beef and Yorkshire pudding—and the rest of the time it was fairly boring. If I had written a fantasy cookbook then, it simply couldn't have reflected the variety of culinary specialties I have had the great satisfaction of consuming since I departed England for the shores of America.

My hands-on involvement in the world of food and cooking began shortly after I arrived in New York. The year was 1963, and it was one heck of a cold winter. I had a tiny apartment on East 33rd Street: a one-room place, with the kitchen located inside a closet, and a fold-

down bed that fell out of the wall. Wanting to spend as little as possible of my weekly pittance on feeding myself, I decided to save money by turning on the stove and cooking at home. My first meal was to be a steak and french fries. I turned everything to the highest temperature, put the potatoes in a pan and the steak under the broiler. Having no previous experience with matters of a culinary nature, I busied myself with several other projects, paying no attention to my cooking. After ten minutes or so, a huge, billowing cloud of black smoke consumed the room, and the stove was shooting flames right out of the closet. Disaster! The flames spread so rapidly, everybody in the building ran out in the street to safety. Eventually, the fire department came, though the fire was out long before they arrived. I realized I would probably have to move out of the apartment as it no longer had a working kitchen—and everyone in the building considered me a risk to their safety as long as I had an appetite. But I vowed to learn how to cook properly, and I eventually got the hang of it. Now I consider myself a fairly accomplished cook, with a sizable recipe file of delicious yet easy-to-prepare foods that I can put together with friends all pitching in and having lots of fun in the process. Even my three sons enjoy my cooking, so it passes that crucial test!

As host and executive producer of the *Lifestyles of the Rich and Famous* television show, I have shared memorable eating experiences, some of them silly and fun, with friends. When I visited Roseanne and Tom Arnold in Los Angeles, we munched peanut butter and jelly sandwiches and sipped tea while filming a segment.

On the flip side of the coin, Sirio Maccioni and Chef Daniel Boulud of Le Cirque restaurant in New York threw one unforgettable party in honor of my twenty-fifth anniversary in America. For that oc-casion, they created the most delicious menu that I have ever tasted.

Of course, there have been many other sumptuous meals over the years. Whether taking tea with royalty or dining at the tables of the greatest chefs in the world, I have never stood on ceremony. If I wanted to know about a recipe, I simply asked. Everyone loves to share recipes—even the rich and famous.

Over the past ten years of filming *Lifestyles of the Rich and Famous*, I was actually compiling this cookbook in the back of my mind. Always observing, always asking about the cuisine. Unbeknownst to anyone, I made mental notes on every aspect of thousands of amazing meals I have had the pleasure of consuming. The arrangement of the food and the plates themselves caught my eye—in fact, many times, I've wished I had a camera to record the dishes as they were served to me. I often regretted not having enough time to poke my head in the kitchen long enough to walk away with a copy of the recipe tucked in my pocket. Finally, the time arrived to gather recipes from our friends who've appeared on the *Lifestyles* television show over the years. And here, for our tenth anniversary, is *The Lifestyles of the Rich and Famous Cookbook*.

You're holding in your hands nearly 200 delicious recipes, plus cooking and entertaining tips from some of the most fascinating people you'll ever meet. These celebrities and celebrated names are from the worlds of film and television, the arts, business, society. And yes, even royals and nobles make appearances throughout the pages. Included also are the recipes and photographs from several special gastronomic events. Everything here is fresh, fun, new, exciting, and never seen before. You'll see, through hundreds of behind-the-scenes photographs, what happens when *Lifestyles of the Rich and Famous* gets into the kitchen.

Chapter after chapter of unique recipes will certainly give you a wide variety of delightful new lunch and dinner meals to re-create

at home. The beautiful photographs of the food will let you feast with your eyes first, and the easy-to-follow instructions assure you of the same delectable results. Take full advantage of the many wonderful recipes—invent your own unique menus by borrowing recipes from a variety of different chapters. Dress up a dinner that starts off, for example, with Brooke Shields's Spring Rolls from the Celebrity Gourmet Cook-Off on page 66. The next course might be Elizabeth Taylor's wedding supper entrée—Roast Chicken with Morel Sauce —or Johnny Carson's delectable Whitefish. Pick a salad from Martha Stewart's Fall Menu. Finish off with Lemon Tarts from baseball legend Steve Garvey. It's all guaranteed to start some very lively conversations.

Another creative approach to the use of the book is to plan a theme party—such as one featuring an interesting array of desserts. There's a sumptuous chocolate cake with cherry and wine sauce on page 74, which would go perfectly with fine Champagne. Robert De Niro and Whoopi Goldberg thought it was absolutely fantastic at a Cannes Film Festival party.

Much like our *Lifestyles of the Rich and Famous* television show, this cooking-and-entertaining book is also a travel journal. We covered the world seeking the extravagant, the unseen, the unusual— special events and parties that offered not only wonderful culinary creations but interesting presentations in locations you would be certain to enjoy. Ultimately, we wanted to provide a book of delicious recipes along with a collection of *useful* entertaining ideas—gathered, as only *Lifestyles* can, directly from some of today's most celebrated people and special events. You'll join with these new friends, and get to know them through their personal interpretations of home cooking, entertaining, and party planning. It's great to have someone do all the experimenting for you.

Some of those recipes are even my own. I didn't want to be left out of such a superb opportunity to share recipes, and I wanted to show off my talents in the kitchen, which have improved greatly since the fire of '63! My friends and house guests all know me for my Rich and Famous Chicken recipe, which you'll find on page 154. The real secret to perfecting this recipe, as anyone who has ever made a stock will know, is all in the soup bones. But in my special stock, Essence of Silver and Gold, it's not only the bones. One of the essential ingredients is Champagne—a whole bottle of Cristal goes into the cooking pot. Now, if this is a bit excessive for you, simply save the Cristal for another occasion, and add a bottle of less expensive bubbly. Whatever I cook, it has to be easy, fun, and involve people, which is why I designed my kitchen with an island surrounded by stools. One hour from start to finish is my only rule when picking out a recipe or creating a new one.

With this book in your kitchen, you have everything you'll need to liven up your cooking-and-entertaining events. There is plenty of opportunity to mix and match your way through the stellar collection of recipes.

Above all, enjoy and have fun. Satisfy your own Champagne Wishes and Caviar Dreams right in your own home, as often as possible.

Bon Appétit!

Robin Leach

New York
April 1992

5

Introduction

◆ ◆ ◆ ◆ ◆ ◆ ◆ ◆ ◆ ◆

Over the past ten years, the *Lifestyles of the Rich and Famous* television show has treated its viewers to tours through princely palaces and multimillion-dollar houses from Beverly Hills to Bavaria. This time, we're taking you on a culinary tour through the recipe files and party books of those who have made an art of entertaining, and of celebrities who simply love to cook.

In creating *The Lifestyles of the Rich and Famous Cookbook*, we discovered that the rich and famous are no different from the rest of us when it comes to cooking and entertaining. They love to cook and throw unforgettable parties. As the social "season" approaches, hard-working hostesses are never found on a tennis court or yacht's bow. In fact, one socialite said, "Guests come first, last, and always, because I want them to remember *my* party at the end of the season. And

the competition is stiff, believe me." With casual simplicity being the mark of the nineties, it is only natural that we found many celebrities and celebrated personalities expressing themselves at the backyard grill when making meals for friends and family. But wherever we went, once the cameras stopped clicking, these extraordinary people invited us to sit down at their tables, share a glass of wine, and sample their fare. Whether you want a sumptuous feast or a tasty nibble, you'll find this book has assembled an incredible array of recipes—from fancy party fare and low-calorie interpretations of the classics to tasty, quick-to-fix favorites—prepared and served in a variety of personal styles. We've tried to convey the excitement of being there, of seeing the splendor and the details of being a guest in the homes and kitchens and at the soirees.

Among the events where we found the rich and famous were charity galas. In New Orleans, Prince and Princess Michael of Kent—members of the royal family of Great Britain—were guests of the English-Speaking Union. We also went to fund-raising parties for the March of Dimes and the New York Public Library.

Cruising south along the Mexican Riviera, Ernest and Tova Borgnine and twenty-eight other couples reaffirmed their wedding vows aboard the super-luxury yacht the *Sea Goddess*. The wedding cake was from a recipe Tova's mother brought from Norway.

At the Cannes Film Festival, Whoopi Goldberg and a host of other stars helped Robert De Niro celebrate receiving France's prestigious Award of Creativity.

We've also gone to Monaco, to London, and to Los Angeles for the wedding of the decade. On October 6, 1991, Elizabeth Taylor and Larry Fortensky exchanged their vows under a gazebo decorated with fragrant white and yellow flowers. May their love last forever!

With the theme of Champagne Wishes and Caviar Dreams, it's

only natural for *The Lifestyles of the Rich and Famous Cookbook* to give special attention to these delicacies. First, we drank Champagne with Claude Taittinger, scion of the House of Champagne Taittinger, in Reims, France. Then we visited Armen Petrossian of the Petrossian caviar dynasty. You'll find their wonderful Champagne and caviar recipes in our "Casual Entertaining" chapter.

That's also where you'll find the lunch menu from Marylou Vanderbilt Whitney, who invited us to her home in Saratoga Springs, New York, for her first luncheon of the 1991 racing season.

Martha Stewart, writer of eight books on cooking, entertaining, and gardening, contributed a fall supper menu. Martha's apple pie is especially satisfying when the air becomes crisp.

Ivana Trump insisted we go out to her Connecticut country home—a sprawling white colonial house on a lake—because, she said, the kitchen was more charming than the one in her Trump Plaza apartment. She also invited us to a party for fifty of her best girlfriends, held in the magnificent White and Gold Suite at the Plaza Hotel.

Super-star chef Wolfgang Puck and his wife, architectural interior designer Barbara Lazaroff, gave us a tour of their famed L.A. eateries, Spago, Eureka, Chinois on Main, and the newest, Granita, in Malibu, as well as a very special sampling of their signature dishes from each restaurant. Spago's star-studded clientele has long known the secret of Wolfgang's legendary pizzas, and now you will, too!

Do the rich and famous eat Mexican food? Yes, absolutely, when they're visiting Isabel Goldsmith at her ever-so-private compound, Las Alamandas, in Mexico. Isabel has restyled and revamped ordinary Mexican food; her dishes are light, calorie-reduced versions that she calls Nouvelle Mexican Cuisine à la Las Alamandas. Her intriguingly exotic recipes are perfect served at any al fresco buffet.

At home, we found many of our celebrities doing the things that made them celebrities in the first place—Randy Travis and Skitch Henderson composing music, Barbara Taylor Bradford writing her best-selling novels—along with cooking casual fare. Most everyone whose recipes and cooking tips are represented in the "Relaxing at Home" chapter chose a simple and familiar menu to re-create for us. Bruce Jenner demonstrated his grilling skills, while Candace Garvey surprised her husband, Steve, with a romantic dinner at dusk. Several of these menus are so casual, the ingredients are probably in your cupboard and fridge right now.

Even though Dina Merrill grew up in the biggest house in Palm Beach, she's traded in that lifestyle—her uncomplicated parties with friends and family at her Hamptons hideaway are perfectly simple, and her menu is simply perfect.

Actress Jackie Zeman, who plays Bobbie on *General Hospital*, installed a grill in her kitchen so she could make her favorite grilled fish, chicken, veggies, and fruit any time. Jackie's recipes are truly California Cuisine with a homey touch.

The last chapter is where you'll find some of the most special recipes in this entire collection. Joan Collins offers us her best Spaghetti Bolognese; brilliant designer Valentino shares a chic risotto; Elle Macpherson—the beautiful Australian model—keeps her shape with Smoked Salmon Bruschetta; and a spicy shrimp dish sends Florence Griffith Joyner running to the kitchen.

Our goal was to make this book as lively and interesting as the past ten years of the *Lifestyles of the Rich and Famous* television program has been. As a celebration of our first decade, we toast you, our viewing audience and new friends, with *The Lifestyles of the Rich and Famous Cookbook*, and hope it entertains you as well as provides you with a new twist for your own personal culinary pursuits.

Extravagant
Affairs

◆ ◆ ◆ ◆ ◆ ◆ ◆ ◆ ◆

The Royal Cuisine of Monaco

◆ ◆ ◆ ◆ ◆ ◆ ◆ ◆ ◆ ◆

"MONACO REGULARS KNOW THE STYLISH
WAYS TO ARRIVE—BY YACHT INTO THE
SMALL HARBOR OR BY PRIVATE HELICOPTER
FROM NICE. SOME DROP IN JUST FOR
DINNER."

Ever since 1297, the Grimaldi family has ruled the tiny principality of Monaco. Handsome Prince Rainier has made it the ultimate playground of Europe. The lovely Princesses Caroline and Stephanie are almost as famous as their beautiful mother was, and people make wagers on whom Albert, the business-minded heir to the throne, will pick for his fairy-tale princess bride.

Jet-setting visitors to Monaco have plenty to keep themselves occupied. By day, amusements such as yachting, *haute couture* shopping, and sunbathing at the pool of the Belle Epoch–style Hôtel de Paris are part of the stylish scene. At night, the atmosphere quickly changes. Everyone, dressed in the finest attire, heads for the casinos, the discos, or one of the many legendary restaurants along the French Riviera.

In nearby Nice and Cannes are some of the world's most acclaimed restaurants. Yet the most elegant restaurant and most innovative gastronomic experience on the Riviera is right in Monte Carlo, at the Louis XV Restaurant in the Hôtel de Paris. This grand dining room, presided over by chef Alain Ducasse, has received accolades from food critics the world over. The Michelin guide, Europe's harbinger of taste and the bible of gastronomes, awarded the Louis XV three stars for excellence—the highest tribute.

On the night of the three-star celebration, Monaco's royal family enjoyed Ducasse's ten-course menu of pure culinary magic, matched by his selection of special wines.

The Louis XV Restaurant simply offers a grand twist to a great old tradition. The royal family of Monaco has a standing invitation, and their table is always ready.

THE MENU

◆ ◆ ◆ ◆ ◆ ◆

CHILLED LOBSTER BOUILLON
RISOTTO WITH PANCETTA
CRISPY-SKIN SEA BASS
GLAZED VEAL ROAST
MASCARPONE SORBET

OPPOSITE: *The glittering Monte Carlo Casino and Hôtel de Paris were opened in the 1860s, and beckon fun-loving, high-society visitors from all over the world.*

CHILLED LOBSTER BOUILLON

2 small lobsters, about 1 pound
  each
3 tablespoons olive oil
½ garlic clove, minced
3 shallots, finely chopped
1 small onion, finely chopped
2 medium tomatoes, quartered
2 tablespoons Cognac
⅔ cup dry white wine
2 quarts water
2 teaspoons salt
1 tablespoon whole black
  peppercorns
⅔ cup light cream
1 Belgian endive, very thinly
  sliced
1 ounce (or more, to taste) osetra
  caviar
Several sprigs fresh chervil

Bring a large pot of water to a boil. Add the lobsters, bring back to a boil, and cook rapidly for 20 seconds. Drain and cool slightly. Remove one of the tails and set aside to use for the garnish. Using a large chopping knife, chop the lobsters as finely as possible, including the carapace and bones.

Place the olive oil in a large sauté pan and set over moderately high heat. Add the chopped lobster and sauté for 5 minutes, stirring constantly. Add the garlic, shallots, onion, and tomatoes. Sauté for 2 to 3 more minutes, or until the vegetables begin to soften. Add the

Cognac and white wine. Increase the heat to high and boil until the liquid has evaporated, stirring constantly. Add the water, salt, and peppercorns. Reduce the heat to moderate and simmer for about 35 minutes or until reduced by one-third. Strain through a fine sieve, pressing hard on the solids to extract as much flavor as possible. Cool the bouillon to room temperature, cover, and refrigerate for at least 6 hours.

Remove the shell from the reserved lobster tail and cut the flesh into tiny dice. Add the cream to the chilled bouillon and stir well to blend. Pour into chilled, shallow bowls. Garnish with the diced lobster, endive, caviar, and chervil.

SERVES 4.

OPPOSITE: *Chef Alain Ducasse says, "My cuisine was born out of a need to make food taste as good as it possibly can. Flavors remain pure. The Chilled Lobster Bouillon is a perfect example: the flavor is totally 'intense' and uncluttered with other ingredients."* ABOVE: *The harbor has grown to accommodate hundreds of sleek yachts belonging to the rich and famous.*

Melt the butter in a large saucepan over moderately high heat. Add the onion, marrow, saffron, and rice. Stir until the rice is coated with butter and heated through, about 2 minutes. Add the wine, increase the heat to high, and stir until the wine is absorbed, about 2 minutes.

Reduce the heat to moderately high and add ½ cup of the stock. Stir until the stock is absorbed. Add another ½ cup of stock and repeat this process, continuing until all the stock is used, about 15 minutes.

Remove the risotto from the heat. Stir in the sliced squash blossoms, the cheese, and the cream. Season with salt and pepper to taste. Transfer to a shallow serving bowl. Drizzle the olive oil over the risotto and sprinkle with the pancetta. Serve at once.

SERVES 4.

TOP: *Risotto with Pancetta.* ABOVE, FROM LEFT: *Prince Albert, Prince Rainier, Alain Ducasse, and Princess Caroline. A royal meal at the Louis XV might begin with a dozen types of breads and end with handmade chocolates decorated with edible gold-foil imprints. In between, extraordinary soups, meats, handmade pastas, and fish are served on hand-painted plates trimmed with 24-karat gold.* RIGHT: *Chef Ducasse designed the multimillion-dollar, super-modern kitchen from the floor up.*

RISOTTO WITH PANCETTA

2 tablespoons unsalted butter
½ small onion, finely chopped
½ cup beef marrow, cut into small dice (optional)
Pinch saffron threads (about 1 teaspoon)
1 cup Arborio rice
½ cup dry white wine
2 cups chicken stock, preferably homemade
12 small squash blossoms, trimmed and thinly sliced
2 tablespoons freshly grated Parmesan cheese
⅓ cup heavy cream, whipped
Salt and freshly ground pepper
1 to 2 tablespoons olive oil, or to taste
3 to 4 slices pancetta (or bacon), fried crisp, crumbled

CRISPY-SKIN SEA BASS

½ cup coarse salt
8 medium tomatoes, quartered and
   seeded
1 teaspoon sugar
¼ cup olive oil
½ cup small olives (preferably
   French Picholines)
2 cups vegetable oil
16 to 20 small leaves fresh basil,
   rinsed and patted dry
4 6-ounce sea bass fillets, skin
   attached
6 tablespoons (¾ stick) unsalted
   butter
1 tablespoon red wine vinegar
Salt and freshly ground pepper

Preheat the oven to 175° F. Spread the coarse salt over the bottom of a baking sheet. Arrange the tomatoes on top, sprinkle them with the sugar, then drizzle with 2 tablespoons of the olive oil. Place in the oven and bake for 2 hours.

Pit the olives and chop them finely.

Pour the vegetable oil into a frying pan or skillet and set it over high heat. When the oil is very hot but not smoking, drop in the basil leaves. When the leaves come back to the surface, remove them with a slotted spoon and drain on paper towels.

In a large bowl, combine a large amount of ice cubes with a small amount of water. In a medium saucepan, melt 4 ta-blespoons of the butter over moderately high heat. Watching closely, cook the butter until it starts to turn a deep golden brown. Immediately submerge the pan in the ice water for about 1 minute to stop the cooking. When the butter has cooled, stir in the vinegar and set aside.

In a non-stick sauté pan large enough to hold the fish in one flat layer, melt the remaining 2 tablespoons of the olive oil with the remaining 2 table-spoons of butter over moderately high heat. Add the fillets, skin side down, and cook until crisp, 3 to 5 minutes. Use a spatula to dislodge the skin and gently turn the fillets over. Continue cooking on the other side for about 3 more minutes.

Carefully remove to individual serving plates. Surround with the browned butter, and garnish with the tomatoes, chopped olives, and fried basil. Season with salt and pepper to taste. Serve at once.

SERVES 4.

◆ ◆ ◆ ◆ ◆ ◆ ◆

ABOVE: *Crispy-Skin Sea Bass is garnished with tomatoes and fried basil. For centuries, fresh fish and wine-marinated meats, as well as a wide variety of fresh vegetables, fruits, and herbs, have graced the tables of Monegasque citizens and royals.*

GLAZED VEAL ROAST

1 whole veal shank, about 4
   pounds
1 carrot, peeled, halved, and thinly
   sliced
1 celery stalk, peeled and thinly
   sliced
1 medium onion, finely chopped
1¼ cups chicken stock
Several sprigs fresh thyme, or
   1 teaspoon dried
Salt and freshly ground pepper
2 pounds Swiss chard, cleaned and
   trimmed
1 tablespoon lemon juice
3 medium tomatoes
2 tablespoons unsalted butter
4 to 5 scallions, trimmed and
   thinly sliced
2 tablespoons red wine vinegar (see
   note)

Preheat the oven to 325° F.
Place the veal in a large casserole or Dutch oven with a lid.
Surround with the carrots, celery, and onion. Add 1 cup of
the chicken stock and the
thyme, and season with salt
and pepper, to taste. Cover and
place in the oven. Cook until
tender, about 2 hours, checking
frequently; add additional stock
as needed to prevent scorching.

Meanwhile, bring a pot of
salted water to a boil. Separate
the green leafy part of the
Swiss chard from the stem.
Cut the greens into thin slices
and reserve in a bowl filled
with water and the lemon
juice. Cut the stems into 1-inch
pieces. Plunge the stems into
the boiling water, bring back
to a boil, drain, and set aside.

Cut the tomatoes in half and
gently squeeze out the seeds.
Cut into ¼-inch dice and set
aside.

In a medium saucepan, melt
the butter. Add the chard
stems, tomatoes, and scallions.
Stir over moderately high heat
until warmed through, about
3 minutes. Add the remaining
¼ cup of chicken stock and increase the heat to high. Drain
the chard greens and add to the
pan. Increase the heat to high
and stir until the greens have
just wilted, about 30 seconds.
Remove from the heat and add
the vinegar. Season with salt
and pepper to taste and set
aside until the veal is ready to
serve.

Remove the veal from the
casserole or Dutch oven and
keep warm. Strain the cooking
liquid through a fine sieve,
pressing down hard on the
vegetables to extract as much
flavor as possible. Wipe out the
casserole and return the veal to
it. Pour the strained cooking
liquid over the veal and return
the casserole to the oven, uncovered. Increase the oven
temperature to 450° F. Cook
until the veal is "glazed," about
10 minutes. Remove the veal to
a large serving platter.

Reheat the reserved vegetable
mixture over moderately high
heat. Transfer to the serving
platter, attractively surrounding
the veal. Serve from the platter, cutting thick slices for each
person, accompanied by the
vegetable garnish.

SERVES 4.

NOTE: Alain Ducasse uses a special French vinegar, *vinaigre de
vieux vin*, available in the United
States in some specialty food
stores. If unobtainable, substitute
any high-quality red wine
vinegar.

◆ ◆ ◆ ◆ ◆ ◆ ◆

ABOVE, LEFT: *Glazed Veal Roast
with Swiss chard.*

ABOVE: *Says Alain Ducasse, "I want everyone to experience my cuisine. Although my restaurant is quite formal, the food would also be at home on a big wooden table in a simple country kitchen." Three-star chef Ducasse hopes you will someday enjoy a meal in his gilded dining room. The restaurant is booked up to six weeks in advance, so remember to make your reservations early.* RIGHT: *At the Belle Époch–style Hôtel de Paris, the Louis XV dining veranda,* RIGHT, *becomes the royal box seat for the annual Grand Prix race.*

MASCARPONE
SORBET

1¾ cups water
¾ cup sugar
1½ cups plain yogurt
1 cup mascarpone (see note)
2 tablespoons freshly squeezed
    lemon juice

Combine the water and the
sugar in a medium saucepan.
Over high heat, bring to a boil
and cook for 10 minutes or until clear and syrupy. Remove
from the heat, cool to room
temperature, pour into a mixing bowl, and cover and chill
at least 4 to 5 hours.

In a large mixing bowl,
combine the yogurt, mascarpone, and lemon juice. Add
1⅓ cups of the chilled syrup.
(Reserve any extra for another
use.) Beat with a wire whisk
until blended. Transfer to an
ice-cream maker and freeze according to the manufacturer's
instructions. Serve with sweetened fresh berries or fruit, if
desired.

SERVES 6.

NOTE: Mascarpone is a fresh
cheese available in many specialty
food stores or by mail order.

ABOVE: *Mascarpone Sorbet is one of
the most delightful desserts from the
Ducasse kitchen: not too sweet, not
too rich, and just flavorful enough to
satisfy. Famed cookbook author and
New York Times* columnist Craig
Claiborne *says this is one of his
favorites, and declared Ducasse a
master chef.*

Nighttime in Monaco means entertainment; evening is perhaps the most dazzling time in this fairy-tale land. People descend upon the Sporting Club, Monte Carlo's six-story, open-air "fun" center on the Mediterranean. It's a complex where you can disco-dance at Jimmyz, gamble at the casino, eat in exotic restaurants, or sip Champagne, nibble caviar, and listen to the world's biggest musical acts at the Salle d'Étoile. CLOCKWISE FROM TOP LEFT: *Prince Rainier, Princess Caroline, and Prince Albert arrive at the Sporting Club; Ray Charles; Tina Turner; Ursula Andress and John Forsythe; Whitney Houston; Prince Albert and Elton John at the World Music Awards; Albert and Caroline leading off the dancing for the evening.*

Congratulations, Elizabeth and Larry

◆ ◆ ◆ ◆ ◆ ◆ ◆ ◆ ◆ ◆

"AT WHAT OTHER WEDDING RECEPTION COULD YOU FIND NANCY REAGAN, VALENTINO, DIANE VON FURSTENBERG, MOVIE MOGUL BARRY DILLER, MICHAEL JACKSON, AND EVA GABOR?"

It was the wedding of the decade. The bride wore a Valentino dress of yellow lace and held a bouquet of fragrant yellow and white flowers. The groom—tall, blond, and handsome—was very nervous. Almost everyone in America would have liked to receive one of the 165 invitations to witness Elizabeth Taylor and Larry Fortensky exchanging vows in a white gazebo at Michael Jackson's fantasyland estate.

THE WEDDING FEAST

◆ ◆ ◆ ◆ ◆ ◆

SMOKED SALMON

LOBSTER SALAD ON ARTICHOKES

ROAST CHICKEN WITH MOREL SAUCE

FETTUCCINE WITH SEAFOOD

CHOCOLATE TULIPS

OPPOSITE: *The beautiful bride was given away by her son Michael Wilding and her best friend, Michael Jackson. Everyone in attendance wished the newlyweds all the happiness that love can bring. It was a joyous day.*

by one of Los Angeles's most talented and sought-after florists, David Jones. In the center of every table was an antique plant stand. At the top of the stand was a large arrangement of Queen Anne's lace. Trailing down the sides were double-faced, picot-edged lavender and mauve satin ribbons. On the bottom was a mound of violets and variegated ivy. Very simple and very elegant.

Around the base of the five-tiered chocolate mousse wedding cake, Jones placed a wreath of stephanotis, gardenias, and white roses.

The wedding didn't start exactly on time. Only after a thirty-minute delay did guests get their first look at the stunning bride. She was escorted down the green to the gazebo by two of the most cherished men in her life—her eldest son, Michael Wilding, and superstar Michael Jackson—who jointly gave the bride away. Best man José Eber and maid of honor Norma Heyman looked on as Elizabeth and Larry became husband and wife.

The gazebo and the huge white tent where the wedding dinner was held were lavishly decorated

The magnificent celebration dinner was served on gold-trimmed dishes. The very happy new couple led off the dancing, and soon guests were whirling around the dance floor. The best Champagne was served until the evening's end. Hollywood insiders called it a most romantic wedding. Truly a *delicious* affair. Our congratulations to Elizabeth and Larry Fortensky!

SMOKED SALMON

8 ounces smoked salmon, sliced
   very thin
4 tablespoons (½ stick) unsalted
   butter, softened
¼ teaspoon salt
⅛ teaspoon freshly ground pepper
4 to 6 thin slices dark bread
1 small lemon
Several sprigs fresh dill

Arrange the salmon slices on 4
chilled individual serving
plates. In a small bowl, work
the softened butter and the salt
and pepper with a fork until it
is smooth and spreadable.
Transfer to a small ramekin
and smooth the surface of the
butter with the back of a small
knife. Place the filled ramekin
on a serving tray. Remove
crusts from the bread, halve the
bread slices, and arrange attractively around the ramekin. Cut
the lemon in half lengthwise
and cut each half into quarters.
Garnish each plate with lemon
wedges and sprigs of dill. Pass
the tray of bread and butter on
the side.

SERVES 4.

At the reception, hors d'oeuvres
passed on silver trays included:
Asparagus Tips with Lemon Caviar
Mousseline, Cucumber Cups with
Ratatouille, Mini Vol-au-Vent with
Wild Mushrooms, Shrimp
Quesadillas with Roasted Red Pepper

Salsa, Paillette au Fromage, and
Tartlets with Sun-Dried Tomatoes
and Smoked Mozzarella.
   Besides the Smoked Salmon,
ABOVE, and Lobster Salad on
Artichokes, OPPOSITE, the amusette
course featured vermicelli with lemon,

crème fraîche, and beluga caviar. The
first course was Sea Scallops and
Shrimp. We have teamed it up with
fettuccine; at the wedding feast,
Tomato Concasse, Mustard Chive
Beurre Blanc, and Herb Buttered
Toast were the accompaniments.

LOBSTER SALAD ON ARTICHOKES

4 large artichokes
1 lemon, halved crosswise
2 tablespoons olive oil
1 tablespoon red wine vinegar
1 teaspoon Dijon mustard
2 tablespoons heavy cream
¼ teaspoon salt
⅛ teaspoon freshly ground pepper
½ pound cooked lobster meat, cut
    into ½-inch chunks and chilled
1 tablespoon finely chopped chives
8 medium leaves of Boston lettuce,
    washed, dried, and chilled

To prepare the artichokes, break off the stem end of each and bend back the outer leaves one by one until they are dislodged from the fleshy base. Discard the leaves. Continue until you reach the tender yellow-green leaves underneath. Cut off and discard the top two-thirds of the artichoke, leaving only the flat base. Using a paring knife, trim away the tough bottom vestiges of outer leaves. Working in a spiral from the stem end, trim the artichoke bottom into a smooth round. Rub the artichokes frequently with the lemon halves throughout this process to prevent discoloration.

Meanwhile, bring a large pot of salted water to a simmer. Add the artichokes and cook over moderately high heat until tender, about 30 minutes. Drain on paper towels. When cool enough to handle, use a small spoon to scoop out the chokes, or inner fibers. The artichokes are now ready to fill.

In a medium mixing bowl, combine the oil, vinegar, mustard, cream, salt, and pepper. Whisk until smooth and well blended. Add the lobster and gently stir to coat. Taste for seasoning and add additional salt and pepper, if desired.

Divide the lobster salad among the 4 artichokes. Sprinkle each with chopped chives. Arrange 2 lettuce leaves on 4 individual serving plates and place a filled artichoke in the center. Serve at once.

SERVES 4.

ROAST CHICKEN WITH MOREL SAUCE

1 whole free-range chicken, 3½ to
    5 pounds
2 tablespoons unsalted butter,
    softened
½ teaspoon salt
¼ teaspoon freshly ground pepper
1 small onion, halved
¾ pound fresh morels (1½ ounces
    dried)
½ cup dry white wine
1 cup chicken stock
1½ cups heavy cream
Salt and freshly ground pepper
1 tablespoon freshly chopped
    parsley

Preheat the oven to 450° F. Trim the chicken of any excess fat and clip the tips off the wings. Pat the chicken dry with paper towels. Smear the butter over the entire surface and season with the salt and pepper. Place the onion in the cavity and set the chicken, breast side up, in a roasting pan. Place the pan in the oven and immediately lower the temperature to 350° F. Cook until the juices run clear when a fork is inserted into the thickest part of the thigh, 1 to 1½ hours. Baste often with the pan juices.

Clean the fresh mushrooms or soak the dried ones in a cupful of hot water until reconstituted, about 10 minutes (save the liquid if using dried). Rinse well and finely chop. If using dried morels, strain the soaking liquid through a sieve lined with a double thickness of cheesecloth and reserve.

Remove the chicken to a platter and cover with foil to keep warm. Skim the fat from the roasting pan and set the pan over high heat. Pour in the wine and stir with a wire whisk to dislodge any bits stuck to the bottom of the pan. Boil over high heat until only a tablespoon or so of liquid remains. Pour in the chicken stock and continue boiling until it has been reduced by half. Pour into a small saucepan and add the morels.

Cover the saucepan and cook the morels over moderately low heat until they are very tender, about 10 minutes if they are fresh and 20 minutes if dried. Uncover and add the cream and the strained mushroom juices if used. Increase the heat to high and boil until the sauce has reduced by about half and has thickened to the consistency of thick custard. Season with salt and pepper to taste.

Cut the roast chicken into 8 pieces and arrange on a serving platter. Spoon the sauce over it and garnish with chopped parsley. Serve at once.

SERVES 4.

FETTUCINE WITH SEAFOOD

2 tablespoons unsalted butter
½ pound medium shrimp, peeled
    and deveined
½ pound bay scallops
2 cups heavy cream
1 pound fettuccine
1 ounce (30 grams) caviar,
    preferably Beluga
Salt and freshly ground pepper

Melt the butter in a medium skillet over moderately high heat. Add the shrimp and toss or stir until pink, about 2 minutes. Add the scallops and cook for 1 minute longer. Pour in the cream, partially cover the skillet, and cook until the shrimp and scallops are firm, about 3 more minutes. Using a slotted spoon, remove the shrimp and scallops to a plate and cover with foil to keep warm. Reduce the cream over high heat by half. Return the shrimp and scallops to the reduced cream and set aside.

Cook the pasta according to package instructions. Gently reheat the shrimp and scallops over very low heat. Drain the pasta well and place in a warmed mixing bowl. Add the cream sauce and the caviar to the pasta, and toss gently to blend. Season to taste with salt and pepper. Serve at once.

SERVES 4.

OPPOSITE: *Roast Chicken with Morel Sauce.*

As the main course, a whole baby chicken, stuffed with morel mousse, was served to each of the wedding guests. A mélange of sautéed vegetables accompanied the baby chicken, though broccoli, as shown on page 28 with our adaptation, Roast Chicken with Morel Sauce, is a wonderful partnering of flavors. Puree of pumpkin and potato with fresh thyme rounded out the wedding's main course.

CHOCOLATE TULIPS

4 egg whites, at room temperature
1¼ cups all-purpose flour
1 cup confectioners' sugar
5 tablespoons (⅝ stick) unsalted
*   butter, melted and cooled*
2 tablespoons cocoa
1 tablespoon heavy cream
Ice cream and sorbets

In a medium mixing bowl, whisk egg whites briefly just to break down. Add the flour and sugar and whisk until blended and smooth. Stir in the butter, cocoa, and cream. Cover and let the batter sit for about 30 minutes.

Preheat the oven to 450° F. Butter 2 large nonstick baking sheets. Drop tablespoonfuls of the batter about 5 inches apart on the baking sheets. Using the back of a spoon, spread the batter out as thin as possible to measure 3 to 4 inches in diameter. Bake until the wafers are just brown around the edges, 2 to 3 minutes. Watch carefully, as they burn easily.

Remove the baking sheets from the oven. Working quickly, use a spatula to transfer the wafers to cover the end of an upturned drinking glass whose bottom measures 2 to 3 inches in diameter. While the wafer is still warm, use a ramekin to gently press down to form a tulip-shaped wafer. Leave the ramekin to cool on the glass with the ramekin on top. Lift gently to unmold. The wafers must be hot to mold them into shape. If they cool during the process, run them back into the oven for 30 seconds to 1 minute to warm them and render them pliable. Continue this process until all the batter is used. Wipe the baking sheets, cool, and rebutter between each batch.

Just before serving, place the tulips on individual serving plates. Fill each with small scoops of vanilla ice cream and sorbets.

Baked tulips will keep overnight in an airtight container and may be frozen for up to a month.

MAKES 10 TO 12 TULIPS.

Lady Weinberg

◆ ◆ ◆ ◆ ◆ ◆ ◆ ◆ ◆

"A CERTAIN UNEXPECTED TWIST IS PART OF
MY ENTERTAINING STYLE. GUESTS ARE
ALWAYS TO BE AMUSED AND BE DELIGHTED
WITH SURPRISES."

Lady Weinberg, also known as Anouska Hempel, is a visionary regarding food, fashion, and hostessing. Blake's, her exclusive town house–hotel in London, offers rooms (which she calls "sets") to complement the moods of her guests. Blake's is also known for its unique restaurant, where diners—including Prince Charles and Princess Diana—are amused by creative presentations. One of the most popular selections on the menu is the Fabergé Chicken, a chicken breast shaped into an egg that, when cut open, reveals a center of cream-of-ginger sauce.

"I devised all sorts of strange dishes for Blake's restaurant menu," Lady Weinberg said, "including dishes that mixed Japanese-style raw fish with Italian pasta. Now everyone does it. The Sushi Pavé is a fantasy terrine I created by reorganizing ordinary sushi ingredients to make it a visual experience as well as a taste experience. People are completely fascinated by the Sushi Pavé, sometimes hesitating to eat it because it is so unusual to look at.

THE MENU

◆ ◆ ◆ ◆ ◆

SUSHI PAVÉ
RASPBERRY ALMOND CREAM
PISTACHIO CAKE
PISTACHIO MERINGUES

OPPOSITE: *Inside Lady Weinberg's Pudding Room, the decor is richly beautiful, dark, and restful. Whether she is decorating, designing* haute couture *clothing, or creating magnificent table settings, Lady Weinberg's unique style is delightfully different.*

"At home, I create themes incorporating a variety of elements, using my *objets d'art* on the table with foods that are color-coordinated.

"The night we introduced my 'Green and Pink' theme party, my husband, Mark, and I had eight for dinner. After the meal, everyone strolled to the living room. There was glorious music, and when no one was expecting an encore, the Pudding Room doors were thrown open. Dozens of tiny flickering oil lamps beckoned the guests to enter. Inside was an utterly sophisticated and eclectic array of unique desserts, sweets, and drinks—the table was a work of art. None of the silverware or glasses matched. I served one of the cakes in clear glass boxes. Everything was totally unique.

"This unusual entertaining theme was drawn from my own fantasy world," she stressed. "I take my fantasies apart and put them back together in a hundred different ways. Then, I'm satisfied."

SUSHI PAVÉ

⅓ cup wasabi (see note)
8 medium sea scallops
8 langoustines, cooked and peeled
¼ pound fresh turbot, sliced thinly
4 very small sprigs fresh basil,
  washed and patted dry
4 sprigs fresh dill, washed and
  patted dry
1 to 2 tablespoons vegetable oil,
  for brushing
2 cups uncarbonated mineral water
1 envelope gelatin
½ cup pickled ginger, patted dry
2 bunches chives
1 sheet toasted nori (see note)
½ teaspoon freshly ground cloves
¼ teaspoon red pepper flakes
1 small scallion, white part only,
  julienned

In a pastry bag fitted with a
¼-inch tube, pipe the wasabi
into small drops on a baking
sheet lined with wax paper.
Freeze until solid.

Cut each of the scallops horizontally into 3 slices. Remove
the flesh from the langoustines
and trim. Lightly brush the
scallops, langoustine pieces,
turbot, basil leaves, and dill
sprigs with the vegetable oil.

Place ¼ cup of the water in a
small saucepan. Sprinkle the
gelatin over and dissolve for
1 minute. Over low heat,
warm through to dissolve
completely. Do not boil. Place
the remaining water in a medium mixing bowl set over a
larger bowl, full of ice. Pour in
the dissolved gelatin and stir

until the aspic is the consistency of heavy syrup.

In 4 lightly oiled molds that
measure 3 by 3 inches (or
1-cup-capacity glass baking
dishes or ramekins), pour half
of the aspic. Chill in the refrig-

ABOVE: *Lady Weinberg in the
Pudding Room of her townhouse. Her
country house, she says, is the
complete opposite.*

erator until slightly set, about 15 minutes. (Remove the bowl with the remaining aspic from the bowl of ice and set it aside in a warm area. It should remain liquid enough for pouring when you are finishing the pavé. If it has turned solid, pour into a saucepan and gently reheat over very low heat. Do not boil.) Remove the molds from the refrigerator and arrange the wasabi, scallops, langoustines, turbot, basil leaves, dill sprigs, and several pieces of the ginger attractively on top. Place a layer of chives through the center. Refrigerate until set, about 2 hours.

When the aspic-filled molds have set, pour the remaining aspic into a medium mixing bowl set over a larger bowl,

full of ice. Stir until thick and syrupy. Pour on top of the set aspic and place in the refrigerator. Refrigerate until completely solid, 2 to 3 hours.

Turn the pavé out by rubbing a hot cloth around the outside of each mold. Cut the toasted nori into thin strips and tie each pavé with a bow. Place on a plate, garnish with the remaining ginger, cloves, and red pepper flakes. Place a strip of scallion through the bow.

SERVES 4.

NOTE: Wasabi is a green paste often used as a pungent condiment in Japanese cooking. Nori is a flat sheet of compressed seaweed, dark green in color. Both are available in Oriental food markets.

ABOVE: *Lady Weinberg said, "My food and entertaining themes are all drawn from my fantasy world, including this 'floating' sushi. It makes a wonderful appetizer or main course at a luncheon. We also serve it at Blake's, my hotel in London."*

RASPBERRY ALMOND CREAM

1 16-ounce package ginger snaps
10 tablespoons (1¼ sticks)
  unsalted butter, cut into small
  pieces
1 teaspoon vanilla extract
1¼ cups lightly roasted almonds
2 cups milk
⅔ cup sugar
2 envelopes unflavored gelatin
½ cup cold water
10 egg yolks
2 cups heavy cream, whipped
3 tablespoons amaretto
2 pints fresh raspberries, rinsed,
  drained, and dried completely

Lightly brush an 8-to-9-inch
springform pan, 2 inches deep,
with vegetable oil, and set
aside.

In the bowl of a food processor, combine the ginger snaps,
butter, and vanilla; blend until
smooth. Set aside.

In a medium-sized, heavy
saucepan, combine the al-
monds, milk, and ⅓ cup of the
sugar. Bring to a simmer over
moderately high heat. Reduce
the heat to moderate and simmer for 10 minutes.

◆ ◆ ◆ ◆ ◆ ◆ ◆

LEFT: *Lady Weinberg's special
touches—shimmering glass and
sensual objects adorning the table—are
a delight to the eye.*

Sprinkle the gelatin over the cold water. Let sit for 5 minutes to dissolve.

In a large mixing bowl, whisk the egg yolks with the remaining sugar until pale. Pour a little of the almond milk into the egg mixture, whisking briefly to blend, then pour the egg mixture into the saucepan. Reduce the heat to low and stir constantly until the mixture resembles the consistency of heavy cream, about 5 minutes. Do not boil, or the eggs will curdle. Remove from the heat, cool about 2 minutes, then stir in the dissolved gelatin.

Pass the mixture through a fine mesh sieve into a large mixing bowl. Cool at room temperature for 10 to 15 minutes, then set over a large bowl of ice water. Stir with a wooden spoon until the mixture begins to thicken. When the mixture is completely cooled and has the consistency of thick custard, fold in the whipped cream and the amaretto.

Fill the pan with one third of the mixture. Sprinkle with one third of the ground ginger-snap mixture, then cover with a layer of raspberries. Repeat with the remaining thirds of almond cream, ginger-snap mixture, and raspberries. Cover with plastic wrap and refrigerate for at least 12 hours, but no more than 2 days.

SERVES 8 to 10.

PISTACHIO CAKE

2 cups superfine sugar
1 cup honey
6 tablespoons light corn syrup
¼ cup water
2 pounds peeled, dry-roasted
  pistachio nuts
Petals of 8 red roses
2 egg whites
1¼ cups confectioners' sugar
Fresh rose petals, for garnish

Lightly brush an 8-to-9-inch springform pan, 2 inches deep, with vegetable oil and set aside.

In a medium saucepan, over moderate heat, combine the superfine sugar, honey, corn syrup, and water. Sir until the sugar has dissolved. Increase the heat to moderately high and cook, without stirring, until the syrup reaches the hard crack stage, 300° F, on a candy thermometer. Immediately remove from the heat and stir in the pistachios. Pour into the prepared pan and cool. Cover with plastic wrap and let set overnight.

Brush the rose petals with the egg whites. Arrange in a single layer on a large baking sheet and sprinkle with the confectioners' sugar. Leave to dry overnight in a warm place. When completely dry, crush to a powder with a mortar and pestle. Remove the cake from the pan and sprinkle with the crushed rose petals. Serve on a bed of fresh rose petals.

SERVES 8 to 10.

ABOVE: *Another unique creation, Pistachio Cake with candied rose petals, is actually a "confection," and is served in a cakelike wedge.*

PISTACHIO MERINGUES

FOR THE MERINGUES
4 egg whites
1 cup confectioners' sugar, sifted
1 vanilla bean, split in half

FOR THE ITALIAN MERINGUE
½ cup water
1 cup sugar
4 egg whites

FOR THE FILLING
8 egg yolks
¾ cup sugar
2 cups milk
1 cup pistachio paste (see note)
1 envelope gelatin
¼ cup cold water
1 cup heavy cream

To prepare the meringues, preheat the oven to 225° F. Line a non-stick baking sheet with parchment paper and set aside.

In a large, clean bowl, beat the egg whites until stiff. Fold in the sugar. Scrape the vanilla beans down the middle with the tip of a sharp knife and fold into the whites. Using a pastry bag fitted with a plain, ½-inch-wide tip, pipe out cookies that measure about 1½ inches in diameter onto the parchment-lined sheet. Bake until firm and lightly colored, about 1 hour. Remove the cookies from the parchment to racks and let cool completely.

For the Italian meringue, combine the water and the sugar in a small saucepan over moderately high heat, stirring

to dissolve. Increase the heat to high and cook until the mixture forms a thick syrup, 238° F on a candy thermometer. In the bowl of an electric mixer, beat the egg whites until soft peaks form. With the beaters in motion, slowly pour the syrup into the whites. Continue beating until the whites

ABOVE: *In England, meringues are very popular at tea and dessert. Pistachio Meringues are the most beautiful shade of green and rest on a bed of pistachios. Open the jar and have a cookie—if only in your imagination!*

are firm and glossy.

To prepare the filling, beat the egg yolks with half of the sugar in a small bowl. In a medium saucepan, combine the remaining sugar, milk, and pistachio paste. Bring to a simmer over moderate heat. Pour half of the pistachio mixture over the egg yolks and stir to blend. Pour this mixture back into the saucepan and reduce the heat to low. Stir gently until the custard is thick enough to coat the back of a wooden spoon. Do not overcook.

In a small bowl, sprinkle the gelatin over the cold water. Let dissolve for 5 minutes. Add to the custard and stir to mix in. Allow to cool completely.

When cool, fold the Italian meringue into the pistachio custard mixture. Whip the cream to form stiff peaks, then fold in. Cover and refrigerate until the mixture is the consistency of a soft cream, about 1 hour.

To assemble the meringues, place about 2 tablespoons of filling on the smooth side of half of the meringue cookies. Top each with the remaining halves, smooth side down. Gently press together, allowing the filling to spill out slightly.

MAKES ABOUT 12 1½-INCH FILLED MERINGUES.

NOTE: Imported pistachio paste is sometimes available in specialty food stores. Its appearance is rare, however. To make your own, grind 2 cups peeled, blanched pis-

tachios in a food processor with 2 tablespoons granulated sugar. With the blade in motion, pour in 1 tablespoon light corn oil. Process until smooth. Makes about 1 cup of paste.

TOP: *Each place setting is different in some way.* ABOVE: *Green Sleeves Roses from the Weinbergs' cutting garden at their country house.*

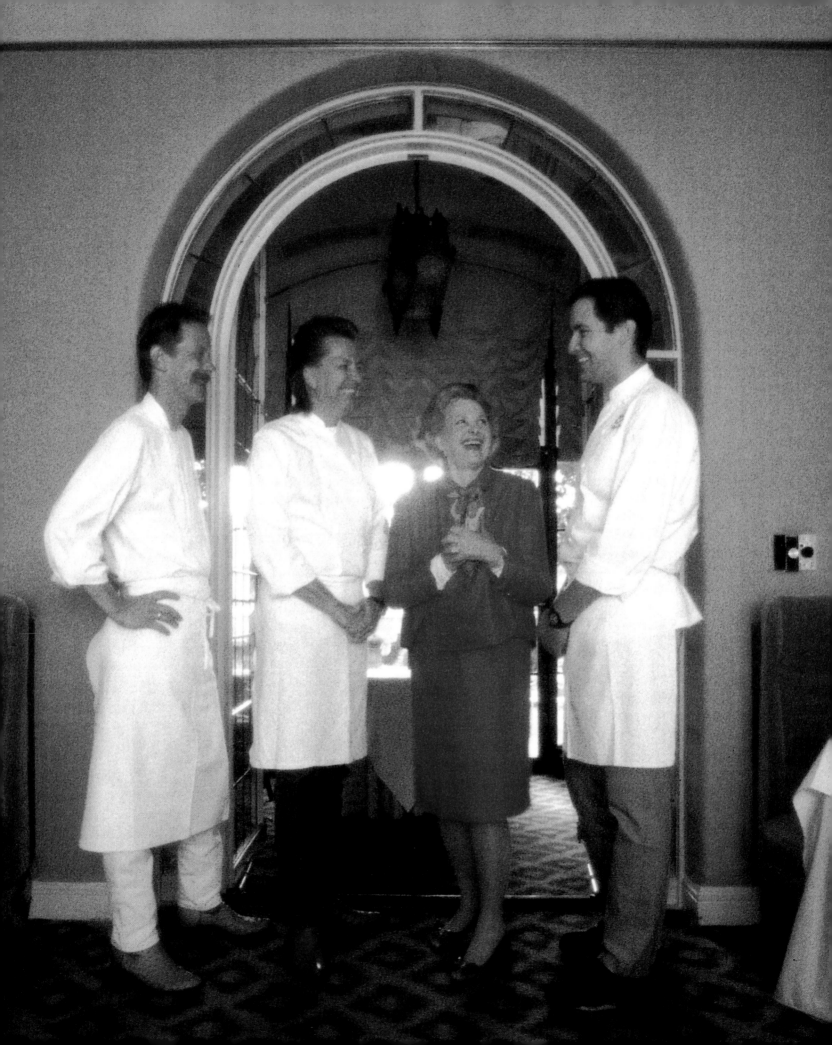

Caroline Hunt

♦ ♦ ♦ ♦ ♦ ♦ ♦ ♦ ♦ ♦ ♦

"I HAVE SO MANY GUESTS I COULD NEVER DO ALL THE COOKING."

Caroline Hunt, the gracious Texas hotelier and gastronome, has had a number of very special guests at her dining table. Queen Elizabeth II and Prince Philip, the Duke of Edinburgh, came for Jubilee Dallas, a 150th birthday celebration held, in part, at Caroline Hunt's stunning Crescent Court Hotel. Over the years, other well-known guests have included Margaret Thatcher, the members of the Economic Summit, and actor Larry Hagman.

Planning a sit-down dinner for Her Majesty, a royal entourage of twenty, and fifty of her own most important friends was no small task, even for Caroline Hunt. However, planning a menu to please the queen, who reportedly never eats in public and politely departs after the main course, was another story. A superb cook herself, Caroline Hunt is seldom ruffled by culinary challenges. For this occasion, however, she called the executive chef of her hotel dynasty, Dean Fearing, who is credited

---

THE MENU

♦ ♦ ♦ ♦ ♦ ♦

WOOD GRILLED VEAL LOIN
TOMATO RANCHERO SAUCE
CRISP TORTILLA AND JICAMA SALAD
BANANA SOFT "TACOS"

OPPOSITE: *Caroline Hunt with chefs Dan O'Leary, Dean Fearing, and Jeff Triola. Though Caroline enjoys cooking, with her Rosewood Hotel Corporation to oversee, she leaves it up to those who have more time and experience.*

---

with putting Southwestern cuisine on the culinary map and making The Mansion on Turtle Creek a five-star restaurant.

That night, in the Crescent Court's grandest dining room, with Limoges and Lalique gracing the tables and Dean Fearing directing the kitchen staff, Her Majesty couldn't resist. Not only did the Queen eat the masterful entrée of Wood Grilled Veal Loin with Black Bean and Sweet Corn Purees, but she quietly proclaimed, "I will stay for dessert!" Imagine the mood in the kitchen when the chefs found they were twenty desserts short! Fortunately, the ingredients were on hand, and everyone was treated to Fearing's signature dessert, Banana Soft "Tacos."

Smiling a special sweet smile, Caroline said, "I have always enjoyed cooking. Now, though, with five hotels to oversee, including my new hotel, the Lanesborough in London, I leave it to those who have more time. I'd rather give the parties!"

TOP: *Caroline Hunt loves to entertain, whether the occasion is a lavish charity fund-raiser or a quiet high tea at Lady Primrose, her English tearoom at the Crescent Court Hotel, with friend and partner Vivian Young and manager Lori Kosberg.* ABOVE: *This busy hotelier even found time to collect enough pumpkin recipes to publish this charming cookbook on the subject in 1984.* OPPOSITE: *Dean Fearing, executive chef of the restaurant at The Mansion on Turtle Creek, created this unique recipe for grilled veal. His restaurant is considered one of the best in the United States.*

WOOD GRILLED VEAL LOIN

1 cup dried black beans
3½ cups chicken stock
1 medium onion, coarsely chopped
3 garlic cloves, minced
2 to 3 slices raw, smoked bacon, chopped
2 serrano chilies, chopped
1 sprig fresh epazote (available in Latin American markets)
Salt and freshly ground pepper
4 ears fresh sweet corn
¼ cup bacon fat (or vegetable oil)
1 shallot, finely chopped
1 tablespoon freshly squeezed lemon juice
2 tablespoons corn oil
4 6-ounce veal loin steaks, slightly flattened

Place the beans in a large, heavy saucepan. Add cold water to cover and soak for 8 hours or overnight. Drain and rinse under cold water. Return the beans to the saucepan and add the chicken stock, onion, half of the garlic, the bacon, serrano chilies, epazote, and salt and pepper to taste. Bring to a boil, reduce the heat to moderate, and simmer until the beans are tender, about 1 hour. Transfer the beans to a food processor and puree until smooth. Add additional chicken stock to thin, if necessary; there should be about 2 cups puree. Return the puree to the saucepan and keep warm.

Shuck the corn and remove the silk. Cut down the center of the kernels in each corn row with a paring knife. Scrape the kernels off the cob with the back of a chopping knife, retaining all the liquid and pulp. Heat the bacon fat in a medium saucepan over moderately high heat. Add the corn, shallot, and the remaining garlic. Reduce the heat to moderately low and simmer until softened, 10 to 15 minutes, stirring often. Season with lemon juice and salt to taste. Keep warm.

Light a charcoal fire and let the coals burn down to a gray ash. Rub a bit of the corn oil on a grill and set over the coals. Brush the remaining oil over the veal steaks and season with salt and pepper to taste. Grill the steaks for 2 to 3 minutes per side, turning 90 degrees halfway through each side to form a *quadrillage*, or grill markings; the veal will be slightly rare.

Heat four dinner plates. Place a steak on each one with about 2 tablespoons of each puree. Serve with Tomato Ranchero Sauce and Crisp Tortilla and Jicama Salad.

SERVES 4.

TOMATO RANCHERO SAUCE

2 tablespoons vegetable oil
4 ripe tomatoes, seeded and
    coarsely chopped
1 yellow onion, halved and peeled
½ pound veal shank bones, cut
    into 1-inch sections
3 shallots, coarsely chopped
1 yellow onion, peeled and
    coarsely chopped
1 celery stalk, coarsely chopped
½ carrot, peeled and coarsely
    chopped
1 poblano chili, stem and seeds
    removed, coarsely chopped
2 garlic cloves, finely chopped
3 cups chicken stock
4 sprigs cilantro
1 cup veal demi-glace (bottled
    demi-glace is available in
    specialty food stores)
½ each small red, green, and
    yellow bell peppers, peeled,
    seeded, and cut into medium dice
Juice of ½ lime
Salt to taste

In a large sauté pan, heat 1 tablespoon of the oil over high heat until it just begins to smoke. Add the tomatoes and onion, and sauté just until the onion is transparent and the tomatoes have released their liquid; set aside to cool.

Preheat the oven to 400° F. Place the veal bones in a roasting pan and roast until golden brown, about 35 minutes, stirring frequently. Remove the

bones with a slotted spoon and set them aside.

In a large saucepan, heat the remaining vegetable oil just until it smokes. Add the shallot, onion, celery, carrot, and poblano chili. Sauté until the vegetables are well browned. Add the garlic and the roasted bones, stirring well, then add the chicken stock. Bring to a boil, reduce the heat, and simmer until the mixture has reduced by half, about ½ hour. Add the cilantro and demi-glace, and simmer for an hour. The volume should measure about 2 cups; if there is too much, boil to reduce; if too little, add additional chicken stock.

Meanwhile, grind the cooled tomato-onion mixture through a food mill fitted with a medium plate. Set aside.

Strain the sauce through a large sieve. Add the tomato-onion mixture, diced peppers, lime juice, and salt. The sauce should yield about 2½ cups; if quantity is too great, boil to reduce. If not enough, add stock to equal this amount. Set aside and keep warm until ready to serve. Serve with grilled veal loin steaks.

MAKES ABOUT 2½ CUPS.

◆ ◆ ◆ ◆ ◆ ◆ ◆

LEFT: *At Shopping the English Countryside, the gift shop at the Crescent Court Hotel, one can find a hundred different teapots, antiques, and treasures from the English countryside. Each piece is personally selected by Caroline Hunt and Vivian Young on their yearly shopping trip.*

◆ ◆ ◆ ◆ ◆ ◆ ◆

CRISP TORTILLA AND JICAMA SALAD

4 corn tortillas
4 blue corn tortillas★
4 ancho corn tortillas★
5 cups vegetable oil
½ cup jicama, julienned
½ each small red, green, and
    yellow bell peppers, peeled,
    seeded, and julienned
½ cup mizuna leaves, packed
¼ cup cilantro, packed
3 tablespoons corn oil
1½ tablespoons freshly squeezed
    lime juice
2 serrano chilies, seeded and finely
    chopped
Salt to taste

Make three tortilla stacks and cut each stack in half. Restack the tortillas, forming three half-moon stacks, and slice crosswise into ⅛-inch strips. Separate the strips and combine all three types of tortillas into one big pile.

In a deep fryer, heat the vegetable oil to 325° F. When it is hot, add half of the tortillas. Stirring constantly, fry for 35 seconds or until crisp. Do not overcook or the tortillas will lose their color and burn. Remove from the oil and drain on paper towels. Fry and drain the remaining tortillas. Reserve.

In a large bowl, combine the jicama, bell peppers, mizuna, cilantro, corn oil, lime juice, chilies, and salt. Toss to mix and adjust the seasonings if necessary.

Gently toss with the tortilla strips. Be careful not to break them, but make sure they are well coated with the dressing. Serve immediately with grilled veal loin steaks.

SERVES 4.

* Use plain corn tortillas if others are unavailable.

ABOVE: *Tea at Lady Primrose is a tradition among Dallas debutantes and their mothers. The tray of sandwiches and tiny scones is as pretty as a picture, and divinely delicious. If you're in the neighborhood, stop by for tea.*

ABOVE: *After tea at Lady Primrose, stop to buy some treasures at Shopping the English Countryside.* BELOW: *Follow these easy steps, along with the recipe instructions, to create Banana Soft "Tacos," another of Dean Fearing's fun and fancy Southwestern-style recipes.*

BANANA SOFT "TACOS"

2 cups all-purpose flour, sifted
   twice
1 tablespoon sugar
Pinch salt
1 cup milk
2 large eggs, beaten
2 large egg yolks, beaten
4 tablespoons (½ stick) unsalted
   butter, melted
2 tablespoons cognac
4 tablespoons (½ stick) unsalted
   butter
½ cup + 2 tablespoons brown
   sugar, packed
1 tablespoon freshly squeezed
   orange juice
1 tablespoon Grand Marnier
3 medium bananas, peeled and
   sliced ½-inch thick
½ pint strawberries, washed and
   stemmed

In a medium bowl, combine the flour, sugar, and salt. Slowly beat in the milk, eggs, and egg yolks. Stir in the melted butter, then the cognac. Let sit for 15 to 20 minutes.

Lightly butter an 8-inch sauté or crêpe pan and place over medium heat. Pour in approximately 2 tablespoons of the

batter and swirl in a circular motion to cover the bottom of the pan evenly. Cook on one side until the crêpe is lightly browned, 2 to 3 minutes, then turn and cook for an additional 1 to 2 minutes. Continue until all the batter is used. Stack the crêpes between layers of wax paper to prevent sticking. You should have 12 to 16 crêpes; extras can be frozen for another use.

In a small saucepan over medium heat, stir the butter and ½ cup of the brown sugar until liquefied and smooth. Add the orange juice and the Grand Marnier. Reduce the heat to low and cook, stirring occasionally, until the syrup has thickened, about 5 minutes. Remove from the heat and add the sliced bananas, gently stirring to glaze.

Cut half of the strawberries into ½-inch dice and set aside. In a blender, puree the remaining 2 tablespoons of brown sugar with the remaining berries. Pour the pureed mixture over the diced strawberries and stir to combine.

Preheat the broiler. With a slotted spoon, transfer 6 or 8 slices of banana to the center of

each crêpe and loosely roll into a cylinder; reserve the liquid that the bananas have cooked in. Place two rolled crêpes on individual ovenproof serving plates. Brush a small amount of the banana cooking liquid across the top of the crêpes and place under the preheated broiler until lightly browned, about 2 minutes. Divide the remaining banana slices among the crêpes and garnish with the strawberries on the side. Serve at once with Papaya Salsa (recipe follows) on the side.

SERVES 4 to 6.

PAPAYA SALSA

1 papaya, peeled, halved, and
  seeded
3 tablespoons sugar
1 teaspoon cinnamon

Cut half of the papaya into ¼-inch dice. In a blender, puree the remaining papaya with the sugar and cinnamon until smooth. Pour the puree over the diced papaya and stir to combine.

MAKES ABOUT 1½ CUPS.

ABOVE: *Banana Soft "Tacos,"*
served on a plate with an
appropriately Southwestern motif.

CLOCKWISE FROM TOP LEFT: *Model Cecilia Nord, Robin Leach, and host Fred Deutsch; Fred "schmoozes" with guests; hosts Penny Drue Baird and Fred Deutsch; library patrons toast their "Rich and Famous" evening.*

New York Public Library Party

♦ ♦ ♦ ♦ ♦ ♦ ♦ ♦ ♦ ♦

"WHEN I PLAN A CHARITY PARTY, THE FIRST THING I ASK MYSELF IS 'WHAT WILL MAKE EIGHTEEN PEOPLE PAY NEARLY ONE THOUSAND DOLLARS FOR A SEAT AT *MY* DINNER TABLE?' "

Every two years, on an evening in December, the Volunteers of the Public Library of New York City throw the biggest bash imaginable. Fifty fund-raising parties are given simultaneously in homes across the city, each with an amusing and entertaining theme. The parties range from a dinner planned and attended by the celebrated author and cook Julia Child to one entitled "Octopussy: An Evening of James Bond." Library supporters place their requests months ahead in hopes of attending the party of their dreams.

Library volunteer Penny Baird, creator of the "Lifestyles of the Rich and Famous" theme party, said, "This is the fourth party I have given for the library and I haven't had a vacant seat yet. I've noticed that people respond best to themes they can get involved in. Previously, my theme was Babar, and Laurent De Brunhoff, the author of the famous elephant's current adventures, attended. Many of the guests showed up with stacks of Babar books and stuffed toys for Laurent to autograph.

> ## THE MENU
>
> ♦ ♦ ♦ ♦ ♦
>
> CURRIED TUNA TARTARE
> ROASTED BLACK SEA BASS WITH SALSIFY
> BRAISED RABBIT WITH PAPPARDELLE
> APPLE, APPLE, APPLE!

"The 'Lifestyles of the Rich and Famous' theme was one I had thought about for quite a while. At first I wanted to have rich and famous 'types' played by look-alike actors, who would make a surprise entrance. But when Robin Leach agreed to be the special guest, I felt the party would be a great success. I knew that guests would be curious to meet Robin and hear his globe-trotting stories."

Penny continued, "I asked my favorite restaurant, Le Cirque, to donate the food. Their chef, Daniel Boulud, created the most delicious menu.

"To top off the elegance, only Cristal Champagne was served, compliments of Louis Roederer. It was truly an evening of rich and famous experiences. When eighteen total strangers become incredible friends over dinner, you know you've created a very successful party."

She added, with a smile, "I love to have people in my home and 'wow' them with good food and the spirit of the evening. I *live* for parties."

CURRIED TUNA TARTARE

FOR THE CURRY SAUCE
2 tablespoons water
1 tablespoon curry powder
1 tablespoon mayonnaise
1 teaspoon Dijon mustard
1 tablespoon mango chutney
2 tablespoons freshly squeezed
   lemon juice
2 drops Tabasco
1/8 teaspoon salt

FOR THE TUNA TARTARE
12 ounces very fresh tuna
1 small bunch round red radishes,
   cleaned and trimmed
1 celery stalk
1 bunch fresh chives
Salt and freshly ground pepper

FOR THE CELERY SAUCE
1/2 cup vegetable oil
1 small onion, thinly sliced
2 teaspoons curry powder
2 cups chicken stock
1/2 small all-purpose potato, cut
   into 1/4-inch dice (about 1/4 cup)
3 celery stalks, trimmed and sliced
   1/4 inch thick
Pinch salt
8 to 10 celery leaves, rinsed and
   patted dry

To prepare the curry sauce, combine the water and curry powder in a small saucepan over low heat. Cook, stirring, until the mixture forms a smooth paste, about 2 minutes. Transfer to a small mixing bowl. When the mixture is cool, mix in the mayonnaise,

ABOVE: *The curried tuna appetizer was served on Penny's antique Royal Copenhagen dishes. The pattern, Flora Danica, is made in exactly the same way it was in 1790. The table was filled with amusing objects, from Lalique figurines to golden candles.* RIGHT: *The guests toasted master chef Daniel Boulud of Le Cirque Restaurant; they knew the dinner would be a memorable meal. Though French-born and -trained, Boulud is considered one of the top chefs in America. If you can't get to Le Cirque, sample his extraordinary fare in your own home with these easy-to-follow recipes.*

mustard, chutney, lemon juice, Tabasco, and salt. Set aside. (If prepared in advance, refrigerate for up to 2 to 3 days.)

To prepare the tuna tartare, cut the tuna into ¼-inch dice. Set aside.

Cut 3 or 4 of the radishes into paper-thin slices and reserve in ice-cold water for garnish (drain on paper towels before using). Mince the remaining radishes and the celery stalk. Cut chives into 3-inch sticks and reserve for garnish; finely chop the remaining chives.

In a small mixing bowl, combine the diced tuna, curry sauce, minced radishes, celery, and chopped chives. Blend well and season to taste with salt and pepper. Cover and refrigerate until ready to serve.

To prepare the celery sauce, place ½ tablespoon of the vegetable oil in a small saucepan. Add the onions and curry powder and cook over medium heat until the onions have softened, 2 to 3 minutes. Add the chicken stock and the potato and increase the heat to high. Bring to a boil and cook until potatoes are softened, 4 to 5 minutes. Add the celery and salt. Continue boiling until the celery is very soft, about 5 more minutes. Pour into a blender and puree until smooth. Strain through a fine-mesh sieve into a bowl. Cool to room temperature, cover, and refrigerate until well

chilled, about 2 hours. (This can be made up to 2 days in advance.)

Heat the remaining oil in a very small sauté pan. When very hot but not smoking, add the celery leaves and cook until crisp, about 2 minutes. Remove and drain on paper towels.

To assemble the dish, place a 2½-inch round cookie cutter in the middle of a chilled dinner plate. Fill the ring with tuna tartare and press down gently on top to make sure it will keep its shape. Remove the ring and place one-fourth of the radish slices around and over the tartare. Garnish with the fried celery leaves and the chives. Pour the celery sauce around the tartare. Repeat the process with 3 additional chilled plates.

SERVES 4.

◆ ◆ ◆ ◆ ◆ ◆ ◆

TOP: *Only Cristal Champagne was served that evening. The House of Louis Roederer developed it for Czar Alexander II of Russia in 1876.* CENTER AND BOTTOM: *Well known for her splendid and creative table settings, Penny Baird loves details. Her magnificent candle collection— tree branches (TOP), treasure chests, crowns, pillows, gold doubloons, and an enchanted castle—brings amusement and delight to the dinner table. "I bring these candles home from Paris by the armload. They are from the Point à la Ligne candle shop on the Avenue Victor Hugo."*

herb crust starts browning, about 2 minutes.

Arrange the salsify on a serving platter. Place the fillets over and drizzle with any melted butter from the broiling pan. Garnish with sprigs of chervil.

SERVES 4.

NOTE: Red snapper can be substituted for the sea bass, if desired.

♦ ♦ ♦ ♦ ♦ ♦ ♦

ROASTED BLACK SEA BASS WITH SALSIFY

3 tablespoons chopped fresh herbs: chives, chervil, parsley, and rosemary, for example
2 1-inch-thick slices day-old French bread, crusts removed
6 tablespoons (¾ stick) unsalted butter, softened
Salt and freshly ground pepper
1 pound salsify, peeled and sliced on the diagonal ¼-inch thick
4 black sea bass fillets, about 7 ounces each (see note)
1 tablespoon vegetable oil
Several sprigs fresh chervil

In the bowl of a food processor, combine 2 tablespoons of the herbs with the bread and process until bread is reduced to crumbs. Add 5 tablespoons of the butter and a pinch of salt and pepper and process until smooth. Set aside.

Bring a large pot of salted water to a boil over high heat. Cook the salsify until tender, 5 to 7 minutes. Drain and transfer the salsify to a sauté pan, set over medium heat. Toss the salsify with the remaining tablespoon of butter, add the reserved fresh herbs, and season to taste with salt and pepper. Sauté briefly, then remove from heat and cover to keep warm.

Preheat the broiler. Season the sea bass with salt and pepper to taste. In a nonstick sauté pan or skillet, heat the oil until it is hot but not smoking. Place the fish skin side down in the pan, and sear, about 2 minutes. Gently turn and cook the fillets on the other side for about 1 more minute. Transfer to a broiling pan, skin side up, and let cool for about 2 minutes. Spread the bread and herb butter mixture evenly over each fillet. Broil the fish until the

BRAISED RABBIT WITH PAPPARDELLE

1 young rabbit, about 3 pounds, cut into 6 or 8 pieces
Salt and freshly ground pepper
2 tablespoons olive oil
2 small onions, minced
2 medium carrots, peeled and minced
1 small celeriac, peeled and minced
6 garlic cloves, minced
2 medium mushrooms, cleaned and minced
6 fresh sage leaves, minced
2 teaspoons tomato paste
2 teaspoons all-purpose flour
1 cup dry white wine
2 cups chicken stock
1 large tomato, peeled, seeded, and chopped
2 tablespoons unsalted butter
1 pound pappardelle pasta
¼ cup freshly grated Parmesan cheese

Preheat the oven to 425° F. Season the rabbit with salt and pepper. In a flameproof casserole or Dutch oven with a tight-fitting lid, heat the olive oil over moderately high heat. Add the rabbit and, turning frequently, brown the pieces on all sides. Stir in the onions, carrots, celeriac, garlic, mushrooms, and sage with a wooden spoon. Reduce the heat to moderate and cook, partially covered, until the vegetables are softened, about 10 minutes. Add the tomato paste, mix well, sprinkle with the flour, and stir to blend.

Cover the casserole and place in the oven until the taste of the flour has cooked off, 8 to 10 minutes. Stir in the wine and braise in the oven for about 15 minutes. Add the chicken stock, season with salt and pepper, cover again, and braise until the rabbit is very tender, about 45 minutes.

Remove the rabbit to a large platter and set aside to cool slightly. Meanwhile, bring the cooking juices, with the vegetables, to a boil on top of the stove and boil until the juices have been reduced to 1 cup. Add the chopped tomato and season to taste with salt and pepper.

When the rabbit is cool enough to handle, shred the meat into large pieces with your fingers. (Don't bother removing the meat from the neck and rib cage.) Discard the

bones. Add the shredded meat to the sauce and stir in the butter. Mix well and reduce the heat to very low while the pasta cooks.

Bring a large pot of salted water to a boil and cook the pasta according to package instructions. Drain the pasta and pour into a large, warmed serving bowl. Pour the rabbit and sauce over the pappardelle. Mix well and serve immediately, with the Parmesan cheese on the side.

SERVES 4.

OPPOSITE: *Roasted Black Sea Bass with Salsify.* ABOVE: *Braised Rabbit with Pappardelle.*

APPLE, APPLE, APPLE!

*10 medium McIntosh apples (5 to
   6 pounds)*
Juice of 1 lemon
½ cup granulated sugar
1 cup water
1 tablespoon confectioners' sugar

To prepare the sorbet, peel, core, and slice 7 of the apples. Place in a large mixing bowl and toss with half the lemon juice. Crush the apples in a juice extractor and reserve the pulp. In a small bowl, combine the apple juice with half of the granulated sugar. Pour the sweetened juice into the bowl of an electric sorbet maker and, following the manufacturer's instructions, freeze until it is firm. Remove from the machine and keep frozen until ready to serve. The sorbet can be made several days in advance.

To make the apple syrup, mix the reserved apple pulp with the water and the remaining lemon juice in a heavy, nonreactive saucepan. Add the remaining sugar and bring to a boil over high heat. Boil for 2 minutes, strain, and cool. Peel, core, and slice 2 of the remaining apples and cut into very thin slices. Add to the apple syrup.

To caramelize the remaining apple, preheat the oven to 325° F. Peel, core, and thinly slice the apple into 16 rings. Place the rings in a single layer on a large nonstick baking sheet. Bake the rings until lightly browned, about 10 minutes. Increase the oven temperature to broil. Sprinkle the rings with the confectioners' sugar and broil, watching carefully, until the apples are caramelized and glazed, 1 to 2 minutes. Turn the pan around often to ensure even coloring and do not let the apples burn. Cool the apples on the pan, then transfer the rings to an airtight container and freeze for at least 1 hour. The rings can be done 2 to 3 days in advance.

At least 30 minutes before serving, place individual round-bottom serving bowls in the freezer. When ready to serve, remove the sliced apples from the syrup and arrange like a flower on the bottom of each bowl, overlapping the slices from the edge of the bowl to the center. Add about 2 tablespoons of the apple syrup to each bowl. Place a scoop of the apple sorbet in the center. Decorate with the caramelized apple rings pushed lightly into the sorbet.

SERVES 4.

◆ ◆ ◆ ◆ ◆ ◆ ◆

TOP: *One of Chef Daniel Boulud's best-loved desserts—the cool and tart apple sorbet, served on a drizzle of apple syrup and topped with a crisp baked round of apple. So very unique.* ABOVE: *Everyone went home with a golden bag filled with gifts.*

OPPOSITE: *The magnificent table glittered with golden objects, from the charming French candles, to the place settings, to the gold-wrapped Hershey kisses scattered down the length of the table. The "Rich and Famous" table design by hostess Penny Baird, an interior decorator at Dessins, Inc., was a dazzling* tour de force!

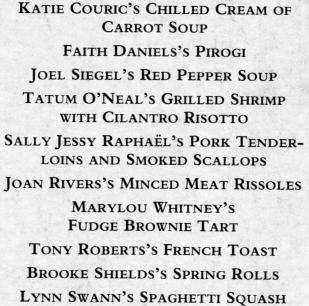

THE RECIPES

◆ ◆ ◆ ◆ ◆

KATIE COURIC'S CHILLED CREAM OF
CARROT SOUP

FAITH DANIELS'S PIROGI

JOEL SIEGEL'S RED PEPPER SOUP

TATUM O'NEAL'S GRILLED SHRIMP
WITH CILANTRO RISOTTO

SALLY JESSY RAPHAËL'S PORK TENDER-
LOINS AND SMOKED SCALLOPS

JOAN RIVERS'S MINCED MEAT RISSOLES

MARYLOU WHITNEY'S
FUDGE BROWNIE TART

TONY ROBERTS'S FRENCH TOAST

BROOKE SHIELDS'S SPRING ROLLS

LYNN SWANN'S SPAGHETTI SQUASH

CLOCKWISE FROM LOWER LEFT: *Katie Couric, Lynn Swann, Ivana Trump, Joan Rivers, Faith Daniels, Joel Siegel, and Brooke Shields.*

Celebrity Gourmet Cook-Off

❖ ❖ ❖ ❖ ❖ ❖ ❖ ❖ ❖ ❖

"A PANEL OF DISTINGUISHED JUDGES
CAME TO EVALUATE THE DISHES CREATED
BY THE CELEBRITY CHEFS. THEY NIBBLED,
THEY TASTED, THEY GRAZED, AND THEN
THEY PUT THEIR WIDE AND VARIED
CULINARY EXPERTISE TO WORK."

Twenty-one charity-minded celebrities donned their aprons to cook appetizer-size tastes of their favorite dishes. Mini-kitchens were constructed in the Terrace Room of the Plaza Hotel especially for the evening, and New York society turned out for the most delicious charity party of the season.

Beautiful Brooke Shields's Vietnamese Spring Rolls came with a choice of hot or spicy sauce. "They're so low in calories, you can eat several," she said, as she handed a taste to each guest.

Actor Tony Roberts focused on breakfast fare, assisted by a bejeweled Ivana Trump, who helped cook and serve. "My mother used to make this French Toast recipe at least once a week," said Tony. "It has everything you shouldn't eat and is very fattening."

Tatum O'Neal created a unique risotto with cilantro, cumin, and corn, topped with marinated and grilled shrimp.

"It only takes a minute to grill the shrimp," said Tatum, as she cooked them on a stovetop grill. The judges, going for her dish in a big way, awarded Tatum the Creative Cookery Award.

During the evening, Tatum shared her secrets for giving a great party. "A terrific party, just like a fabulous recipe, needs the best ingredients. In general, you need lots of great people, and food—*lots* of great food. A big, colorful pasta is my favorite dish if I'm entertaining more than six people."

Sally Jessy Raphaël cooked smoked scallops with pork tenderloin in mustard sauce and won the top prize of the evening, the Food and Wine Award for Overall Excellence.

Katie Couric, co-host of NBC's *Today* show, ladled small portions of her slightly sweet, pale orange Chilled Cream of Carrot Soup. "Naturally simple but elegant dishes that take only a few minutes to prepare are my favorite kinds of foods to serve," she said.

First prize for the Most Masterful Interpretation of a Classic Recipe went to Joan Rivers and her Minced Meat Rissoles.

The prize for the best recipe combining taste, appeal, and creativity landed in the kitchen of Marylou Vanderbilt Whitney—fundraiser and lifelong supporter of the arts—for her delectable, oh-so-chocolaty Fudge Brownie Tart.

Though not among the winners this year, two culinary devotees who won the attention of the patrons with their interesting vegetarian dishes were Lynn Swann and Joel Siegel.

When Faith Daniels tied on her apron, it was her mother's handed-down Pirogi recipe she chose to enter in the Celebrity Gourmet Cook-Off.

The celebrity chefs who spun their culinary magic and the caring New Yorkers who paid $750 per person to sample these taste treats raised over half a million dollars for the March of Dimes.

In a large stockpot or soup kettle, combine the carrots, onion, celery, half of the chicken stock, and salt. Bring to a boil over high heat, reduce the heat to moderate, cover, and simmer until the carrots are tender, about 15 minutes. Transfer to the bowl of a food processor, add the cayenne and rice, and process briefly to mix. With the motor running, pour in the remaining chicken stock and the cream and process until smooth. Transfer to a heat-proof bowl, cool to room temperature, cover, and refrigerate for at least 3 hours or overnight. Serve chilled, garnished with diced pimiento, if desired.

SERVES 4.

Katie Couric, LEFT, *co-host of the "Today" show, made a delectable Chilled Cream of Carrot Soup,* BOTTOM. OPPOSITE: *Faith Daniels, a "Today" regular, seemed comfortable cooking in her glamorous evening gown. Her pirogi were so tasty, many nibblers came back for seconds.*

KATIE COURIC'S CHILLED CREAM OF CARROT SOUP

4 medium carrots, scrubbed and sliced ¼-inch thick
1 medium onion, coarsely chopped
1 celery stalk, thickly sliced
1½ cups chicken stock
1 teaspoon salt
Pinch cayenne pepper
½ cup cooked white rice
¾ cup heavy cream
½ cup diced pimiento

FAITH DANIELS'S PIROGI

FOR THE DOUGH
4 cups all-purpose flour
½ teaspoon salt
2 eggs
1 teaspoon vegetable oil
¼ cup milk
¼ cup water

FOR THE FILLING
6 large all-purpose potatoes, peeled and cut into large cubes
½ pound Longhorn cheese, grated
½ cup (1 stick) unsalted butter, melted
½ teaspoon salt

To prepare the dough, combine the flour and salt in a large bowl. Make a well in the center and add the eggs, oil, milk, and water. Work the flour into the liquid, a small amount at a time, until the mixture forms a stiff dough. Turn out onto a large, floured work surface. Knead until the dough is smooth and shiny. Cover with a damp kitchen towel and set aside for 20 minutes.

Cut the dough into 4 equal pieces. Roll out one piece at a time to a thickness of about ⅛ inch, leaving the others covered. Cut the dough into 3-by-3-inch squares, then cover to prevent drying out. Continue with the other pieces.

To prepare the filling, place the potatoes in a large pot and cover with cold, salted water. Bring to a boil over high heat,

reduce the heat to moderate, and cook until tender, about 25 minutes. Drain and work through a food mill or ricer. While the potatoes are still hot, blend in the cheese, butter, and salt.

To assemble the pirogi, place about 1 teaspoon of the potato mixture in the center of each square of dough. Fold in half diagonally and crimp the edges closed with the tines of a fork dipped in cold water.

Bring a large pot of salted water to a boil. Add the pirogi and boil until they float to the surface, about 15 minutes. Drain the pirogi in a colander, then place in a mixing bowl and toss with butter. Transfer to a platter and serve immediately.

MAKES ABOUT 4 DOZEN PIROGI.

JOEL SIEGEL'S RED PEPPER SOUP

4 red bell peppers (about 2 pounds)
2 tablespoons (¼ stick) unsalted butter
2 pounds (1 bunch) leeks, trimmed, cleaned, and thinly sliced
2 tablespoons all-purpose flour
Salt and freshly ground pepper
4 cups chicken stock
1 cup rosé wine
2 cups heavy cream

Preheat the broiler. Place the peppers on a broiling pan and position about 4 inches from the source of heat, turning the peppers frequently, until they are charred all over. Transfer to a paper bag and tightly seal closed. Let steam in the bag for 30 minutes. Remove from the bag and peel. Cut in half and remove seeds and membranes. Julienne and set aside.

In a heavy stockpot or soup kettle, melt the butter over moderate heat. Add the leeks and cook until softened but not browned, about 5 minutes, stirring frequently. Blend in the flour, and add salt and pepper to taste. Add the strips of peppers, chicken stock, and wine. Increase the heat to high and bring to a boil, then reduce the heat to moderate and simmer for an hour.

Puree the soup in a food processor in several batches. Return to the pot and bring to a simmer over moderate heat. Whip the cream until it forms soft peaks. Gently fold into the soup and heat through. Serve in warmed bowls.

SERVES 6 TO 8.

◆ ◆ ◆ ◆ ◆ ◆ ◆

ABOVE: *Joel Siegel, film critic for ABC Television, created a Red Pepper Soup that was, he said, "so simple to make even I could do it."*

OPPOSITE: *Academy Award–winning actress Tatum O'Neal won the Creative Cookery Award for her shrimp and risotto dish.*

TATUM O'NEAL'S GRILLED SHRIMP WITH CILANTRO RISOTTO

FOR THE SHRIMP
1 cup chicken stock
2 tablespoons red wine vinegar
¼ cup freshly squeezed lemon juice
¼ cup freshly squeezed orange juice
¼ cup brown sugar, packed
1 teaspoon salt
½ teaspoon paprika
2 teaspoons freshly ground pepper
2 teaspoons Dijon mustard
1 teaspoon ground cumin
2 teaspoons ground coriander
¼ small onion, thinly sliced
2 teaspoons olive oil
1½ pounds medium shrimp, peeled and deveined

FOR THE RISOTTO
6 cups chicken stock
3 tablespoons olive oil
1 small onion, thinly sliced
4 shallots, finely chopped
1 garlic clove, finely chopped
2 cups Arborio rice
1½ teaspoons ground cumin
1½ cups loosely packed fresh cilantro, finely chopped
2 medium ears of fresh corn, kernels scraped off the cob
3 tablespoons freshly grated Romano cheese
Salt and freshly ground pepper

To prepare the shrimp, combine the chicken stock, vinegar, lemon juice, orange juice, brown sugar, salt, paprika, pepper, mustard, cumin, coriander, onion, and olive oil in a large mixing bowl. Add the shrimp, toss to coat, cover, and marinate in the refrigerator for about 2 hours. Remove the shrimp from the marinade, pat dry, and grill over a charcoal fire or under a broiler until pink and firm, about 2 minutes per side. Set aside and keep warm.

To prepare the risotto, bring the chicken stock to a simmer in a saucepan. In another large saucepan, heat the oil over moderate heat. Add the onion, shallots, and garlic, and cook until softened, about 3 minutes. Add the rice and stir until the rice is completely coated.

Add the hot chicken stock to the rice mixture, ½ cup at a time, stirring until the liquid is absorbed. Proceed in the same manner until all the stock has been absorbed and the rice is tender, 20 to 25 minutes. Stir in the cumin, cilantro, corn, cheese, and salt and pepper to taste.

Transfer to a serving bowl and top with the shrimp.

SERVES 4.

SALLY JESSY RAPHAËL'S PORK TENDERLOINS AND SMOKED SCALLOPS

1 cup freshly squeezed orange juice
½ cup freshly squeezed lime juice
1 cup sesame oil
6 to 8 garlic cloves, crushed
½ teaspoon freshly ground pepper
½ cup fresh chopped cilantro
2 bay leaves, crumbled
½ tablespoon sugar
2 tablespoons teriyaki sauce
3 tablespoons hoisin sauce
¼ teaspoon red pepper flakes
4 pork tenderloins, about 1 pound
    each, cut in half lengthwise on
    the bias

6 cups heavy cream
2 cups veal demiglace (see note)
6 tablespoons Creole mustard
Salt and freshly ground pepper
¼ to ½ cup peanut oil
2 cups clarified butter
2½ pounds smoked scallops
2½ tablespoons fresh chopped
    cilantro
2 tablespoons freshly squeezed lime
    juice
½ cup roasted sesame seeds
1 8½-ounce tin golden caviar
1 cup sour cream
8 sprigs fresh cilantro
2 ripe papayas, cut into wedges
8 fresh figs, quartered
4 limes, quartered
8 fresh edible flowers or fresh
    orchids

First, marinate the pork. Combine the orange juice, lime juice, sesame oil, garlic, pepper, cilantro, bay leaves, sugar, teriyaki sauce, hoisin sauce, and red pepper flakes in a ceramic or glass baking dish. Mix well. Add the pork, cover with plastic wrap, and refrigerate overnight, turning several times.

Next, prepare the mustard sauce. Over high heat, bring the cream to a full boil in a large, heavy saucepan. Reduce the cream until thick enough to coat the back of a wooden spoon. Whisk in the *demiglace*, add the mustard, and remove from the heat. Strain through a fine mesh strainer and keep warm.

Just before serving, remove the meat from the marinade and pat dry. Season with salt and pepper to taste. Heat the peanut oil in a large sauté pan over moderately high heat. Sauté (about 2 minutes per side for medium rare). Cover and keep warm.

In a separate skillet, heat the clarified butter over moderately high heat. Add the scallops, cilantro, and lime juice and heat just to warm through (since the scallops are already cooked). Remove from the heat and keep warm.

Spoon some of the mustard sauce on 8 serving plates. Top with the pork and scallops, fanned out on opposite sides on each plate. Sprinkle a bit of roasted sesame seeds on the

pork and some golden caviar on the scallops. Garnish each plate with a dollop of sour cream crowned with a sprig of cilantro. Border the left side of each plate with a papaya wedge and a fresh fig, and the right with a wedge of lime. Place an edible flower or fresh orchid in the center.

SERVES 8.

NOTE: *Demiglace* is a rich, concentrated reduction of veal stock. It is available from some mail-order sources and is often found in specialty food stores. Consult a classic French cookbook for directions on making your own.

OPPOSITE: *In addition to hosting her top-rated daily television program, Sally Jessy Raphaël is familiar with the kitchen.* ABOVE: *The Pork Tenderloins and Smoked Scallops, served with mustard sauce, won the Food and Wine Award for Overall Excellence. The recipe was created by Allison Vladimir, a graduate chef of the Culinary Institute of America, and Sally's daughter.*

JOAN RIVERS'S MINCED MEAT RISSOLES

Vegetable oil for frying
2 pounds ground beef
2 medium onions, grated
2 eggs
1 cup olive oil
2 1-inch-thick slices of day-old French bread
2 tablespoons chopped fresh parsley
1 garlic clove, minced
Salt and freshly ground pepper
Flour

Pour about a 1-inch layer of vegetable oil in a large frying pan or skillet. Combine the beef, onions, eggs, and olive oil in a large mixing bowl. Soak the bread briefly in water, squeeze out the moisture, and add to the bowl. Add the parsley and garlic, season with salt and pepper to taste, and blend thoroughly. Make 2-to-3-inch round shapes and flatten by hand to form patties about ½-inch thick. Lightly dredge the patties in flour and shake off the excess. Heat the oil to very hot but not smoking. Cook the patties until well browned, 1 to 2 minutes per side. Serve immediately.

MAKES 16 MEATBALLS.

◆ ◆ ◆ ◆ ◆ ◆ ◆

Marylou Vanderbilt Whitney, ABOVE, *prepared a dense, rich, divine Fudge Brownie Tart,* OPPOSITE TOP. OPPOSITE, CENTER: *Tony Roberts's great French Toast begins with challah bread slices.* OPPOSITE, BOTTOM: *Ivana Trump lent Tony Roberts a hand in the kitchen.*

Joan Rivers, ABOVE, *made Minced Meat Rissoles,* TOP.

MARYLOU WHITNEY'S FUDGE BROWNIE TART

¼ pound (1 stick) unsalted butter
½ cup brown sugar, packed
¼ cup sugar
9 ounces bittersweet chocolate,
  chopped
1 ounce unsweetened chocolate,
  chopped
2 eggs
1½ teaspoons vanilla extract
½ cup all-purpose flour
⅛ teaspoon salt
½ cup coarsely chopped walnuts
1 tablespoon orange liqueur
½ cup chocolate chips

Preheat the oven to 350° F. Butter and flour a 10-inch tart pan with a removable bottom.

In a medium saucepan over moderate heat, combine the butter and the sugars. Cook, stirring constantly, until the butter is melted.

In the bowl of a food processor, combine the bittersweet and unsweetened chocolate and process until finely chopped, 15 to 20 seconds. Add the hot butter-sugar mixture and process for 15 more seconds. Scrape the sides of the bowl and add the eggs and vanilla. Process to combine, about 10 seconds. Add the flour, salt, walnuts, and orange liqueur. Pulse briefly, just to mix.

Spread the batter evenly into the prepared pan and sprinkle the top with chocolate chips. Bake 25 to 30 minutes; a toothpick inserted near the center will come out moist. Do not overbake. Remove the sides of the pan and cool on a wire rack. Cut into wedges and serve.

SERVES 6 TO 8.

♦ ♦ ♦ ♦ ♦ ♦ ♦

TONY ROBERTS'S FRENCH TOAST

2 tablespoons sugar
2 tablespoons ground cinnamon
2 eggs
¾ cup milk
4 1-inch-thick slices stale challah
  bread
2 tablespoons unsalted butter
2 tablespoons vegetable oil
Maple syrup
Butter

In a medium, shallow bowl, mix the sugar, cinnamon, eggs, and milk well. Dip the slices of bread in the mixture to coat lightly.

In a large skillet, melt the butter and oil over high heat. Fry the coated bread until golden brown and crispy, turning once. Drain on paper towels and serve with maple syrup and butter.

SERVES 2.

BROOKE SHIELDS'S SPRING ROLLS

1 pound small shrimp, peeled and deveined
24 rice papers (see note)
24 large Boston lettuce leaves, washed and dried
1 pound fresh bean sprouts
48 to 50 fresh mint leaves
2 to 3 tablespoons vegetable oil
1 garlic clove, minced
½ cup plum sauce (see note)
1 tablespoon water
1 tablespoon honey
½ cup roasted peanuts, finely chopped

Bring a large pot of salted water to a boil. Add the shrimp, bring back to a boil, then drain immediately in a colander. Set aside to cool, then cut each shrimp in half.

Prepare the rice papers according to package directions. When they are softened, individually lay out flat on a large work surface. In the center of each paper, place four shrimp halves, a lettuce leaf, a large pinch of bean sprouts, and three mint leaves. Fold the paper over the filling and roll to form a cylinder that measures 1½ inches wide by 2 inches long.

To prepare the sauce, heat the vegetable oil in a small skillet. Add the garlic and cook over moderate heat until softened but not brown, about 1 minute. Add the plum sauce and water, reduce the heat to low, and cook until the flavors have blended, about 3 minutes. Stir in the honey and peanuts.

Cut the spring rolls in half and serve with the sauce on the side.

MAKES 48 SPRING ROLLS.

NOTE: Rice papers and plum sauce are available in Oriental or specialty food stores. Thin, edible rice papers are made from white rice flour. They usually come in packages of 12.

LYNN SWANN'S SPAGHETTI SQUASH

2 spaghetti squash, halved and
    seeded
2 tablespoons olive oil
2 green peppers, seeded and
    julienned
2 red peppers, seeded and julienned
1 4-ounce bottle sun-dried tomatoes
    packed in olive oil, drained
2 garlic cloves, minced
¼ cup chopped fresh basil
1 tablespoon fresh thyme, chopped
¼ pound French, Greek, or
    Italian black olives, pitted and
    coarsely chopped
¼ cup freshly grated Parmesan
    cheese

In 2 large pots fitted with colanders, add a 1-inch depth of water. Over moderately high heat, steam the squash until tender, about 20 minutes.

Meanwhile, heat the olive oil in a large sauté pan. Sauté the peppers, tomatoes, garlic, basil, thyme, and olives briefly over high heat, then reduce the heat to moderate and cook until the peppers are tender, about 10 minutes, stirring often.

Scoop out the contents of the squash and add to the sauté pan. Toss and stir to heat through. Transfer to a large serving bowl and serve at once, topped with cheese.

SERVES 8.

OPPOSITE, TOP LEFT: *All the ingredients are very fresh—like a rolled salad.* OPPOSITE, TOP RIGHT: *Brooke Shields with a Plaza Hotel chef.* OPPOSITE, BOTTOM: *Brooke likes to serve her Spring Rolls as appetizers or as a light lunch.* ABOVE: *Lynn Swann, assisted by a Plaza Hotel chef, created a colorful Spaghetti Squash that hit the spot with vegetarians.* LEFT: *Elegant attire was* de rigueur *at the March of Dimes Celebrity Cook-Off Benefit.*

The Cannes Film Festival

◆ ◆ ◆ ◆ ◆ ◆ ◆ ◆ ◆ ◆

"ROBERT DE NIRO'S PARTY WAS THE MOST
COVETED INVITATION AT THE FESTIVAL,"
SAID PATRICK TERRAIL, PARTY CONSULTANT.

"You haven't lived until you've seen Cannes during the film festival—there's nothing like it. At four in the morning the streets are packed with people and lined with limos and Rolls-Royces. It's so crazy, people fight to get a seat in one of the movie theaters," said Terrail.

Once a year, Hollywood and the international film world take up temporary residence in the South of France. For seven glamorous days, they schmooze, applaud a new crop of films, see-and-be-seen, and have a great time indulging in France's best foods and wines. And the parties! Invitations to the season's hottest are a must to determine one's status in the industry.

Robert De Niro, the star of *Guilty by Suspicion*, one of 1991's top films, also won the Commandeur des Arts et Lettres, France's coveted award for creative achievement. A lavish party was given for him by Odyssey Films. Odyssey knew only one man could handle this party-planning job—Patrick Ter-

> ## THE MENU
> ◆ ◆ ◆ ◆ ◆ ◆ ◆
> TERRINE OF FOIE GRAS
> JOHN DORY FILLETS AND LANGOUSTINES
> MEDALLIONS OF BEEF
> CELERIAC SLICES WITH ARTICHOKE
> CHOCOLATE SPONGE CAKE

OPPOSITE: *Once a year, when Hollywood invades the South of France, it's no secret why they're there. The Carlton Hotel became a backdrop for favorite films like* Thelma and Louise, *and last summer's "hottest" film,* Backdraft.

rail, a fifth-generation restaurateur and native of France who created the L.A. eatery Ma Maison.

A whole raft of film friends and supporters were invited to this "A" list soiree. Guests included Whoopi Goldberg, as well as studio heads, producers, and France's minister of culture, Jack Lang.

Terrail knows that working the festival is like doing no other party in the world. The invitations cannot be sent out until four days before the party because no one knows who's in town, and so the invitations all have to be hand-delivered to the hotels. "Very few know how to *work* Cannes, but I know my way around—the kitchens, the tiny streets, *and* I speak French," said Patrick Terrail.

One thing Odyssey and Terrail agreed upon was that De Niro's would be *the* party of Cannes 1991, from appetizers to after-dinner drinks. It was—just ask the elusive Mr. De Niro.

TERRINE OF FOIE GRAS

FOR THE TERRINE

½ pound smoked duck breast,
   sliced paper thin (magret de
   canard)
1 whole fresh foie gras (about 1½
   pounds), uncooked
Salt and freshly ground pepper

FOR THE CAULIFLOWER *TOURTE*

½ pound puff pastry
1 small head cauliflower (about
   1½ pounds)
1 tablespoon chopped fresh parsley
1 small truffle, finely chopped
1 egg yolk, beaten with 1 teaspoon
   water

FOR THE GARNISH

Chopped aspic
Several leaves of fresh purslane
3 to 4 legs of confit de canard,
   removed from the bone and cut
   into long, thin strips (see note)
Freshly ground pepper

To prepare the terrine, preheat
the oven to 250° F.

In a 5-cup terrine mold with
a heavy lid, lay strips of the
duck breast on the bottom and
sides. Line the mold com-
pletely, overlapping the strips
and allowing them to overhang
the edges.

Gently cut down the center
of the foie gras and remove the
tough nerves. Season lightly
with salt and pepper. Carefully
close and place in the center of
the terrine. Fold the strips of
duck breast over the foie gras.

Fit the lid on the terrine to firmly seal.

Bring a kettle of water to a boil. Place the terrine in a deep baking pan and add enough boiling water to cover half of the mold. Bake until the internal temperature reaches 115° F to 120° F, about 20 minutes. (Test the temperature by lifting the lid and inserting a thin-needled, quick-reading thermometer for accuracy.) Remove the terrine from the water bath and cool on a rack to room temperature. Refrigerate until ready to serve.

To prepare the cauliflower *tourte,* preheat the oven to 425° F and lightly butter a baking sheet.

Roll out the pastry to a ¼-inch thickness. Cut out six 3-inch circles. Transfer to a baking sheet, cover loosely with plastic wrap, and refrigerate.

Wash and trim the cauliflower into tiny flowerets. Bring a large saucepan of salted water to a boil, and cook the flowerets until they are soft but not mushy, about 3 minutes. Drain well. Place 2 to 3 on one side of each circle of dough. Top with a pinch of parsley and a sprinkling of truffle.

Lightly brush the edges of the dough with the egg wash. Fold the dough over and crimp the edges with a fork to seal. Prick the top with a fork to allow steam to escape. Place on the prepared baking sheet.

Brush each *tourte* with more egg wash and bake until golden brown, 15 to 20 minutes. Keep warm until ready to serve.

To assemble the dish, cut six ½-inch-thick slices from the terrine using a warm knife. Arrange on individual serving plates and garnish with chopped aspic and leaves of purslane. Serve with the warm *tourtes,* long, thin strips of *confit,* and a sprinkling of freshly ground pepper. The remaining terrine will keep in the refrigerator for 3 to 5 days.

SERVES 6 TO 8.

NOTE: *Confit* is duck or goose that has been cooked and preserved in its own fat. Patrick Terrail's recipe calls for *confit* of duck *breasts,* which is difficult to find this side of the Atlantic. While the results are somewhat less attractive, smoked duck breasts or *confit* of duck *legs* provide good results. Both of these are available in specialty food stores and through mail-order sources.

If you would like to prepare your own *confit,* consult the poultry section of a classic French cookbook.

Long before the winners were honored with the coveted Palme d'Or awards, one party was on the drawing board. Jack Lang, France's Minister of Culture, and Robert De Niro were the honored guests at a soiree held in the Carlton Hotel's elegant dining room, OPPOSITE. *Only party planner and restaurateur Patrick Terrail could have made the occasion so special. Patrick spent most of the evening in the kitchen, dressed in his tux, making sure the courses got to the table at exactly the right moment. The Terrine of Foie Gras,* ABOVE, *was served with duck breasts and a cauliflower tourte.*

Course after course, guests were amazed by Terrail's use of France's best ingredients. John Dory Fillets and Langoustines, TOP, and Medallions of Beef, ABOVE, were but two dishes in this most creative menu. OPPOSITE, TOP: Terrail and his staff gather just minutes before the guests arrive. OPPOSITE, CENTER: Terrail greets guest and friend Whoopi Goldberg. OPPOSITE, BOTTOM: The guest of honor, Robert De Niro.

JOHN DORY FILLETS AND LANGOUSTINES

6 very small, young fennel bulbs, about ¼ pound each
2 tablespoons olive oil
Juice of 1 lemon
1 teaspoon coriander seeds
Salt and freshly ground pepper
1 teaspoon saffron threads
2 tablespoons unsalted butter
6 fillets John Dory, ¼ to ½ pound each
12 small langoustine tails, peeled and trimmed
Italian (flat-leaf) parsley sprigs
Fresh cilantro leaves

Preheat the oven to 350° F.

Cut the fennel bulbs in half lengthwise and place them in a baking dish large enough to hold them in one layer. Drizzle with olive oil and sprinkle with lemon juice and coriander seeds. Season to taste with salt and pepper. Cover loosely with foil and bake until the bulbs are softened, 30 to 45 minutes. When they are done, add the saffron, gently stirring to mix. Remove the fennel to a bowl, set aside, and keep warm. Reserve the cooking liquid.

Melt the butter in a large sauté pan. Season the fish with salt and pepper to taste. Over moderately high heat, sauté the fillets until they are firm to the touch and cooked through, about 2 minutes per side. Transfer to individual warmed dinner plates and cover with foil. Place the langoustine tails in the pan and cook over moderately high heat until pink and warmed through, about 2 minutes. Remove to the dinner plates and re-cover with the foil.

Pour the cooking liquid from the fennel into the sauté pan. (You should have about 1 cup liquid; add water if necessary.) Over high heat, boil until the liquid is reduced by half, whisking constantly.

Spoon a small amount of the sauce over the fish and langoustine. Garnish with sprigs of parsley and cilantro. Serve at once with the fennel on the side.

SERVES 6.

◆ ◆ ◆ ◆ ◆ ◆ ◆

MEDALLIONS OF BEEF

1 tablespoon coarsely crushed black peppercorns
6 fillets of beef tenderloin, 1 to 2 inches thick, 4 to 6 ounces each
3 tablespoons unsalted butter
2 tablespoons cognac
½ cup beef stock
Salt and freshly ground pepper

Divide the pepper evenly among the fillets. Using the heel of the hand, gently press the pepper into the meat.

In a large sauté pan, melt 2 tablespoons of the butter over moderately high heat. Sauté the fillets to taste (about 5 minutes on each side for rare). Remove to a warm platter and keep warm.

Pour off the fat from the pan. Carefully add the cognac and light with a match. Allow the flame to subside, then add the beef stock. Increase the heat to high and reduce the mixture until it is thick and syrupy, about 2 minutes. Lower the heat and swirl in the remaining tablespoon of butter. Season to taste with salt and pepper. Spoon a small amount of sauce over each fillet and serve at once.

SERVES 6.

◆ ◆ ◆ ◆ ◆ ◆ ◆

CELERIAC SLICES WITH ARTICHOKE

1 large celeriac (about ¾ pound)
6 artichokes (about ½ pound each)
2 tablespoons unsalted butter
Salt and freshly ground black
*   pepper to taste*

Peel the celeriac and rinse well. Cut in half. With the cut side down, use a sharp knife to cut paper-thin slices from the thickest part of the root. Choose six of the largest, thin-

nest slices. Reserve the remaining celeriac for another use.

Bring a large pot of salted water to a rapid boil. Add the slices to the water, cooking until flexible but still firm, about 2 minutes. Drain and rinse under cold water to stop the cooking process. Drain and pat dry with paper towels.

Remove all the leaves from the artichokes. Cut away the tough bottom part until only the edible heart remains. Trim, rinse well, and slice the heart thinly. In a medium sauté pan over moderately high heat, melt 1 tablespoon of the butter. Add the artichoke slices and sauté until soft, about 7 to 10 minutes. Season to taste with salt and pepper.

Place a small amount of the cooked artichoke hearts in the center of each slice of celeriac. Fold the top over or roll the celeriac and brush the outside with the remaining tablespoon of butter. Keep warm until ready to serve.

SERVES 6.

◆ ◆ ◆ ◆ ◆ ◆ ◆

CHOCOLATE SPONGE CAKE

FOR THE CAKE
4 large eggs
Pinch salt
⅔ cup sugar
2 tablespoons unsweetened cocoa powder
¾ cup all-purpose flour
4 tablespoons (½ stick) unsalted butter, melted and cooled

FOR THE GANACHE
1 cup heavy cream
10 ounces semisweet chocolate, finely chopped
2 tablespoons cognac

FOR THE WINE SAUCE
2 cups strong, dry red wine
½ cup sugar

FOR THE GARNISH
1 12-ounce jar brandied cherries
½ cup heavy cream
2 ounces semisweet chocolate squares

To prepare the cake, first preheat the oven to 350° F. Butter 6 individual stainless steel baking rings that measure 3½ inches in diameter and 2½ inches deep. Place on a buttered baking sheet. Set aside.

In the top of a double boiler over hot but not boiling water, beat the eggs and a pinch of salt; add the sugar and beat until the mixture is light and thick enough to leave a ribbon when the beater is lifted, about 10 minutes. Remove from the heat, add the cocoa, and continue beating until cool.

Sift the flour into the batter a tablespoon or two at a time, and fold in with a spatula as gently as possible. Fold in the butter.

Ladle the batter into the rings. Bake until the cakes shrink slightly from the edges and the tops spring back when lightly pressed, 18 to 20 minutes. Run a knife around the edges of the cake to loosen, and turn out onto a rack to

cool. Clean the rings, butter again, and set aside for assembling the dessert.

To prepare the *ganache,* bring 1 cup of cream to a boil in a small, heavy saucepan over moderately high heat. Remove from the heat and add the chocolate. Transfer the mixture to a large mixing bowl. When cool, beat in the cognac with an electric mixer until the mixture has doubled in volume and holds its shape when beaters are lifted, about 7 to 10 minutes. If the *ganache* is not used immediately, cover it with plastic wrap and refrigerate. Warm over tepid water and gently stir to blend before spreading.

To prepare the wine sauce, bring the wine to a boil over moderately high heat in a nonreactive medium saucepan. Stir in the sugar. Let the mixture reduce by half or until it is thick and syrupy (do not stir). Let cool, then cover and refrigerate for 4 hours or overnight before assembling the dessert.

When ready to assemble the cake, drain the cherries and reserve their juice. Remove the pits and coarsely chop the fruit.

With a serrated knife, slice each cake horizontally into five layers. Brush the top of each slice with the juices from the brandied cherries.

Just before using, whip a half cup of cream until it is very stiff. Gently fold into the *ganache*.

Place a slice of cake in each of the baking rings. Spread about 1 tablespoon of the *ganache* filling and sprinkle with a few of the cherries. Continue until each ring is filled. Refrigerate for 4 hours or overnight.

To serve, spoon a small amount of wine sauce onto individual dessert plates. Tilt the plate to obtain a thin, even pool. Carefully unmold the cakes and place in the center of the sauce.

Using a vegetable peeler, shave thin curls of chocolate off the squares and decorate the cake tops. Serve at once.

SERVES 6.

OPPOSITE: *The pastry chef at the Carlton Hotel demonstrates the preparation of Chocolate Sponge Cake with cherries and wine sauce,* ABOVE. *You'll want to serve this dessert at a Cannes Film Festival party of your own.*

Prince and Princess Michael of Kent

❖ ❖ ❖ ❖ ❖ ❖ ❖ ❖ ❖ ❖ ❖

"Visiting crowned heads are second
nature in New Orleans—but their
Royal Highnesses Prince and Princess
Michael of Kent gave the collective
tiara an extra twinkle."

Prince and Princess Michael of Kent were introduced to New Orleans–style cuisine at a gala with a Mardi Gras theme at London's Claridge House. Chef Kevin Graham of the five-star Windsor Court Hotel in New Orleans brought the ingredients with him from Louisiana to create an authentic meal.

The Kents fell in love with the mood and festivities, as well as with the food. So, naturally, when they were invited by the English-Speaking Union in New Orleans to attend three days of fund-raising activities, they happily accepted.

The Windsor Court Hotel became their home away from home. Here, Chef Graham created another culinary extravaganza in their honor, in the hotel's private dining room, elegantly trimmed in pink and gold. He added a touch of Mardi Gras gaiety to the presentation of each course. The Prince and Princess were again amused and delighted with his *tour-de-force* dinner.

> ## THE MENU
> ❖ ❖ ❖ ❖ ❖ ❖ ❖
> **Quail with Port Sauce**
> **Sugar Cane Pasta**
> **Chocolate Breathless**
> **New Orleans Pralines**
> **Harlequin Masks**

OPPOSITE: *Theirs is a love story: Prince Michael of Kent was born into the Windsor family; Princess Michael is Austrian. Neither religion nor nationality could keep them apart. Today, they reside in London.*

Once the fund-raising activities began, the Kents spent several whirlwind days and nights making personal appearances for the charity. At one grand soiree, themed "A Royal Affair," Her Royal Highness wore a diamond-and-pearl-encrusted tiara—and looked very much like a fairy-tale princess. Everyone present—including Mayor Sidney Barthelemay, and his wife, Mickey—danced the night away, and those who had the chance to dance with the royals considered it a once-in-a-lifetime experience.

"The people of New Orleans may well tell their children one day of the time they met a real princess and prince!" Princess Michael later said.

"In my own small way, I want to be able to change the lives of those whose lives touch mine," said the Princess, referring to her charity work. "I want to let in a little chink of light, a little compassion wherever I can."

QUAIL WITH PORT SAUCE

1½ cups fresh bread crumbs
1½ tablespoons dried thyme
1½ tablespoons dried rosemary
Pinch cayenne pepper
⅓ cup all-purpose flour
3 eggs
3 tablespoons water
12 boneless quail
⅓ cup whole grain mustard
1 cup vegetable oil
⅓ cup clarified butter
3 shallots, finely chopped
1 teaspoon ground coriander
1½ cups demiglace (see note)
¾ cup port
⅓ cup honey
Salt and freshly ground pepper
*1 bunch watercress, washed and
    dried*

In a wide, shallow bowl, combine the bread crumbs, thyme, rosemary, and cayenne. Place the flour in a similar bowl. In a large bowl, mix the eggs and water until well blended. Brush the quail with the mustard, then dust lightly with flour. Dip the coated quail in the egg wash, then dredge through the bread crumbs.

Heat the oil in a large sauté pan over moderately high heat. Sauté the quail until golden brown, about 2 minutes per side. Remove from the pan, drain on paper towels, and keep warm.

Heat the clarified butter in a saucepan over moderate heat. When it is hot, add the shallots and the coriander. Sauté until the shallots are softened, about 2 minutes. Add the *demiglace*, port, and honey. Bring the sauce to a slow boil and cook until it is thick enough to coat the back of a wooden spoon, about 5 minutes. Season with salt and pepper, to taste.

Spoon equal portions of the sauce onto four warmed serving plates. Arrange two quail on each plate and garnish with the watercress.

SERVES 6.

NOTE: *Demiglace* is a rich, concentrated reduction of veal stock. It is available from some mail-order sources and is often found in specialty food stores. Consult a classic French cookbook for directions on making your own.

◆ ◆ ◆ ◆ ◆ ◆ ◆

Chef Kevin Graham created a spectacular meal to set before the Prince and Princess. Sugar Cane Pasta and Quail with Port Sauce are pictured with one of the Windsor Court Hotel's many precious objects, a nineteenth-century English tureen.

SUGAR CANE PASTA

6 sheets fresh pasta, about 6 inches
    long and 4 to 5 inches wide
¼ pound medium shrimp, peeled
    and deveined
1 egg white
Pinch salt
¼ cup heavy cream
Pinch cayenne pepper
⅛ teaspoon freshly ground pepper
2 tablespoons snipped chives
1 tablespoon unsalted butter
1 shallot, finely chopped
1 garlic clove, finely chopped
6 ounces cooked crawfish tails,
    chopped
1 large egg, beaten

Bring a large pot of salted water to a boil. Cook the pasta sheets until just soft, 3 to 5 minutes. Drain in a colander and reserve in flat layers between damp cloths.

Combine the shrimp and egg white in the bowl of a food processor. Add the salt and process until very smooth. Add the cream, cayenne, pepper, and chives. Blend until smooth, about 10 seconds. Transfer to a bowl, cover, and chill for at least 2 hours or overnight.

Melt the butter in a large sauté pan over moderately high heat. Add the shallots and garlic, and cook until the shallots are tender, about 2 minutes. Stir in the crawfish tails, heat through for 1 to 2 minutes, and remove from the heat. Cool to room temperature, then fold the crawfish mixture into the shrimp puree. Spoon into a pastry bag fitted with a plain tube with a 1-inch opening.

Arrange the pasta sheets lengthwise on a flat work surface. Pipe a line of filling down the center of each sheet. Lightly brush the pasta sheet and the filling with the beaten egg.

With scissors or a sharp knife, make about 13 cuts about ½ inch apart, at an angle down both sides of the line of filling to resemble chevrons. Do not cut through the filling. As though making a braid, fold the first top right strip over the filling, letting it cross at an angle. Bring the top left strip over the right strip. Continue crisscrossing strips to the bottom of each pasta sheet.

Meanwhile, bring salt water to a boil in a casserole or baking dish large enough to hold pasta flat. Ease the stuffed pasta pieces, a few at a time, and without crowding, into the pan and cook over moderate heat until the pasta is tender, 3 to 5 minutes. Remove from the water with a slotted spoon and drain on a cloth towel. Repeat the process for the remaining pasta. Transfer to serving plates and serve with a butter or tomato sauce.

SERVES 6.

TOP: *The Kents were presented with keys to the city of New Orleans and made honorary citizens.* MIDDLE: *Princess Michael's dance card was filled with the names of many adoring partners.* BOTTOM: *The Kents and their hosts shared this extraordinary meal in the private dining room of the Windsor Court.*

CHOCOLATE BREATHLESS

½ pound semisweet chocolate, coarsely chopped
1½ cups heavy cream
2 eggs, separated
2 tablespoons water
2 tablespoons dark rum
2 tablespoons plus ⅓ cup sugar
4 egg whites
½ heaping cup confectioners' sugar, plus 1 tablespoon
⅓ cup unsweetened cocoa powder

Place the chocolate in the top half of a double boiler set over hot but not boiling water. Stir occasionally until it has melted. Meanwhile, whip the cream until stiff peaks form. In a large mixing bowl, blend the 2 egg yolks, water, and rum thoroughly, then stir in the melted chocolate.

In a medium bowl, beat the 2 egg whites until foamy. Add 2 tablespoons of the sugar and continue to beat until stiff peaks form. Fold the beaten whites into the chocolate mixture, then fold in the whipped cream. Cover the mousse with plastic wrap and refrigerate while making the chocolate meringue. (The mousse can be made up to 2 days in advance.)

Preheat the oven to 150° F. In a large, deep mixing bowl, beat the 4 egg whites until foamy. Add the ⅓ cup sugar and continue to beat until stiff peaks form. Sift together the confectioners' sugar and cocoa, then fold gently into the meringue. Do not overmix. Spoon the mixture into a pastry bag fitted with a ½-inch plain tube.

Line a baking sheet with parchment or wax paper. Pipe 18 2-inch meringue circles about 1 inch high onto the sheet, and about an inch apart. Pipe long lines with the rest of the meringue. Using a wooden spoon to prop the oven door open about 1 inch, bake the meringue until firm, about 1½ hours. Remove from the oven and let cool on the baking sheet. (The meringue can be made a day in advance and stored in a dry, airtight container.)

When cooled, chop the meringue lines into ½-inch pieces and set aside. Place a meringue disc on a flat work surface and top with a ½-inch layer of chocolate mousse. Add another meringue disc, then another layer of mousse, and another layer of meringue. Frost the top and sides of the stack with mousse, then sprinkle chopped meringue pieces on top. Repeat the assembly with the remaining meringue discs.

To serve, place one Breathless on a dessert plate and dust the top lightly with confectioners' sugar.

SERVES 6.

NEW ORLEANS PRALINES

½ cup (1 stick) unsalted butter
1 cup heavy cream
2 cups granulated sugar
2¼ cups brown sugar, packed
1 pound pecan pieces, coarsely
  chopped

Spread sheets of wax paper on
2 large baking sheets. In a
heavy saucepan over high heat,
combine the butter, cream,
sugar, and brown sugar. Bring
to a boil, then stir in the pecans. Return the mixture to a
boil, then remove from heat.

Drop the praline mixture
from a soup spoon to make
1½-inch circles onto the wax
paper. The mixture will crys-
tallize rapidly, so work
quickly. Let the pralines harden
at room temperature for
6 hours, then store for up to
2 weeks in airtight containers.

MAKES ABOUT 5 DOZEN
PRALINES.

ABOVE: *The official portrait from the Kents' memorable visit to New Orleans was taken in the lobby of the Windsor Court Hotel.* LEFT: *The Windsor Court Hotel prides itself on a multimillion-dollar collection of museum-quality English antiques, including paintings, porcelain, and silver.*

ABOVE: *Kevin Graham adds a touch of Mardi Gras gaiety to every place setting at his award-winning restaurant, The Grill, in the Windsor Court Hotel.* OPPOSITE: *As a finale to the exquisite meal served to the Prince and Princess, trays of charming and delicious dessert tidbits were placed along the length of the table. Everyone had his own Harlequin Mask cookie. "To eat, or not to eat" —it's a tough question.*

HARLEQUIN MASKS

½ cup all-purpose flour
½ cup confectioners' sugar
4 egg whites
⅛ teaspoon cinnamon
½ teaspoon vanilla extract
1 teaspoon cocoa powder
Vegetable oil spray

Sift the flour and sugar into a large mixing bowl. With an electric hand mixer, beat in the egg whites, one at a time, until the mixture forms a smooth paste. Mix in the cinnamon and vanilla. Let the batter rest, covered, for 45 minutes at room temperature.

In a small bowl, mix 2 tablespoons of the batter with the cocoa. Transfer to a pastry bag fitted with a thin tip; set aside.

To make the mask-shaped stencil, draw a mask onto cardboard. Carefully cut the mask out with a sharp knife. Cover a baking sheet with parchment paper and spray lightly with vegetable oil spray. Lay the stencil on top of the parchment paper and trace out a pattern of the shape. With a spatula, spread a thin layer of batter onto the parchment paper within the pattern. Repeat the procedure to make 12 masks in all.

Preheat the oven to 375°F. Pipe a ½-inch band of the chocolate batter along the edge of each mask. With an up-and-down motion, draw a toothpick through the chocolate band to create a decorative effect resembling feathers. Bake the masks until golden, about 10 to 15 minutes.

While the masks are hot, peel them from the parchment paper and place each one on a large round canister to give it a curved shape. Allow the masks to cool on the canisters before handling. Keep them in an airtight container for up to 8 hours.

When ready to serve, prop each mask against a tall champagne or martini glass filled with ice cream or sorbet as desired.

MAKES ABOUT
12 DOZEN COOKIES.

Ernest and Tova Borgnine

◆ ◆ ◆ ◆ ◆ ◆ ◆ ◆ ◆ ◆ ◆

"YOU'RE ON BOARD THE *SEA GODDESS*,
YOU'RE WALKING WITH YOUR BEST GIRL AND
THE MOON IS ON THE WATER, AND YOU'VE
GOT THE EPITOME OF EVERYTHING THAT'S
SWELL IN LIFE . . . AND IT'S TIME FOR
LOVE."

"Let the fantasy trip begin! On behalf of the Cunard Line and the *Sea Goddess*, and Ernest and Tova Borgnine, welcome aboard! We want to extend to you our warmest wishes for the celebration of remarriage and reavowal of love. May this romantic fantasy adventure provide you a week of magical memories," wrote Tova Borgnine to the passengers joining them.

"If you don't happen to have your own private 360-foot yacht, the *Sea Goddess* is a perfect substitute," said Tova. "This is the ultimate Champagne-and-caviar cruise. Anything you want, day or night, is yours just by asking. And it's one of the most luxurious ships afloat."

What made this cruise so special were the twenty-six couples who renewed their marriage vows, plus one couple who married for the first time.

At the ceremony, the deck was adorned with the

THE MENU

◆ ◆ ◆ ◆ ◆ ◆ ◆

CAVIAR WITH CLASSIC GARNITURE
TRUFFLE CONSOMMÉ WITH PUFF PASTRY
POACHED SALMON ON SAFFRON SAUCE
TOVA'S WEDDING CAKE

OPPOSITE: *After eighteen happy years of marriage, Ernest and Tova Borgnine decided it was time to say "I do" all over again—only this time, it would be a ceremony they could only have dreamed about the first time around.*

---

most beautiful collection of dresses ever assembled on a cruise ship. Tova looked elegant in her Bob Mackie gown, and there was an abundance of white lace and ruffles. A ceremonial gazebo of flowers, constructed especially for the occasion, encircled the couples as they tearfully and enthusiastically reaffirmed their vows. "I do's" were exchanged, and everyone joined hands, repeating the promises as directed by Captain Eric Dahl.

Ernest had romance on his mind long before the *Sea Goddess* left port. He had asked Tova for her wedding ring prior to the ceremony so that when the time arrived he could slip it back on her finger. When Tova and Ernest reaffirmed their vows, out from his pocket came a wonderful, glittering *new* diamond ring. "There were no words to express the love in my heart over Ernie's romantic gesture," Tova said.

CAVIAR WITH CLASSIC GARNITURE

8 ounces chilled Beluga caviar
2 hard-cooked egg whites, finely
  chopped
2 hard-cooked egg yolks, finely
  chopped
½ small onion, finely chopped
4 lemon wedges
4 tablespoons sour cream

Arrange the caviar in the center of a large serving tray. Surround with small bowls of egg whites, egg yolks, onion, lemon, and sour cream. Serve with thin slices of buttered toast.

SERVES 4.

ABOVE: *Raul Rodriguez created the gazebo and assembled it on the deck of the* Sea Goddess *the morning of the ceremony. The world's premier float designer, Mr. Rodriguez is best known for his award-winning contributions to the annual Tournament of Roses parade.* RIGHT: *The* Sea Goddess, *in all her splendor.* OPPOSITE, TOP: *The brides and grooms were toasted at sunset, just seconds after the ceremony took place.* OPPOSITE, BOTTOM LEFT: *Couples stand together as Captain Dahl performs the ceremony.* OPPOSITE, BOTTOM RIGHT: *The wedding dinner was created by Tova and the Cunard Line's executive chef, Rudy Sodamin. Tova's only mandate: Watch the calories!*

TRUFFLE CONSOMMÉ WITH PUFF PASTRY

4 cups rich double veal or beef
consommé
2 ounces black truffles, cleaned and
chopped
¼ cup dry sherry
1 pound puff pastry
1 egg yolk
Pinch salt

Preheat the oven to 400° F. In a
large saucepan, combine the
consommé, truffles, and sherry.
Bring to a simmer over low
heat. Ladle into 4 small, heat-
proof bowls. Roll the pastry
out to about ⅛-inch thickness.
Cut out 4 6-inch circles and
place over the soup bowls to
cover. Score the pastry with
the tip of a sharp knife.

Lightly beat the egg yolk
with the salt. Brush the pastry
with a small amount of the egg
wash. Bake until the pastry is
puffed and golden brown,
about 20 minutes. Serve at
once.

SERVES 4.

POACHED SALMON ON SAFFRON SAUCE

4 boneless salmon steaks, 6 to 8
   ounces each
5 cups fish stock
½ teaspoon sea salt
1 bay leaf, crumbled
5 whole white peppercorns
1 cup dry white wine
2 shallots, finely chopped
1 cup heavy cream
6 tablespoons (¾ stick) unsalted
   butter, diced and chilled
1 teaspoon saffron threads
Salt and freshly ground pepper
12 large spinach leaves
4 teaspoons golden caviar

Place the salmon steaks in a sauté pan large enough to hold them in one layer. Pour in 4 cups of the fish stock over moderately low heat. Season with the sea salt, bay leaf, and peppercorns. Bring to a simmer, cover, and cook until the steaks are pale pink and firm to the touch, about 10 minutes. Remove to a plate and keep warm.

Meanwhile, prepare the saffron sauce. In a small, heavy saucepan, combine the wine, shallots, and the remaining cup of fish stock. Bring to a boil over high heat and reduce until only 2 tablespoons of liquid remain. Add the cream and boil over high heat until reduced by about half. Strain the sauce through a sieve and wipe out the pan. Return the sieved mixture to the pan. Working on and off the heat, whisk in the butter bit by bit until the

TOP: *On the* Sea Goddess, *there's always a beautiful view.* ABOVE: *Chef Freddy Napotnik and his first-rate kitchen staff.* RIGHT: *Some guests just can't stay away from the kitchen! Ernest is as comfortable in the galley as he is on deck.* OPPOSITE, TOP: *Tova was made honorary "godmother" of the* Sea Goddess—*an unbelievable honor.* OPPOSITE, BOTTOM: *In the* Sea Goddess's *dining room, the best silver and china don't gather any dust.*

sauce is thick and emulsified. Add the saffron and season with salt and pepper to taste. Set the sauce over a larger pot of barely simmering water until ready to serve.

In a large saucepan, bring a large amount of salted water to a boil. Add the spinach leaves, bring back to a boil, then drain immediately. Refresh the leaves under cold water and drain on paper towels.

Place 3 spinach leaves on each plate. Top with a salmon steak and surround with one fourth of the sauce. Garnish with 1 teaspoonful of the caviar. Serve at once.

SERVES 4.

Preheat the oven to 375° F. Butter a 9-inch round cake pan that measures 3 inches deep.

Grind the walnuts to a powder in a food processor. In a large mixing bowl, whisk the egg yolks with the sugar and water until foamy. Gently stir in ½ cup of nuts, flour, baking powder, and cornstarch just until blended.

In a clean bowl, whisk the egg whites until they form stiff peaks. Fold the whites into the batter and pour into the prepared pan. Bake until the cake springs back slightly when touched in the center, 40 to 50 minutes. Remove and cool on a wire rack.

When the cake is completely cooled, carefully cut in half horizontally with a serrated knife. Spread lingonberries on top of each layer.

Whip the cream until stiff. Fold in the rest of the nuts. Coat the top of one layer with the whipped cream. Place the other layer on top and completely cover the top and sides of the cake with whipped cream.

SERVES 8 TO 10.

TOVA'S WEDDING CAKE

1½ cups walnuts
6 eggs, separated
1½ cups confectioners' sugar
2 tablespoons warm water
½ cup all-purpose flour
1 teaspoon baking powder
¼ cup cornstarch
2 cups lingonberry preserves
3 cups heavy cream

Executive Chef Rudy Sodamin, ABOVE, *an Austrian-born culinary genius, is also an artist in his presentation and has published a book about turning food into art. The cake he created was even more magnificent than Tova had hoped. Each person was served a slice topped with a charming sugar swan,* LEFT.

Love was in the air! Tova and Ernest led the couples in celebrating their renewed vows.

F. Warrington and Eles Gillet

♦ ♦ ♦ ♦ ♦ ♦ ♦ ♦ ♦ ♦

"I START WITH A PARTICULAR MENU, AND
THEN CHANGE IT A DOZEN TIMES."

"I don't just wake up in the morning and decide to have twenty-two of our best friends over for dinner that night," stated Eles Gillet, doyenne of the Palm Beach party scene. "I start planning about six to eight weeks in advance to have a party like Warry's sixtieth-birthday dinner. The invitations usually go out three weeks in advance. At the height of the season in Palm Beach, the invitations have to be followed up with a call," Eles asserted.

To watch Eles Gillet, one would think throwing a large, lavish party required no special skill—the festivities simply unfold. While most of the Palm Beach set might start their party plans by calling a caterer, Eles consults her computer, where every detail—from the menu to the color of the tablecloths—of every party she's given in the last ten years is catalogued. (Before the computer every bit of information went into party diaries.) She researches everything: the guest list, the theme, the location (dining room, tent, or poolside, for starters), even the exact recipes (from one of the 24 volumes of cookbooks she's compiled). Many of the recipes are her own creations—Eles is one woman who knows her way around a kitchen, though she leaves much of the cooking to her chef, Dorothy, these days.

"Warry always picks the wines. He also takes charge of the seating arrangements—I think he does this by intuition, because he knows just how to get the best party chat happening between guests."

Suddenly Eles disappeared. Shortly before the guests were to arrive, and looking unbelievably relaxed and refreshed, she reappeared dressed to kill.

Eles and Warry spent the next few hours enjoying their party as though they were invited guests.

> ## THE MENU
> ♦ ♦ ♦ ♦ ♦ ♦ ♦
> COLD AVOCADO SOUP
> LOBSTER TAIL AND SHRIMP FLAMBÉ
> HARICOTS VERTS IN PHYLLO
> PORTOBELLO MUSHROOMS
> MANGO AND CHOCOLATE SORBETS

OPPOSITE: *One of the premier party-giving couples in Palm Beach, Eles and Warrington recently gave a fund-raising soiree for the British Game Conservancy —with the Duke of Westminster, Gerald Grosvenor, as the honored guest.*

COLD AVOCADO SOUP

1 large, ripe avocado
2 cups cold chicken broth,
    preferably homemade
2 generous tablespoons white rum
½ teaspoon mild curry powder
½ teaspoon salt
Freshly ground pepper to taste
1 cup half-and-half
¼ pound fresh lump crab meat
    (optional)
1 medium lemon, thinly sliced

Halve the avocado and remove
the pit. Peel and cut the meat
into large chunks.

In a blender, combine the
avocado, chicken broth, rum,
curry powder, salt, and pepper.
Blend until smooth. Add the
half-and-half and blend to mix.

Pour the soup into four
chilled bouillon cups. Add a
large piece of crab, if desired,
and garnish with lemon slices.
Serve with toasted crackers.

SERVES 4.

◆ ◆ ◆ ◆ ◆ ◆ ◆

LOBSTER TAIL AND SHRIMP FLAMBÉ

6 Florida lobster tails, 1 to 1½
    pounds each★
2 tablespoons unsalted butter
2 tablespoons olive oil
2 pounds medium shrimp, shelled
    and deveined
2 shallots, finely chopped
3 to 4 garlic cloves, finely chopped
1 cup cognac
1 8-ounce can tomato sauce
2 cups dry white wine
1 teaspoon chopped fresh tarragon
1 tablespoon chopped fresh parsley
Old Bay Seasoning, to taste
1 bay leaf
Salt and freshly ground pepper
1½ pounds squid ink pasta
1 to 2 cups croutons (optional)

Using kitchen shears, trim all
the loose flaps from the lobsters. Cut the tails crosswise
into thirds, and cut down the
center of the front and back,
leaving the shell intact.

In a large sauté pan over
moderately high heat, melt the
butter and olive oil. Add the
lobster, shrimp, shallots, and
garlic. Sauté until the seafood is
pink and firm, and the vegetables have softened slightly,
about 5 minutes.

Meanwhile, bring the cognac
to a simmer in a small saucepan
over moderate heat. Immediately pour the cognac into the
sauté pan. Standing back, carefully light the mixture; high
flames will appear and then
quickly subside. Stir and toss
the mixture until the flames
disappear. Remove the seafood
and keep warm.

Add the tomato sauce, wine,
tarragon, parsley, Old Bay seasoning, and bay leaf into the
sauté pan. Over high heat, boil
the sauce until it has thickened,
about 7 to 10 minutes. Season
to taste with salt and pepper.
Add the sautéed lobster and
shrimp.

Bring a large pot of salted
water to a boil over high heat.
Add the pasta and bring back
to a boil, cooking according to
the package instructions. Serve
at once on a large platter or on
individual serving plates with
the lobster, shell side up, and
shrimp with sauce. Garnish
with croutons fried in butter
and olive oil, if desired.

SERVES 6.

★ Florida lobster season starts August 1. If
Florida lobsters are unavailable, substitute
Maine lobsters. Remove the claws and tail
from the body of Maine lobsters and discard
the body. Cut and prepare the tails as de-
scribed above. The claws can be left whole
and well cracked, in the shell, or the tender
flesh can be removed.

OPPOSITE: *Cold Avocado Soup started the meal.* BELOW: *Happy Birthday, Warry, from "Lifestyles of the Rich and Famous"!* RIGHT: *A specially made chocolate mousse cake ended the birthday feast.*

LEFT: *The theme of the centerpiece was fragrant flowers and fruit, with nectarines and roses.* ABOVE: *Guests included thirty-two of Eles and Warry's very best Palm Beach friends and neighbors.*

HARICOTS VERTS IN PHYLLO

1½ pounds haricots verts (small green beans)
1 16-ounce package frozen phyllo dough
½ cup (1 stick) unsalted melted butter

Wash and rinse the beans, but do not trim the ends. In a vegetable steamer with a removable rack, steam the beans over high heat until tender, 5 to 7 minutes. Refresh under cold, running water and drain well.

Defrost phyllo according to package directions. Remove to a large work surface. Unwrap and cut a 4-inch-wide strip through all thicknesses.

Preheat the oven to 400° F and butter a large baking sheet. Working with one 4-inch-wide strip at a time (keeping the remaining strips covered with a damp towel), brush the length with a small amount of butter. Fold the dough in half lengthwise and brush again with butter. Lay a small handful (about 12) of the beans on top of the strip of dough. Roll around twice, cutting off excess. Repeat the process until all the beans are wrapped in a band of dough.

Place on the baking sheet. Cover the exposed ends of the beans with foil to prevent burning. Bake until the dough is browned and crisp, about 10 minutes. Remove from the baking sheet and keep warm.

Remove one sheet of the remaining phyllo dough at a time to a damp kitchen towel, narrow side toward you. Brush with butter and cut into 3-inch strips. Working quickly, crimp the center of each strip together to form a bow, making one bow per bunch of beans. Place on the baking sheet and bake until golden brown, 5 to 7 minutes. Watch carefully, as they burn quickly.

Set one bow atop each bundle of beans before serving. These bows can be made a day in advance and stored overnight in airtight containers.

SERVES 6.

OPPOSITE: *The birthday dinner.* BELOW: *James serves with such panache!* ABOVE: *Eles brought a wheel of her favorite special Cheshire cheese all the way from England in a suitcase, because it was not obtainable in Florida.*

◆ ◆ ◆ ◆ ◆ ◆ ◆

PORTOBELLO MUSHROOMS

1 pound large portobello mushrooms
2 tablespoons unsalted butter
2 tablespoons olive oil
1 large garlic clove, minced
½ teaspoon salt (or to taste)
1 tablespoon Madeira wine

Wipe the mushrooms clean, trimming off any sandy ends. In a large sauté pan over moderately high heat, melt the butter and oil. Add the mushrooms and the garlic. Gently stir until cooked through and softened, about 2 minutes. Season with salt and Madeira. Heat through and serve at once.

SERVES 4.

TOP: *Dark chocolates in a white chocolate box.* CENTER: *The family silver.* BOTTOM: *Eles has no fewer than forty sets of dishes that she mixes and matches to create incredible place settings. Hand-painted dishes, handed down from her mother, are absolute favorites.*

MANGO AND CHOCOLATE SORBETS

FOR THE MANGO SORBET
2 large mangoes
1½ cups water
¾ cup sugar
3 tablespoons freshly squeezed lime
    juice (preferably from Key
    limes)

FOR THE CHOCOLATE SORBET
4 cups water
1½ cups sugar
4 ounces unsweetened chocolate,
    finely chopped

FOR CHOCOLATE SPOON GARNISH
4 ounces semisweet chocolate,
    finely chopped

FOR CHOCOLATE RIBBON GARNISH
4 ounces chocolate, dark or white
2 tablespoons light corn syrup

To prepare the Mango Sorbet, peel the mangoes and cut the pulp off the stones. In a food processor, puree the pulp until smooth. Reserve the stones.

In a medium saucepan over high heat, combine the water and sugar, then add the mango stones and bring to a boil. Boil for 5 minutes. Strain the liquid into a bowl set over ice and cool completely. Add the lime juice and the mango puree.

Freeze the puree in a conventional, hand-cranked ice-cream maker, layering ice cubes and kosher salt according to the manufacturer's instructions.

Crank until the sorbet has set, then leave in the solution of salt and ice until it has hardened.
Makes about 1 quart.

To prepare the Chocolate Sorbet, combine the water and sugar in a large saucepan over moderately high heat, stirring to dissolve. Add the chocolate, reduce the heat to low, and simmer until the mixture is smooth and not grainy, 20 to 30 minutes. Do not let the mixture boil. Transfer to a bowl and thoroughly cool. Pour into an electric sorbet machine and freeze according to the manufacturer's instructions.
Makes about 1 quart.

To prepare the Chocolate Spoons, place the chocolate in the upper part of a double boiler set over warm, not hot or boiling, water. Using a candy thermometer, slowly bring the chocolate to 130° F. It is crucial to stir constantly to prevent separation. Remove the chocolate from the pan with water and let cool to 88° F. Return to the double boiler and keep over warm water.

Dip pretty teaspoons in chocolate so that most of the bowl is covered. Lift and let the excess drip off. Place on plates and chill. Just before serving, use a knife blade or small spatula to remove the spoons from the plate.

Makes enough for 4 to 6 spoons.

To prepare the Chocolate Ribbons, melt the chocolate in the top of a double boiler over simmering water. Stir in the corn syrup, just barely combining; it will immediately seize into a solid mass. Form into a ball and wrap in plastic. Refrigerate for 1 hour.

On a chilled slab of marble (to chill, fill a roasting pan with ice cubes and set on the marble for 15 to 20 minutes before proceeding) or between two sheets of wax paper, roll out half of the chocolate to form a ribbon that measures 3 by 9 by ⅛ inch thick. If the chocolate becomes too sticky, rechill until firm. If it is still too sticky, the marble may be too warm. Cut the rectangle into ribbons; you should have at least 6. Keep chilled until ready to assemble the dessert.

To assemble the dessert, place 1 scoop of Mango Sorbet and 1 scoop of Chocolate Sorbet in a goblet or on a dessert plate. Garnish with the Chocolate Ribbons and serve with a Chocolate Spoon.

SERVES 6

ABOVE: *Half the fun of eating this dessert is licking the chocolate-coated spoon—a perfect party touch.* LEFT: *Eles is an avid gardener.*

Casual
Entertaining

◆ ◆ ◆ ◆ ◆ ◆ ◆ ◆ ◆ ◆

Ivana Trump

❖ ❖ ❖ ❖ ❖ ❖ ❖ ❖ ❖ ❖ ❖

"I THINK PEOPLE ARE STAYING HOME MORE
AND ENTERTAINING WITH THEIR FAMILIES. I
AM ALSO DOING MUCH MORE OF THE SAME."

On a recent visit to Prague, Ivana revisited all the cafés and bistros where she had spent her afternoons eating and drinking espresso as a student. "Czech food is fantastic, but it is fattening," said Ivana with a laugh, "but I have a Czech chef because I really love this cuisine. I like my family to experience our specialties, like Petrovar, which is pork with sauerkraut and dumplings, or chicken paprika, and my favorite, a fabulous Czech goulash. Oh yes, there are incredible soups and, of course, pastries and cakes—they are all terrible for the waistline!

"Most people are surprised to know that the Pilsen Urquell beer of Czechoslovakia is not the only famous drink. Sparkling wine and their red wines, like Georgian beaujolais, are really delicious. My grandmother had a vineyard in Moravia, very close to Austria, so I know about Czech wines."

"I have always loved to entertain at home. This

> A Favorite Recipe
> **BEEF GOULASH**
> *The Girlfriends' Lunch*
> **MOROCCAN GRILLED SALMON**
> **FOIE GRAS IN PHYLLO**
> **POACHED PEARS**

OPPOSITE: *Ivana Trump loves to make an authentic Czech dinner for friends and family.*

part of my life is very organized. In my party notebooks, I have photographs of all the table settings I have created, including tablecloths and skirts, glasses, silverware, and even the flower arrangements. In Palm Beach alone, there are thirty sets of dishes, so I must be completely organized to give dinner parties for twenty or thirty, which I often do. My chef and I always consult on creating the meal.

"Every December, I give a holiday luncheon for my girlfriends. This party is usually for about sixty people. It's one of the few chances I have to get together with my dear friends. They come from London, Chicago, Paris—everywhere. This year, the White and Gold Suite at the Plaza was a perfect place for my holiday lunch. Kerry Simon, the chef of the Edwardian Room, created a special menu that was very low in calories but also festive—the perfect combination for a ladies' luncheon, as I have discovered through experience."

Preheat the oven to 375° F. Lightly dust the beef with the flour and paprika. Set a 3- or 4-quart-capacity Dutch oven or flameproof casserole over high heat and melt half of the butter with the oil. Add the beef and sauté until browned, stirring constantly. Reduce the heat to moderately high and add the onions and garlic. Cook until the onions are translucent, 3 to 5 minutes. Add water to cover (about 2 cups) and the marjoram and salt to taste. Place the casserole in the oven and cook, uncovered, until the beef is very tender, 1 to 1½ hours, stirring frequently. Add more water if needed to prevent scorching.

Thirty minutes before the goulash is done, add the green pepper and tomato.

Just before serving, cook the noodles in a large pot of boiling, salted water, according to package instructions. Drain and toss with the remaining 2 tablespoons of butter.

Season the stew to taste with additional salt. Serve at once with the hot, buttered noodles.

SERVES 6.

ABOVE: *In the dining room of her Connecticut mansion, Ivana serves her Beef Goulash,* TOP, *on a Valentino-designed serving piece.* OPPOSITE, TOP: *Ivana prepares to greet her guests for a holiday luncheon in the Plaza Hotel's elegant White and Gold Suite.* OPPOSITE, BOTTOM RIGHT: *The Moroccan Grilled Salmon is low-calorie but flavored with an exotic array of spices.* OPPOSITE, BOTTOM LEFT: *Some ingredients found in Ivana's kitchen.*

BEEF GOULASH

2 pounds beef shank or chuck, cut into 1-inch cubes
2 tablespoons all-purpose flour
1 to 3 teaspoons sweet Hungarian paprika
4 tablespoons (½ stick) unsalted butter (or lard)
2 tablespoons vegetable oil
2 medium yellow onions, minced
1 garlic clove, crushed
Pinch dried marjoram
Salt
1 small green pepper, cored, seeded, and minced
1 medium tomato, peeled, seeded, and chopped
1 pound egg noodles

MOROCCAN GRILLED SALMON

1 large carrot, julienned
1 teaspoon freshly squeezed lemon
  juice, or to taste
1½ pounds skinless center-cut fresh
  salmon
1 teaspoon ground anise
1 teaspoon chili powder
1 teaspoon ground cumin
1 teaspoon ground coriander
Salt and freshly ground pepper
1 tablespoon olive oil

Steam the julienned carrot in a vegetable steamer until tender, about 5 minutes. Transfer to a bowl and sprinkle with the lemon juice. Set aside in a warm area.

Preheat the broiler. Cover the broiling pan with aluminum foil and brush with a small amount of olive oil.

Cut the salmon into 4 equal portions. Combine the anise, chili, cumin, and coriander in a small bowl. Mix well. Arrange the fish on the broiling pan and sprinkle the top side with the spice mixture. Season to taste with salt and pepper. Dribble the tablespoon of olive oil evenly over the four fillets.

Broil the fish, seasoned side up, until lightly browned, about 4 minutes. Gently turn and cook the other side until the fillets are firm to the touch, about 3 more minutes. Divide the carrot strips between 4 individual serving plates. Place a salmon fillet on top and serve at once.

SERVES 4.

FOIE GRAS IN PHYLLO

ABOVE: *Foie Gras in Phyllo is one of Chef Kerry Simon's brilliant creations.* OPPOSITE: *The White and Gold Suite at the Plaza Hotel was the location of the special holiday luncheon Ivana gave for fifty girlfriends. Tables were beautifully set for the occasion, and each guest was greeted with a charming gift at her place, a golden bag filled with Annick Goutal fragrances.*

½ pound cooked foie gras
¼ cup heavy cream
¼ teaspoon salt
⅛ teaspoon freshly ground pepper
¾ cup port
Finely grated zest of 1 small lemon
Finely grated zest of 1 small orange
Juice of 1 small lemon
Juice of 1 small orange
4 or 5 whole black peppercorns
1 shallot, thinly sliced
½ cup canola oil
4 sheets phyllo dough
1 teaspoon clarified butter
1 teaspoon finely chopped herbs (parsley, thyme, chervil, or oregano)
1 teaspoon pink peppercorns
2 chives, cut into ¼-inch pieces

Puree the foie gras in a food processor until very smooth. Transfer to a small bowl. In a separate bowl, whisk the cream until it forms stiff peaks. Fold the cream into the foie gras and season with the salt and pepper. Spoon this mixture into a pastry bag fitted with a number-6 plain tip. Refrigerate until ready to use.

In a small nonreactive saucepan, combine the port, the zests and juices of the lemon and the orange, the black peppercorns, and the shallot. Boil over high heat until reduced to ¼ cup. Remove from the heat and cool completely, then strain into a small bowl. Whisk in the oil and set aside.

Preheat the oven to 350° F. Lay 1 sheet of phyllo dough out flat on a large work surface. Sprinkle with a small amount of clarified butter and fresh herbs. Place another layer of phyllo dough and sprinkling of butter and herbs on top. Repeat this procedure one more time and top with the last sheet of dough. Cut out 20 circles of the layered dough, using a 3-inch cookie cutter. Transfer to a nonstick baking sheet and cook until golden, about 8 minutes. Remove the circles to a wire rack and let them cool for 15 to 20 minutes.

Pipe out about 1 tablespoon of the foie gras mixture on one of the cooled circles. Top with another circle and the same amount of foie gras, then top with another circle. Repeat once more for a total of 4 circles with a tablespoonful of foie gras in each layer. Continue with the remaining circles and foie gras.

Place these layered foie gras pastries in the center of 4 individual serving plates. Surround with a heaping tablespoonful of the citrus vinaigrette. Garnish with the pink peppercorns and chives.

SERVES 4.

ABOVE: *Party planning is important to Ivana Trump, especially when it comes to devising the perfect menu. An example of her style is this group of recipes, which she developed with the chef of the Edwardian Room. The dessert was especially flavorful— Poached Pears with a raspberry sauce.*

POACHED PEARS

1 bottle (about 3½ cups) hearty
    wine, preferably Zinfandel
1 1-inch piece of lemon zest
1 tablespoon freshly squeezed
    lemon juice
¼ cup sugar
2 cinnamon sticks
4 medium Bartlett pears, peeled
2 cups fresh raspberries
4 sprigs fresh mint

In a medium nonreactive sauce-pan, combine the wine, lemon zest, lemon juice, sugar, and cinnamon sticks. Add the pears. Bring this mixture to a boil over high heat, reduce the heat to medium, and poach the pears until the tip of a knife can easily be inserted. The time will depend on the ripeness of the pears; poaching pears can take from 15 to 45 minutes. Test frequently to ensure that the fruit is firm yet tender, but not mushy. Remove the pears to a plate or platter, let cool slightly, then cover with plastic wrap and refrigerate for at least 2 hours.

Over high heat, reduce the poaching liquid until it is thick-ened and syrupy; only about ½ cup liquid should remain. Puree the raspberries in a food processor until smooth. Strain through a fine mesh sieve to remove the seeds. Add the raspberry puree to the wine mixure and cook until thick-ened over moderately high heat, about 5 minutes. Transfer to a bowl and let cool to room temperature. Cover and chill for about 2 hours before serv-ing. Makes about 2½ cups sauce. The pears can be poached and the sauce can be made up to 2 days in advance.

Place the pears in 4 shallow bowls. Spoon some of the sauce over each pear and gar-nish each bowl with a sprig of mint. Serve any remaining sauce on the side.

SERVES 4.

ABOVE: *Rare antique Capo di Monte dishes and Venetian glassware grace the table at Mar-a-Lago in Palm Beach.*

Successful parties are all in the details. Special touches, like fresh flowers, RIGHT, and party favors at each place setting, LEFT, are often the most cherished memories of a wonderful get-together.

Wolfgang Puck and Barbara Lazaroff

◆ ◆ ◆ ◆ ◆ ◆ ◆ ◆ ◆

"A RESTAURANT IS AN INTIMATE PART
OF PEOPLE'S LIVES. HERE, THEY
CELEBRATE MANY IMPORTANT MOMENTS.
IT'S PART OF THEIR EMOTIONAL
HISTORY. AND OURS, TOO."

Wolfgang Puck and architectural interior designer Barbara Lazaroff —married since 1983— have created an amazing restaurant empire. Critics and patrons have placed them on the top of the list—from Spago, California's first open-kitchen pizza restaurant; to the Asian-influenced Chinois on Main in Santa Monica; to Eureka, an authentic brewery and charcuterie in West Los Angeles; to the dreamy, oceanic experience of their latest restaurant, Granita, in Malibu.

While Barbara designs and builds the restaurants, Wolfgang challenges himself with creating a new and unexpected menu. "We work with the same general concept, but our jobs are very different," said Barbara. "Wolfgang can change and revise the menu along the way, even after the restaurant opens. My in-

THE RECIPES

◆ ◆ ◆ ◆ ◆ ◆

Spago
**BLACK FOREST HAM AND
GOAT CHEESE PIZZA**
SPICY CHICKEN PIZZA
SHRIMP AND SUN-DRIED TOMATO PIZZA
**WHOLE WHEAT PIZZA WITH
CHANTERELLES AND EGGPLANT**

Eureka
TORTILLA LASAGNA
CHILI GRILLED CHICKEN
YELLOW TOMATO MOLE SAUCE

Chinois on Main
SIZZLING SCALLOPS

Granita
APPLE FENNEL TART

OPPOSITE: *Barbara and Wolfgang at their West Los Angeles restaurant, Eureka.*

terior has to maintain a contemporary look for at least ten years. I'm at the job site every day when we're building, so every detail is exactly as I want it. At Granita, I laid all the colored sea stones and shells into the bar top. I work right alongside the craftsmen and artisans. I'm as comfortable at my construction site as Wolf is in his kitchen."

After fourteen years of working together to create four of California's finest restaurants, not to mention single-handedly inventing "California Cuisine," the Puck-Lazaroff team isn't slowing down.

What's next? Barbara wistfully said, "One of these days, we hope to find the time to redesign our own kitchen at home." Wolfgang agreed with a nod as he ran back to the kitchen.

TOP RIGHT: *Superagent Irving Lazar's annual post–Academy Award parties are always held at Spago.*
TOP LEFT: *Larry Hagman, Barbara, Maj Hagman, and Wolfgang.*
ABOVE: *Wolfgang Puck takes a break with Elizabeth Taylor, George Hamilton, and Barbara.*

BASIC PIZZA DOUGH

1 teaspoon salt
1 tablespoon honey
2 tablespoons olive oil
¾ cup cool water
1 envelope active dry yeast
¼ cup warm water
3 cups all-purpose flour

In a small mixing bowl, combine the salt, honey, olive oil, and the cool water. Mix well. In a separate bowl, sprinkle the yeast over the warm water and let proof for 10 minutes.

Place the flour in the bowl of a food processor. With the motor running, slowly pour the honey mixture through the feed tube, then pour in the dissolved yeast. Process until the dough forms a ball around the blade.

Transfer the dough to a lightly floured surface and knead until smooth. Place in a buttered bowl and allow the dough to rest, covered, for 30 minutes.

Divide the dough into 4 equal parts. Form each piece into a smooth ball, flatten slightly, and place on a plate. Cover each plate with a damp towel and refrigerate. One hour before baking, let the dough come to room temperature.

Lightly flour a work surface. Flatten each ball of dough into a 6-inch circle; use your fingertips to make the outer edge slightly thicker than the center. Turn the dough over and repeat. Lift the dough from the work surface and stretch the edges, working clockwise to form a circle 7 to 8 inches in diameter. Repeat with the other 3 pieces. Garnish pizzas as desired.

MAKES 4 PIZZAS.

BLACK FOREST HAM AND GOAT CHEESE PIZZA

1/4 cup plus 2 tablespoons olive oil

2 small eggplants, thinly sliced
    lengthwise

4 circles Basic Pizza Dough
    (previous page)

1 teaspoon red pepper flakes

1 cup freshly grated Italian fontina
    cheese

2 cups freshly grated mozzarella
    cheese

1 cup cubed goat cheese

4 ounces thinly sliced Black Forest
    ham, julienned

1 bunch fresh basil, chopped

Heat 1/4 cup of the olive oil in a large skillet. Over moderately high heat, sauté the eggplants until lightly browned, about 1 minute on each side. Drain on paper towels.

Place a pizza stone inside the oven and preheat to 500° F. Lightly dust a wooden pizza paddle with flour or semolina. Working with one circle at a time, place the pizza dough on the paddle.

Brush each pizza with about 1/2 tablespoon of olive oil. Sprinkle each with the pepper flakes, fontina, mozzarella, eggplant, goat cheese, ham, and basil.

Using the paddle, slide one pizza at a time onto the stone and bake until the cheeses are bubbling, 10 to 12 minutes. When done, transfer to a cutting board and cut into wedges. Serve on warmed plates, garnished with additional sprigs of fresh basil if desired.

SERVES 4.

Wolfgang's signature pizzas are nearly as popular before they are baked as they are when fresh from the oven. BELOW: *Henry Winkler gives Wolfgang a hand.* BOTTOM LEFT: *Cher and Barbara compare headdresses.* BOTTOM RIGHT: *Don Johnson and Barbara.*

Offering some sage advice, Wolfgang said, "If you want to cook good food, you need only a good sauté pan, a sharp knife, and the freshest ingredients you can find. It's not difficult to cook like me." ACROSS THE TOP: *Wolfgang demonstrates how to make his highly acclaimed pizza.* CENTER: *Barbara designed and created Spago's open interior from floor to ceiling.* BOTTOM: *The Spago staff in the kitchen.*

SPICY CHICKEN PIZZA

¼ cup plus 2 tablespoons olive oil
2 boneless, skinless chicken breasts, about 4 ounces each, cut into long strips
1 jalapeño pepper, seeded and finely chopped
1 cup sliced mushrooms
1 small red pepper, seeded and julienned
Salt and freshly ground pepper
¼ cup freshly ground cilantro
4 circles Basic Pizza Dough (page 112)
1 cup freshly grated Italian fontina cheese
2 cups freshly grated mozzarella cheese
½ cup trimmed, sliced scallions

In a large sauté pan, heat the ¼ cup olive oil over high heat. Add the chicken, jalapeño, mushrooms, and red pepper, and sauté until the peppers are softened and the chicken is partially cooked, about 5 minutes. (The chicken will continue cooking in the oven.) Remove from the heat, season with salt and pepper to taste, stir in the cilantro, and set aside to cool.

Place a pizza stone inside the oven and preheat to 500° F. Lightly dust a wooden paddle made especially for this purpose with flour or semolina. Working with one circle at a time, place the pizza dough on the paddle.

Brush each pizza with about ½ tablespoon of the remaining olive oil. Sprinkle each with a quarter of the fontina and mozzarella. Top with a quarter of the cooled chicken mixture and a sprinkling of scallions.

Using the paddle, slide one pizza at a time onto the stone and bake until the cheeses are bubbling, 10 to 12 minutes. When each pizza is done, transfer to a cutting board and cut into wedges. Serve on warmed plates, garnished with additional sprigs of fresh cilantro if desired.

SERVES 4.

SHRIMP AND SUN-DRIED TOMATO PIZZA

4 circles Basic Pizza Dough (page 112)

2 tablespoons olive oil

1 cup freshly grated Italian fontina cheese

2 cupes freshly grated mozzarella cheese

2 garlic cloves, minced

1 medium Bermuda onion, thinly sliced

¼ cup chopped fresh basil

20 to 24 medium shrimp, peeled and deveined

¼ cup sun-dried tomatoes, thinly sliced

Place a pizza stone inside the oven and preheat to 500° F. Lightly dust a wooden pizza paddle with flour or semolina. Working with one circle at a time, place the pizza dough on the paddle.

Brush each pizza with ½ tablespoon of the olive oil. Top each with fontina and mozzarella, leaving a ½-inch border around the edge. Sprinkle with the garlic, onion, basil, shrimp, and tomatoes.

Using the paddle, slide one pizza at a time onto the stone and bake until the cheeses are bubbling, 10 to 12 minutes. When each pizza is done, transfer to a cutting board and cut into wedges. Serve on warmed plates, garnished with additional sprigs of fresh basil, if desired.

SERVES 4.

◆ ◆ ◆ ◆ ◆ ◆ ◆

AT RIGHT: *Barbara and Steven Spielberg at the party for his movie* The Color Purple; *Barbara, Jimmy and Rosalynn Carter, and Wolfgang at Spago; Stevie Wonder and Wolfgang.*

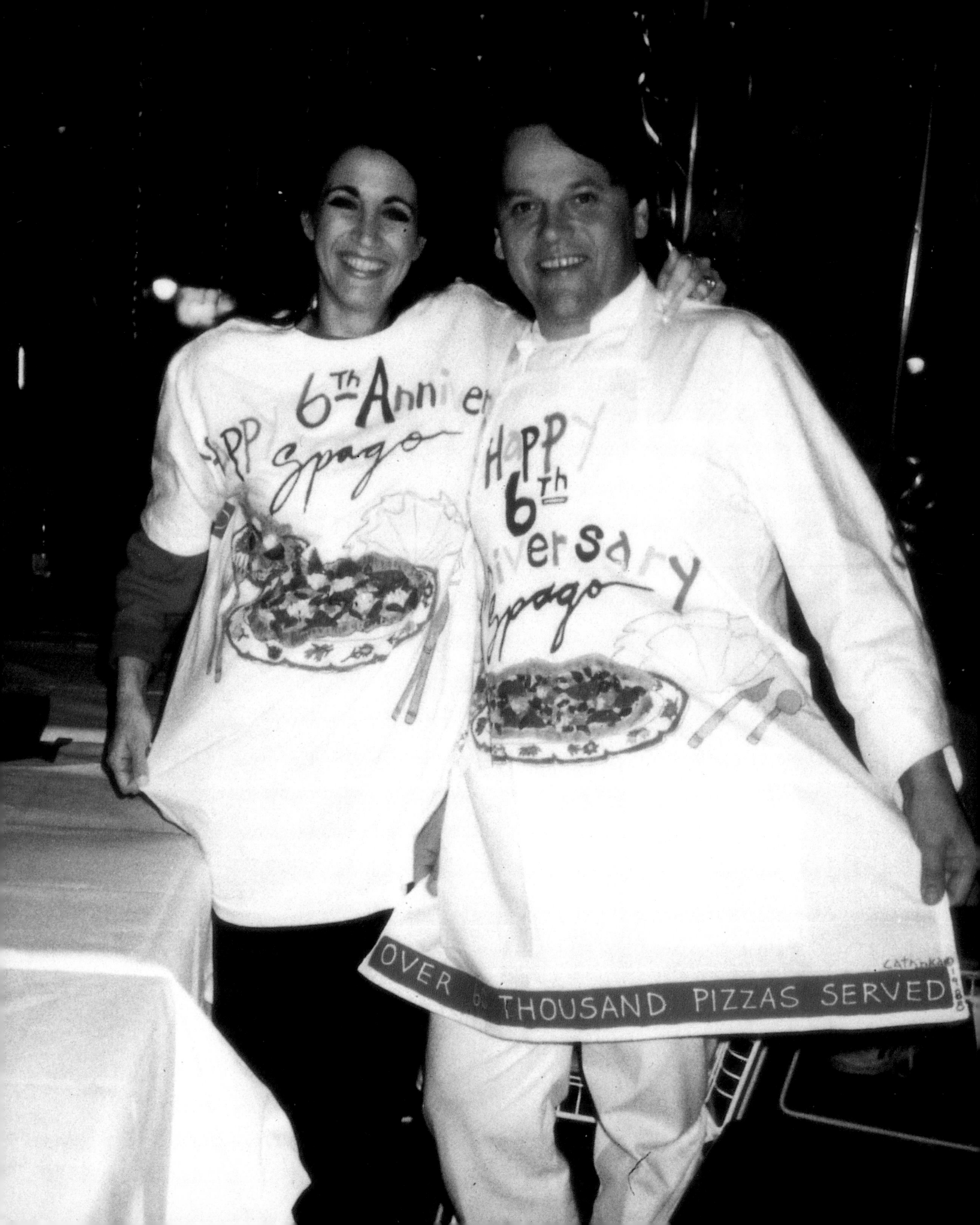
Spago
Spago
OVER
THOUSAND PIZZAS SERVED

WHOLE WHEAT PIZZA WITH CHANTERELLES AND EGGPLANT

FOR THE WHOLE WHEAT DOUGH
1 envelope active dry yeast
¼ cup warm water
1 cup cool water
1 tablespoon olive oil
1 tablespoon honey
Pinch salt
3¾ cups whole wheat flour

FOR THE TOPPING
⅓ cup olive oil
*2 medium eggplants, trimmed and
    sliced ¼-inch thick*
Salt and freshly ground pepper
*½ pound chanterelle mushrooms,
    cleaned and sliced ¼-inch thick*
*2 cups freshly grated mozzarella
    cheese*
*¼ pound fresh goat cheese, cut into
    ¼-inch cubes*
3 to 4 garlic cloves, minced
*1 medium leek, cleaned, trimmed,
    and thinly sliced*
4 plum tomatoes, thinly sliced
*1 tablespoon finely chopped fresh
    sage*
1 tablespoon chopped fresh oregano
Fresh thyme sprigs

In a small bowl, sprinkle the yeast over the warm water and let proof for 5 to 10 minutes. In a separate bowl, combine the cool water with the olive oil, honey, and salt. Place the flour in the bowl of a food processor. With the motor running, slowly pour the olive oil mixture, then the yeast, through the feed tube. Process until the dough forms a ball around the blade. Transfer to a buttered bowl, cover, and let rise until doubled in bulk.

Punch the dough down and knead it on a lightly floured work surface for about 1 minute. Divide it into 4 equal parts and roll into tight balls. Place on a tray, cover with a damp towel, and let rest for several hours or overnight in the refrigerator.

Roll or stretch each ball into a circle 7 to 8 inches in diameter.

Place a pizza stone in the oven and preheat to 500° F. Lightly dust a wooden pizza paddle with flour or semolina. Working with one circle at a time, place the pizza dough on the paddle.

In a small sauté pan, heat about 2 tablespoons of the olive oil over moderately high heat. Sauté the eggplant until tender, adding more olive oil if necessary to prevent sticking. Season with salt and pepper to taste. Remove the eggplant from the pan and set aside. Add the chanterelles and sauté until slightly wilted, adding more olive oil if needed. Season with salt and pepper to taste. Remove the chanterelles from the pan and set aside.

Brush each pizza with about 1 teaspoon olive oil. Top each with mozzarella and goat cheese, eggplant, and chante-relles. Sprinkle with the garlic and leeks, and top with the sliced tomatoes. Lightly dust each with the sage and oregano.

Using the paddle, slide one pizza at a time onto the stone and bake until the cheeses are bubbling, 10 to 12 minutes. When each pizza is done, transfer to a cutting board and cut into wedges. Serve on warmed plates, garnished with sprigs of fresh thyme if desired.

SERVES 4.

OPPOSITE: *Barbara and Wolfgang observed the tenth anniversary of Spago in January 1992. The Spago staff and alumni are invited annually for a private pizza party to help celebrate another successful year.*
ABOVE: *At home in their living room with son, Cameron, and dog, Mellon, one of twenty-eight pets.*

In a large sauté pan, heat half of the oil over moderate heat. Fry the tortillas a few at a time until they are softened but not crisp, 1 to 2 minutes. Drain on paper towels. Heat the remaining oil in a small sauté pan or skillet. Add the onions and cook over moderately high heat until lightly colored, 5 to 7 minutes, stirring frequently. Drain on paper towels and set aside.

Preheat the oven to 350° F. Arrange 3 of the tortillas on the bottom of a 9-by-13-inch baking dish. Layer with one third of the onions, ¼ cup of the chile sauce, one third of the ricotta, one third of the Jack cheese, and one third of the goat cheese slices. Sprinkle over one third of the cilantro, garlic, and tomato. Top with 3 more tortillas and repeat with another layer of the ingredients in the same order. Top with the final 3 tortillas. Cover with the remaining ¼ cup of chile sauce and bake until the sauce is bubbling and the cheeses are melted, about 20 minutes. Serve at once.

SERVES 6.

TORTILLA LASAGNA

¼ cup corn oil
9 corn tortillas, 4 inches in
   diameter
2 large onions, thinly sliced
1 cup chile sauce
1 cup ricotta cheese
1 cup freshly grated Monterey Jack
   cheese
½ pound log goat cheese, sliced
   ¼-inch thick
1 bunch cilantro, trimmed, and
   finely chopped
2 garlic cloves, finely chopped
3 large tomatoes, peeled, seeded,
   and diced

◆ ◆ ◆ ◆ ◆ ◆ ◆

TOP: *Tortilla Lasagna and Chili Grilled Chicken are two of Eureka's specialties.* CENTER: *Behind Barbara are Eureka's million-dollar copper brewing kettles.* BOTTOM: *Eureka features a creative array of charcuterie: wild boar bratwurst, shellfish paella sausage, and smoked almond duck sausage.*

CHILI GRILLED CHICKEN

1 frying chicken, 3½ to 5 pounds,
  cut into 8 pieces
1 tablespoon chili powder, or to
  taste
1 garlic clove, minced
¼ cup freshly squeezed orange
  juice
3 tablespoons freshly squeezed
  lemon juice
3 tablespoons freshly squeezed lime
  juice
2 tablespoons olive oil
2 teaspoons cracked pepper
2 tablespoons fresh chopped
  cilantro
Salt

Start a charcoal fire and let the coals burn down to a gray ash, and preheat the oven to 350° F. Pat the chicken dry.

In the bowl of a food processor, combine the chili powder, garlic, orange juice, lemon juice, lime juice, olive oil, pepper, and cilantro, and process until smooth. Rub this mixture onto the chicken, being sure to coat it entirely.

Place the chicken on the charcoal grill about 5 inches above the coals. Grill the chicken until all sides appear slightly charred, turning frequently, about 15 minutes. Transfer to a large roasting pan, cover loosely with foil, and finish cooking in the oven until tender, about 30 more minutes. Remove and keep warm until ready to serve. Serve with Yellow Tomato Mole Sauce (recipe follows).

SERVES 4.

◆ ◆ ◆ ◆ ◆ ◆ ◆

Barbara and Tina Turner, TOP, *and James Garner and Wolfgang,* CENTER. BELOW: *The mechanics of the brewer's art and film classics like* Metropolis *and* Modern Times *influenced Eureka's design.*

TOP: *Conceived and created by architectural and interior designer Barbara Lazaroff, the Felliniesque interior of Chinois on Main has been featured in every design magazine in the country. Renowned for her innovative concepts, Barbara lectures across the country on the various aspects of restaurant creation.* ABOVE: *Barbara and Vincent Price share an intimate moment at the Chinois Halloween party.*

YELLOW TOMATO MOLE SAUCE

1 tablespoon vegetable oil
1 small onion, minced
4 garlic cloves, minced
2 medium yellow tomatoes (about ½ pound each), cored and quartered
1 small yellow pepper, cored, seeded, and julienned
2 cups chicken stock
1 cinnamon stick
1 dried ancho chili, coarsely chopped
1 jalapeño pepper, seeded and coarsely chopped
1 tablespoon toasted pecan pieces
1 tablespoon toasted sunflower seeds
1 tablespoon toasted sesame seeds
1 bunch cilantro, trimmed
Salt and lemon juice

In a small saucepan, combine the oil, onions, and garlic. Cook over moderate heat until the onions are softened, about 5 minutes. Add the tomatoes, pepper, and stock, and increase the heat to moderately high.

Place the cinnamon stick, ancho chili, jalapeño, pecans, sunflower seeds, and sesame seeds in a large square of cheesecloth, bring up the corners, and tie securely with kitchen string. Add to the saucepan and simmer until the sauce has thickened slightly and is quite spicy, 30 to 40 minutes.

Remove the spice bag and discard. Remove the saucepan from the heat. Tie the stems of the cilantro to form a tight bundle. Add to the sauce and cover. Steep for 5 minutes. Remove the bundle of cilantro and discard.

Pour the sauce into the bowl of a food processor and process until smooth. Strain through a fine mesh sieve, and season with salt and lemon juice to taste. Serve with Chili Grilled Chicken.

MAKES ABOUT 1½ CUPS SAUCE.

◆ ◆ ◆ ◆ ◆ ◆ ◆

OPPOSITE, TOP: *Sizzling Scallops.* OPPOSITE, CENTER: *Barbara and Jimmy Stewart.* OPPOSITE, BOTTOM: *Going all out, Barbara dressed to match the Asian decor at Chinois; Wolfgang stayed with his traditional whites.*

SIZZLING SCALLOPS

1 garlic clove, minced
1 teaspoon grated fresh ginger
1 tablespoon miso paste
10 black peppercorns, crushed
½ cup rice wine vinegar
¾ cup light peanut oil
1 teaspoon soy sauce, or to taste

Peanut oil for frying
8 small all-purpose potatoes,
*   peeled and julienned*
Salt and freshly ground pepper
½ cup potato starch
2 pounds sea scallops, quartered
4 heads radicchio, coarsely chopped
1 bunch cilantro, trimmed and
*   finely chopped*
¼ pound enoki mushrooms,
*   trimmed*
Juice of 1 lime

To prepare the salad dressing, combine the garlic, ginger, miso paste, peppercorns, and vinegar in the bowl of a food processor. Process briefly to blend. With the blades in motion, slowly pour in the oil. Add the soy sauce and set aside.

Pour enough oil into a skillet to measure 2 inches deep. Heat over moderately high heat until hot but not smoking. Add the potatoes and cook until golden brown, about 5 minutes. Drain on paper towels and season with salt and pepper to taste. Keep warm until ready to serve. Keep the oil hot.

Place the potato starch on a large plate. Pat the scallops dry and dredge in the starch, shaking off excess. Fry in the oil until golden brown, about 2 minutes. Drain on paper towels and season to taste with salt and pepper.

In a large mixing bowl, combine the scallops, radicchio, cilantro, and mushrooms. Sprinkle with the lime juice, and season with salt and pepper to taste. Pour the salad dressing over and toss. Serve on a platter with the potato sticks.

SERVES 6 TO 8.

TOP: *Barbara said, "Granita is not about fish, but is about the water, the tide, shells, and the ever-changing qualities of the ocean." Combine Barbara's unique imagination with her "anything's possible" attitude, and you have Los Angeles's most interesting and visually extravagant restaurant—and thanks to Wolfgang, the food's wonderful, too!* ABOVE: *The entrance to Granita is a prelude to its evocative interior.*

APPLE FENNEL TART

1 pound Puff Pastry Beaumanière (recipe follows)
⅓ cup plus 1 teaspoon granulated sugar
2½ sticks unsalted butter, cut into tablespoons
1 large bulb fennel, about 1 pound, trimmed and julienned
1 tablespoon Pernod
6 Granny Smith or Gravenstein apples, peeled, cored, and quartered
1 cup dark brown sugar, packed
½ cup confectioners' sugar
Fresh sprigs of fennel

Roll the pastry out to ⅛-inch thickness and cut 4 4-inch circles. Transfer to baking sheet and refrigerate for 1 hour.

Preheat the oven to 350°F. Prick the pastry circles with a fork and sprinkle with 1 teaspoon of the granulated sugar. Bake until golden brown, about 15 minutes.

Meanwhile, melt 6 tablespoons of the butter in a medium saucepan. Add the fennel and the ⅓ cup granulated sugar and stir to blend. Cook over low heat until caramelized, about 10 minutes, stirring occasionally. Add the Pernod and cook for 1 additional minute. Set aside.

Place 1 tablespoon of the butter in each of 4 4-inch individual tartlet molds. Rub to coat the bottom of the molds with the butter. Top with the apple pieces, rounded side down. Dot each mold with 2 more tablespoons of the butter and sprinkle each with ¼ cup of the brown sugar. Place tartlets on a baking sheet and bake until the apples are tender, about 25 minutes.

Remove the tartlets from the oven. Preheat the broiler. Top each tartlet with ¼ of the fennel mixture and place one puff pastry circle on top. Invert the tartlet onto the baking sheet so that the pastry circle is on the bottom. Sprinkle confectioners' sugar over the apples and place under the broiler. Watching carefully, turn and adjust the pan so that the tops of the tartlets are evenly caramelized.

Transfer the tartlets to 4 individual serving plates. Garnish with sprigs of fennel and top with ice cream, if desired.

PUFF PASTRY BEAUMANIÈRE

2 tablespoons salt
8 to 9 cups pastry flour
1 to 1¼ cups ice water
35 tablespoons unsalted butter (4 sticks + 3 tablespoons)
Additional flour for dusting

In the bowl of an electric mixer fitted with a dough hook, combine the salt, flour, water, and 1¾ sticks (14 tablespoons) of the butter. Turn at slow speed until dough is elastic, about 2 to 3 minutes.

Place the remaining 21 tablespoons butter on a work surface. With your hands, knead the butter into a smooth, malleable square that measures 8 inches. Use the heel of the hand, wiping off the excess water that exudes as you knead. Work quickly, as the butter should not become too soft.

Flour another work surface and roll the dough into a square large enough to enclose the block of butter. Place the butter in the center of the dough and fold the dough over the butter so it is enclosed. Tap lightly to get rid of excess air, and pinch the pastry edges closed, sealing the gaps.

Roll the pastry into a long rectangle that measures ¾-inch thick, 12 inches wide, and approximately 20 inches long. Roll evenly and in one direction as much as possible. Brush off any excess flour with a large pastry brush and fold the dough into thirds. Give the dough a quarter turn and repeat the rolling and folding once. Cover the dough with a towel and let it rest in the refrigerator for at least 20 minutes.

Complete 2 more "turns" and again let the dough rest, covered, in the refrigerator. Then complete 2 more "turns." The dough is now ready to use.

MAKES 2 POUNDS.

TOP: *Apple Fennel Tart is one of the restaurant's most popular desserts.*
RIGHT: *From her initial vision of the restaurant's design to its opening day, Barbara is a "hands-on" participant in every aspect.*

Claude Taittinger

◆ ◆ ◆ ◆ ◆ ◆ ◆ ◆ ◆ ◆

"I WAS BORN IN A TIME WHEN EVERYTHING
WAS CHANGING, ESPECIALLY THE CHAMPAGNE
AT THE HOUSE OF TAITTINGER."

"I am my own best—or worst—critic, which is why I make my Champagne only for my wife, Catherine, and for myself. We share half a bottle before dinner every night. We concentrate on every aspect of it— the lightness, the flavor, the effervescence, and, of course, how it looks in the glass.

"In the twenties, it was my father who decided to change the way Champagne was made, by using only white grapes. His experiment was a perfect success. And suddenly Champagne was a light, pale, and elegantly bubbly drink. The new Taittinger Champagne became a symbol of the good life, and inspired the design of new, lighter menus at Champagne fêtes all over France.

"My Champagne is even lighter and more delicate than that of my father's day. A Blanc de Blancs, it's made of one-hundred-percent Chardonnay grapes. My innovations have been of a different nature, especially in bottle design. Over the past decade, I have selected some of the world's greatest

> ### THE MENU
>
> ◆ ◆ ◆ ◆ ◆ ◆
>
> PANACHÉE OF THREE FISH
> ROAST CRAYFISH
> RED FRUIT CHARLOTTE

OPPOSITE: *Though the Taittinger family acquired their House of Champagne after World War I, its origins date back to 1723. It is one of the oldest Champagne houses in existence today.*

artists to decorate a special series of signed and numbered bottles of my best wine."

Though not a cook, Claude revealed the gastronomic secrets of his family kitchen. "Most of the time, we live a simple country life. On Sunday, Catherine takes over the kitchen and cooks wonderful peasant-style food, which I love. Several times a year, and always in the fall, we have a celebration —a Champagne Fête—at our family estate, La Marquetterie, in Reims. Our dear friends and family come from Paris, and the mood of the party is gloriously high-spirited. The chef from the Crillon, our hotel in Paris, prepares the best menu, and we drink the best Taittinger Champagne."

When asked the secret of his endless enthusiasm for an amazing variety of activities and interests, including food, writing history books, sports, and, of course, Champagne, Claude Taittinger replied, "You must love what you're doing, and drink Champagne every day."

PANACHÉE OF THREE FISH

8 tablespoons (1 stick) unsalted
  butter, cut into small pieces and
  chilled
2 shallots, finely chopped
½ cup Champagne
1 tablespoon heavy cream
Salt and freshly ground pepper
1 pound John Dory fillets
1 pound turbot fillets
1 pound mullet fillets

In a small, heavy nonreactive saucepan, melt 1 tablespoon of the butter over moderately low heat. Sauté the shallots until they are softened, about 2 minutes, stirring constantly. Pour in the Champagne and cook over moderately high heat until the liquid is reduced to 2 to 3 tablespoons, about 5 minutes. Add the cream and reduce again, to about 2 tablespoons.

Working on and off the heat, add the remaining pieces of butter bit by bit, whisking constantly until the sauce is thick and emulsified. Do not allow the pan to become too hot or the sauce will curdle. Remove from the heat and season with salt and pepper. The sauce can be kept warm over hot but not boiling water for about one half hour.

Season the fillets to taste with salt and pepper. In a large, nonstick sauté pan over moderately high heat, pan-"roast" the fish until golden and crunchy outside and tender and moist inside, about 2 minutes per side. Handle the fillets carefully when turning, to prevent the fish from breaking apart.

Serve the fish on warmed dinner plates with a small amount of sauce.

SERVES 6 to 8.

◆ ◆ ◆ ◆ ◆ ◆ ◆

LEFT, CENTER: *Claude and Catherine share a Champagne moment. It was in the cellars of the castle of La Marquetterie in the late 1600s that Brother Oudart, whose portrait appears at* LEFT, *discovered the process by which still Champagne wine becomes a sparkling wine. Today, La Marquetterie is the official Taittinger family estate.*

Claude offers these suggestions, ABOVE, *to make the most of a flute of Champagne: Refrigerate the bottle at 45°F for about one hour before serving to make sure the wine is thoroughly chilled. Wait until you are just about to serve the Champagne before opening the bottle. Open the Champagne with the cork angled away from you, and twist off the cork, keeping your hand on it at all times—loud explosions and the loss of the Champagne are unnecessary. Immediately fill a champagne flute to contain the bouquet and the bead—the terms for the size and quality of the bubble. Familiarize yourself with the color, experience the fragrance, then take the first sip. After savoring, take another sip, and the pleasure is all yours. Toast, "Vive le Champagne!"*

Serve richer, full-bodied Champagnes with meals; select lighter Champagnes for aperitifs. ABOVE, FAR RIGHT: *Claude toasts with the director of marketing. The House of Champagne Taittinger is the only remaining privately held Champagne house of its size in the world.* LEFT: *Panachée of Three Fish is served with a Champagne-shallot sauce.*

Trim the asparagus to 4 inches from the tips. In a large pot set over high heat, bring a large amount of salted water to a rapid boil. Add the asparagus and bring back to a boil. Cook until the tops are just tender, about 3 minutes. Transfer to a colander and refresh under cold water, then drain well on paper towels.

Preheat the oven to 425° F.

Remove the shells from the crayfish if necessary. Place the crayfish tails in a single layer in a large baking dish, then pour the melted butter over them. Season with salt and pepper to taste. Roast until the tails are bright pink and the butter bubbles, about 10 minutes, stirring often to distribute the heat and prevent the crayfish from sticking.

Arrange the asparagus in spokes on individual serving plates. Remove the crayfish with a slotted spoon and divide among the plates, placing them in the center. Drizzle each plate with a few spoonfuls of the oil, and garnish with chopped truffles, if desired.

ABOVE: *Roast Crayfish with truffle oil, surrounded by asparagus, is a perfect meal to serve with Champagne.*

ROAST CRAYFISH

2 pounds very thin asparagus
3 to 4 pounds crayfish tails
2 tablespoons unsalted butter, melted
Salt and freshly ground pepper
½ cup truffle oil
1 small truffle, finely chopped (optional)

SERVES 4 to 6.

ABOVE AND OPPOSITE, BELOW: *La Marquetterie, the Taittinger family estate, is at Épernay, in the Champagne region of France.* RIGHT: *Inside the caves at La Marquetterie, hundreds of thousands of bottles age.* FAR RIGHT: *In 1983, Claude Taittinger launched the Collection Series of Brut Champagne to commemorate the 250th anniversary of the House of Champagne Taittinger. These bottles, designed by Roy Lichtenstein, Victor Vasarely, Arman, André Masson, and Marie-Elena Vieira da Silva, have been signed and numbered by the artists.*

RED FRUIT CHARLOTTE

FOR THE CHARLOTTE
¾ cup sugar
¼ cup water
2 tablespoons Kirschwasser (or
    similar eau-de-vie)
6 egg yolks
1 cup milk
1 cup heavy cream
1 envelope gelatin
1 pint (2 cups) fresh raspberries
24 lady fingers

FOR THE RASPBERRY COULIS
1 pint raspberries
2 tablespoons confectioners' sugar
2 teaspoons freshly squeezed lemon
    juice

First, prepare the charlotte. In a small, heavy saucepan, combine ½ cup of the sugar with 2 tablespoons of the water. Bring to a boil, stirring constantly, to dissolve the sugar. When it is dissolved, boil undisturbed until a thin syrup has formed, about 2 minutes. Remove from the heat and stir in the Kirschwasser. Set aside and let cool.

In a large bowl, beat the egg yolks with the remaining sugar until thick and light. In a heavy saucepan, scald the milk. Whisk half of the hot milk into the yolk mixture, then pour this back into the pot of remaining milk and whisk. Stir over moderately low heat until the custard coats the back of a wooden spoon, about 5 minutes. Remove from the heat and strain into a bowl.

Whip the cream until stiff peaks form. Put the remaining 2 tablespoons of water in a small bowl. Sprinkle in the gelatin and let dissolve for 5 minutes. Stir the gelatin into the custard and mix well. (If lumps appear, strain the custard through a fine mesh sieve.) Set the bowl over ice water in a larger bowl, stirring constantly until the mixture starts to thicken. Fold in the whipped cream and the raspberries. Remove the bowl of custard from the bowl of ice water and set aside. Gently fold the custard from time to time until you are ready to fill the mold.

Brush the lady fingers with the cooled syrup. Use about 16 to line the sides and bottoms of a 6-cup charlotte mold, then fill with the custard mixture. Top with the remaining lady fingers. Cover the mold with plastic wrap and refrigerate for 12 to 24 hours.

To prepare the coulis, combine the raspberries, the sugar, and the lemon juice in the bowl of a food processor fitted with a metal blade. Purée until very smooth, then strain through a fine mesh sieve to remove the seeds. Refrigerate until ready to use.

When ready to assemble the dessert, gently run a warmed knife around the inside of the chilled mold. Center a serving platter over the mold, and carefully turn over, tapping the mold lightly to ensure that the charlotte is loose. Surround with a small amount of the coulis. Cut the charlotte into wedges to serve. Pass the remaining coulis in a serving bowl.

SERVES 6 to 8.

♦ ♦ ♦ ♦ ♦ ♦

ABOVE, LEFT: *Claude consults with his winemaker on every detail of the Champagne that carries his name. While some might be satisfied to leave the decisions to those who watch over the bottles, Claude spends at least half his time at the vineyard and in the cellars.* OPPOSITE: *Red Fruit Charlotte is served in the dining room at the five-star Crillon Hotel in Paris—part of the Taittinger family's holdings.*

Martha Stewart

♦ ♦ ♦ ♦ ♦ ♦ ♦ ♦ ♦ ♦

"I'M FORTUNATE THAT I DEVELOPED A
CAREER FOCUSING ON THE HOME AND
GARDEN, BECAUSE I'M A HOMEBODY FIRST
AND FOREMOST."

As a child in Nutley, New Jersey, Martha Stewart learned to garden with her father. He instructed her how to prune roses, propagate flowers, and keep weeds from overwhelming the vegetables. "I'll always remember what my father taught me," she said.

From her mother, a schoolteacher and homemaker, Martha learned the basics of cooking, baking, canning, and sewing. "This gave me a solid foundation."

Martha used this knowledge from her formative years when she and her own family moved to Westport, Connecticut. She created a catering company, which eventually led to eight books and several videos on cooking, entertaining, and decorating. Martha's success grew even more with regular television appearances and a bimonthly "lifestyle" magazine that was launched in 1991.

When sharing her insights into combining ordinary objects with skill and artistry, Martha keeps no secrets from her readers. In her magazine, *Martha Stewart Living*, she advises, "Dishes of delicious-looking foods can be served alongside unique yet familiar and comforting decorations—seashells transformed into Christmas tree ornaments and baubles, and holiday wreaths adorned with silken gold-mesh ribbons instead of the usual red velvet." Her particular style encourages entertaining at home—with everything being elegant and memorable. How-to instructions and superb recipes, accompanied by beautiful photographs, make Martha's inspired settings easy to re-create.

"In the nineties, we are going to take more time to enhance our surroundings and get closer to our friends and family. I think the garden will become more important. Gardening is a family-oriented activity that anyone can do, and is one of the most rewarding pastimes. You can always cook what you grow to make fresher, tastier, and more memorable meals at home."

A FALL MENU

♦ ♦ ♦ ♦ ♦ ♦ ♦

BIBB LETTUCE SALAD
GRILLED BRIE ON FRENCH BREAD
SESAME CHICKEN IN ACORN SQUASH
OLD-FASHIONED BOTTOM-CRUST
APPLE PIE

OPPOSITE: *Martha Stewart, who loves animals, poses with Roscoe, a Himalayan cat. At Turkey Hill Farm, Martha's home, her cats and dogs often follow her around the grounds and the gardens.*

GRILLED BRIE ON FRENCH BREAD

1 small loaf French bread
2 tablespoons (¼ stick) unsalted
* butter, softened*
1 teaspoon Dijon mustard
¼ pound Brie
1 tablespoon finely chopped chervil
* or parsley*

Preheat the broiler and set the broiling pan about 4 inches from the heat source. Slice the loaf of bread diagonally into ¾-inch slices, figuring approximately 3 to 4 slices per person.

In a small bowl, blend the butter with the mustard. Spread each slice of bread with a small amount of the butter mixture.

Cut the Brie into thin slices and place 1 or 2 slices of Brie on each slice of bread. Put the bread slices on the broiling pan and place under the broiler for about 2 minutes, or until the cheese is hot and bubbly. Sprinkle each slice with a pinch of the chopped chervil or parsley. Serve with Bibb Lettuce Salad.

SERVES 4.

BIBB LETTUCE SALAD

4 small heads Bibb lettuce
1 garlic clove, halved
3 tablespoons olive oil
1 tablespoon freshly squeezed
* lemon juice*
Freshly ground pepper

Separate the lettuce leaves and wash in several changes of cold water. Spin dry in a salad spinner and remove to dry completely on paper towels. Transfer to plastic bags and refrigerate for at least 2 hours before serving.

Rub 4 individual serving plates with the garlic halves. Arrange the chilled lettuce leaves on the plates. Sprinkle the olive oil and lemon juice evenly over the lettuce. Season with pepper to taste. Serve with Grilled Brie on French Bread (recipe follows).

SERVES 4.

SESAME CHICKEN IN ACORN SQUASH

1 1-inch piece fresh ginger, peeled
    and thinly sliced
2 tablespoons sesame oil
3 garlic cloves, peeled and halved
Pinch red pepper flakes
1 teaspoon chili powder
½ cup white wine
¼ cup soy sauce
2 whole chicken breasts, boned,
    skinned, and cut into ¾-inch
    strips
2 acorn squash, halved lengthwise
3 carrots, peeled and sliced
20 snow peas
1 small head broccoli, cut into
    small flowerets
½ cup all-purpose flour
2 tablespoons black sesame seeds
2 tablespoons white sesame seeds
3 tablespoons unsalted butter

Mix the ginger, sesame oil, garlic, red pepper flakes, chili powder, wine, and soy sauce in a shallow bowl. Add the chicken and refrigerate overnight (or for at least 30 minutes at room temperature).

Preheat the oven to 350° F. Put the squash halves, cut side down, in two 9-by-13-inch baking pans. Add ½ inch of water to each and bake until the squash is tender, 30 to 40 minutes.

Meanwhile, bring a large pot of salted water to a boil. Blanch the carrots until tender, about 3 minutes. Drain, refresh under cold running water, and drain again. Blanch the snow peas in the boiling water for about 1 minute. Drain, refresh, and drain again. Blanch the broccoli until tender, about 2 minutes. Drain, refresh, and drain again. Set the blanched vegetables aside.

About 15 minutes before the squash is done, remove the chicken to a plate or platter and set aside. Strain the marinade into a small bowl and set aside. Combine the flour and the black and white sesame seeds in a small, shallow bowl. Roll the chicken strips in the mixture.

Melt the butter in a 10-inch skillet and sauté the chicken for 2 to 2½ minutes per side, or until golden. Remove the chicken and set aside. Pour off the excess butter and crumbs.

Deglaze the skillet with ¼ cup of the strained marinade. Bring the marinade to a boil and add the carrots, snow peas, and broccoli to the pan. Cook over moderate heat just long enough to reheat the vegetables.

Add the chicken strips and toss well. Place each squash half on a dinner plate, cut side up, and add the chicken and vegetables; let them spill over the squash halves. Serve at once.

SERVES 4.

OPPOSITE, TOP: *Martha demonstrates how to make and care for topiaries.* OPPOSITE, BOTTOM: *Working in her favorite spot, the garden, at home in Westport.* ABOVE: *Martha's recipe for Sesame Chicken in Acorn Squash takes advantage of this very autumnal vegetable. "We are accustomed to baked acorn squash with brown sugar, butter, and bacon, or steamed and served with nothing but salt and pepper and butter. But here, the squash halves are filled with crunchy sesame chicken strips and Chinese vegetables that are prepared while the squash bakes." This colorful main course is served on a pottery plate made by Martha's daughter, Alexis.*

Old-fashioned Bottom-Crust Apple Pie

FOR THE PASTRY
8 tablespoons (1 stick) cold
*   unsalted butter, cut into*
*   small pieces*
1 cup all-purpose flour
1 teaspoon sugar
½ teaspoon salt
3 to 4 tablespoons ice water

FOR THE FILLING
4 tart apples, peeled, cored, and
*   thinly sliced*
½ cup plus 2 tablespoons sugar
1 teaspoon cinnamon
2 tablespoons (¼ stick) unsalted
*   butter*
Pinch ground mace
Pinch grated nutmeg
Confectioners' sugar
1½ cups heavy cream

To prepare the pastry, combine the butter, flour, sugar, and salt in the bowl of a food processor. Process just until the mixture resembles coarse meal. Add the ice water bit by bit until the dough pulls away from the bowl and forms a solid mass; this process should take less than 1 minute.

Transfer the dough to a floured work surface. Gather the dough into a ball, flatten it slightly, and roll into a 12-inch circle. Fit the pastry into an 8-inch pie plate and chill for 20 minutes.

Preheat the oven to 375° F. Fill the chilled crust with the apple slices, then sprinkle with ½ cup sugar and the cinnamon. Dot with the butter. Sprinkle with the mace and nutmeg, and then fold the overhanging

pastry edges over the apples.

Bake for 45 minutes, or until the apple filling is bubbly and the crust is golden. Cool slightly, then slide the pie out of the dish and onto a serving plate. Sprinkle the crust with the confectioners' sugar.

Just before serving, whip the cream with the remaining 2 tablespoons sugar until soft peaks are formed. Serve the pie with the whipped cream.

MAKES 1 8-INCH PIE.

◆ ◆ ◆ ◆ ◆ ◆ ◆

ABOVE: *Martha takes a relaxing walk with her dog ZuZu.* OPPOSITE: *Martha serves her unusual but very easy apple pie on an old English breadboard. A circle of pastry dough, several inches larger than the pie plate, is filled with apples and spices, and then the edges are simply folded over the fruit. A yellowware bowl holds freshly whipped cream.*

Isabel Goldsmith

◆ ◆ ◆ ◆ ◆ ◆ ◆ ◆ ◆ ◆ ◆

"I INVITE YOU TO COME DOWN TO LAS ALAMANDAS AND HAVE A MEXICAN FLING."

To have this special drink, you must travel south to Mexico, down the coast to a compound of four pristine, pastel-painted *casas*, which Bolivian tin heiress Isabel Goldsmith calls home when she is not attending to her more formal lifestyle in London and Paris. This compound, named after the yellow wildflower that grows in the region, was originally meant to be a place to invite friends and family to romp on the beach and relax far from the world of cars and phones and fax machines. Still without all three, it is now not only Isabel's private domain but a very exclusive seaside resort hotel halfway between Puerto Vallarta and Manzanillo.

A visit to Las Alamandas places you somewhere between paradise and your favorite Mexican restaurant, with only one exception: Isabel has rethought and restyled Mexican cuisine so she and her guests can enjoy all the wonderful flavors and

---

THE MENU

◆ ◆ ◆ ◆ ◆ ◆

CHICKEN TACOS
STUFFED BANANA CROQUETTES
OCTOPUS SALAD
CARROT SOUP
ALAMANDAS-STYLE FISH
MEXICAN APPLE PIE

OPPOSITE: *Since Isabel Goldsmith decided to open Las Alamandas, her incredibly beautiful private compound, to guests from around the world, her "Nouvelle Mexican" menus are talked about from Hollywood to Gstaad.*

---

still look absolutely great in a bathing suit. All who have had the pleasure of sitting down to a dinner of Isabel's Nouvelle Mexican Cuisine in her open-air dining room surrounded by a patio, with the clear blue Pacific just on the other side, can vouch that she hasn't sacrificed flavor. Most of the ingredients are grown in private gardens located on the 1,400-acre compound. And when fish is served, as it frequently is, you can be sure that it has been taken from the ocean only hours before the grill is fired up in the open-air *palapa*.

When the sky turns the color of the blazing pink drink, that's the time to indulge in a sampling of their amazing Nouvelle Mexican hors d'oeuvres and, of course, a Mexican Fling.

"But you must come down here to try it, because the liquid from the coconut must be totally fresh or the results will not be the same."

TOP: *Isabel frequently stops in the kitchen to discuss the upcoming meal with the chefs.* ABOVE: *Relax in a hammock overlooking the Pacific.* OPPOSITE, TOP: *Most meals begin with an array of appetizers. Chicken Tacos are served with margaritas.* OPPOSITE, BOTTOM: *Colorful handmade Mexican crockery is used for nearly everything at Las Alamandas.*

CHICKEN TACOS

2 boneless and skinless chicken
 breasts, about 4 ounces each
Salt and freshly ground pepper
2 tablespoons olive oil
2 medium tomatoes, cut into
 ½-inch dice
1 medium onion, finely chopped
1 garlic clove, finely chopped
4 bay leaves
12 small soft corn tortillas
2 cups vegetable oil
Sour cream
Guacamole
Salsa Mexicana

Season the chicken fillets with salt and pepper to taste. Place in a small skillet and add just enough water to cover. Over moderately high heat, bring to a boil. Reduce the heat to moderately low and simmer, covered, until firm to the touch, about 5 minutes. Cool, then shred into long, thin strips.

Heat the olive oil in a medium sauté pan or skillet over moderately high heat. Add the tomatoes, onion, garlic, and bay leaves. Reduce the heat to medium and cook until the onions are softened, 7 to 10 minutes. Add the chicken and simmer, partially covered, for 15 minutes. Remove from the heat and discard the bay leaves.

Place about 1 tablespoon of the chicken mixture in the center of each tortilla. Roll and secure with a toothpick.

In a moderately large skillet, heat the vegetable oil to 375° F. Working with only a few tacos at a time, fry them until golden brown, about 5 minutes, turning frequently. Do not overcrowd the pan or the tacos will not brown properly. Drain on paper towels.

To serve, cut the tacos in half and place on a large ceramic serving platter, accompanied by bowls of sour cream, Guacamole, and Salsa Mexicana (recipes follow).

SERVES 4.

GUACAMOLE

2 medium tomatoes
1 small onion
2 serrano chilies, halved and seeded
  (see note)
2 tablespoons chopped fresh
  cilantro (or to taste)
2 ripe avocados
½ teaspoon salt (or to taste)
1 tablespoon freshly squeezed lime
  juice (or to taste)

Finely chop the tomatoes, onions, and chilies. Place in a small bowl along with the cilantro. Peel the avocados and add the pulp to the bowl; reserve the pits. Use the back of a fork or spoon to mash the avocado pulp. Add the salt and lime juice and blend well.

If the guacamole is not served immediately, place the pits in the center of the guacamole to prevent discoloration.

MAKES ABOUT 2 CUPS.

NOTE: Because these chilies are hot, wear rubber gloves when handling them.

SALSA MEXICANA

4 medium tomatoes
1 small yellow onion
2 serrano chilies, halved and seeded
  (see note, above)
2 tablespoons chopped fresh
  cilantro
½ teaspoon salt (or to taste)
1 tablespoon freshly squeezed lime
  juice (or to taste)

Finely chop the tomatoes, onion, and chilies. In a small bowl, combine the chopped vegetables with the cilantro, salt, and lime juice, blending well. Let the salsa sit at room temperature for 1 to 2 hours before serving.

MAKES 1½ TO 2 CUPS.

STUFFED BANANA CROQUETTES

2 large plantains, not very ripe
½ teaspoon salt (or to taste)
2 eggs
¼ cup all-purpose flour
1 cup canned refried beans
¼ pound mozzarella cheese, cut into ¼-inch dice
2 cups vegetable oil
1 head romaine lettuce, leaves separated, rinsed, and dried
½ cup sour cream
Green Sauce

Peel the plantains and cut into thick slices. In a medium saucepan over moderately high heat, combine the plantains and the salt. Add water to cover and bring to a boil. Reduce the heat to moderate and cook until tender, 10 to 15 minutes. (The exact cooking time will depend on the ripeness of the plantains. Test frequently for doneness by piercing with a fork; if not very soft, continue cooking until tender.) Pour off the water and place the cooked plantains in the bowl of a food processor and puree until smooth.

In a medium bowl, beat the eggs with the flour. Stir in the plantain puree and blend well.

Using the palm of the hand, form 16 small croquettes or cylinders that measure about 4 inches long and 2½ inches in diameter. Place about 2 tablespoons of the refried beans in the center of 8 of the croquettes and fold the sides over to seal. Fill the remaining 8 croquettes with the mozzarella. Fold the sides over to seal.

In a large skillet, heat the oil to 350° F. Fry the croquettes in pairs until golden, about 30 seconds on each side. Remove and drain on paper towels.

Arrange the lettuce leaves on a large serving platter. Top with the croquettes. Spoon the sour cream over the croquettes. Serve warm with Green Sauce (recipe follows).

SERVES 4.

GREEN SAUCE

½ pounds tomatillos (see note)
3 serrano chilies (see note, page 141)
1 garlic clove, peeled
2 tablespoons finely chopped onion
½ teaspoon salt

Remove the outer leaves of the tomatillos. Over high heat, bring a large pot of water to a rapid boil. Plunge the tomatillos in and bring the water just back to a boil, then drain immediately. Under cold running water, use a paring knife to remove the tough outer skin.

Cut the chilies in half, remove the seeds and the white membrane, and coarsely chop.

In the bowl of a food processor, combine the tomatillos, chilies, garlic, and onion. Add the salt and process in short pulses until the mixture forms a slightly thick sauce, 15 to 20 seconds. Refrigerate until ready to use.

MAKES ABOUT 1½ CUPS.

NOTE: Tomatillos are small green tomatoes available in Latin American markets.

OPPOSITE, TOP: *Every casa, or house, has its own private patio for dining and relaxing.* OPPOSITE: *Casa del Sol is one of the four private casas that make up the compound.* ABOVE: *Isabel insists that all her dishes be "lower" in calories than ordinary Mexican cuisine. There is less cheese but an interesting balance of flavors in her wonderful Stuffed Banana Croquettes.* BOTTOM: *Follow these simple steps, along with the recipe instructions, to make perfect Stuffed Banana Croquettes.*

TOP: *Octopus Salad and Carrot Soup,* ABOVE, *take advantage of the abundance of fresh seafood as well as the vegetables grown in Las Alamandas's private gardens.* OPPOSITE: *Isabel likes to cook fish with lots of traditional fresh herbs and then tops the fish with a highly seasoned sauce to contrast with its delicate, ocean-fresh flavor.*

OCTOPUS SALAD

1 fresh whole and cleaned octopus (about 2 pounds)
1½ medium onions
3 garlic cloves, crushed but not peeled
1 tablespoon sugar
3 medium tomatoes
10 green olives, pitted
1 serrano chili (see note, page 141)
2 tablespoons chopped cilantro
Juice of 1 lime
Juice of 1 orange
Salt and freshly ground pepper
Sliced tomatoes
Avocado wedges
Fresh basil leaves

Place the octopus, one onion, the garlic, and the sugar in a large pot of salted water. Bring to a boil over high heat. Reduce the heat to moderately low and simmer until the octopus is tender, about 2 hours. Drain in a colander and cool, discarding the onion and garlic. Cut the octopus into bite-size pieces and set aside.

Finely chop the tomatoes, the remaining ½ onion, and the olives. Cut the chili in half, remove the seeds and the membranes, and finely chop.

In a mixing bowl, combine the tomatoes, onion, olives, chili, and cilantro. Add the octopus, lime juice, and orange juice, and season to taste with salt and pepper. Cover with plastic wrap and marinate for ½ hour.

To serve, mound the salad in the center of a large serving platter or on individual plates. Garnish with tomato slices, avocado wedges, and basil leaves. Serve with tostados or tortilla chips.

SERVES 4 to 6.

◆ ◆ ◆ ◆ ◆ ◆ ◆

CARROT SOUP

10 medium carrots (about 1½ pounds)
2 garlic cloves, peeled
1 small onion
½ bell pepper, seeded and deveined
3 cups chicken stock
2 tablespoons (¼ stick) unsalted butter
1 cup heavy cream
Salt and freshly ground pepper

Wash the carrots, but do not peel them. Place in a large pot of salted water and bring to a boil over moderately high heat. Reduce the heat to medium and cook until tender, 10 to 15 minutes. Drain and rinse under cold water. Coarsely chop.

In the bowl of a food processor, combine the carrots, garlic, onion, bell pepper, and 1 cup of the chicken stock. Blend until smooth. (Depending on capacity of food processor, this may have to be done in two batches.)

In a soup pot or saucepan, melt the butter. Add the carrot

mixture, remaining chicken stock, and cream. Over medium-high heat, bring to a boil. Season to taste with salt and pepper.

Serve hot or cold with warm bread sticks.

SERVES 4 to 6.

◆ ◆ ◆ ◆ ◆ ◆ ◆

ALAMANDAS-STYLE FISH

2 teaspoons whole black
  peppercorns
2 tablespoons chopped fresh
  oregano (or 2 teaspoons dried)
3 to 4 garlic cloves, peeled
1 teaspoon ground cumin
1 teaspoon coriander seeds
Pinch saffron threads
1 cinnamon stick, broken into
  pieces
1 teaspoon salt
¼ cup unsweetened grapefruit juice
1 large whole red snapper (3 to 4
  pounds)
Rice with Cilantro and Celery
Baked Tomatoes
Boiled Green Beans

In a mortar with a pestle or in the bowl of a food processor, combine the peppercorns, oregano, garlic, cumin, coriander, saffron, cinnamon, and salt. Grind and crush with the pestle, or pulse several times in the food processor, to blend to a

paste. Add the grapefruit juice and mix well. Pour this mixture into a flat glass baking dish. Let dry, uncovered, for 24 to 36 hours. The paste will be thick and fragrant. Remove to a glass jar and store, covered, until ready to use.

Lightly oil and preheat the broiler. Clean the fish or have the fishmonger prepare it for broiling, but leave it whole. Spread the spice mixture all over the fish to entirely cover, inside and out. Broil 4 to 6 inches away from source of heat until cooked through, 5 to

7 minutes on each side.

Serve with Rice with Cilantro and Celery, Baked Tomatoes, and Boiled Green Beans (recipes follow).

SERVES 4.

TOP: *Architectural splendor, pastoral colors, and flowers—including the tiny yellow flowers called* las alamandas—*abound.* ABOVE: *The "Mexican Fling" is a special drink— invented by Isabel herself—which can be made only in Mexico, where the juice and meat of fresh coconuts are blended with other ingredients just seconds after the nuts are cracked open.* OPPOSITE: *Guests who choose not to dine at their casas gather at the open-air restaurant for dinner.*

RICE WITH CILANTRO AND CELERY

1 cup long-grain rice
2 tablespoons unsalted butter
2 cups boiling water
1 tablespoon powdered chicken consommé
1 tablespoon chopped fresh cilantro
1 celery stalk, finely chopped (about ½ cup)

In a medium mixing bowl, cover the rice with hot tap water and soak for 15 minutes. Rinse well under cold running water.

Melt the butter in a small skillet over medium heat. Add the rice and cook until translucent, about 2 minutes, stirring constantly. Pour in the boiling water. Add the consommé powder, cilantro, and celery. Stir to blend. Reduce the heat to low, cover, and simmer until done, about 15 minutes. Stir with a fork, then re-cover and let sit for 5 minutes before serving.

MAKES 2 CUPS.

BAKED TOMATOES

4 small tomatoes (about 1 pound)
2 garlic cloves
2 tablespoons olive oil
Salt and freshly ground pepper

Preheat the oven to 350° F. Line a 9-by-12-inch baking dish with foil and brush lightly with olive oil. About ¼ inch from the top, slice off the tops of the tomatoes. Discard the tops and stand the tomatoes, cut side up, in the pan.

Use a garlic press to make a paste of the garlic, or chop the cloves very finely. Drizzle about ½ tablespoon of olive oil over the top of each tomato, and distribute the garlic evenly over the oil. Season to taste with salt and pepper.

Bake until the garlic is golden brown, about 30 minutes. Cool slightly before serving.

SERVES 4.

BOILED GREEN BEANS

1 pound green beans
1 teaspoon salt

Trim the ends off the beans and cut them into uniform pieces about 1½ inches long. Bring a large pot of water to a boil, and add the beans. Reduce the heat to medium, add the salt, and cook until tender, about 10 minutes. Drain and serve at once.

SERVES 4.

TOP: *Fresh fruit from the orchards and gardens of Las Alamandas—here, just-picked pineapples—is served at almost every meal.* ABOVE: *Each casa has its own color scheme and distinctive architectural detail.*

MEXICAN APPLE PIE

FOR THE PASTRY

1½ cups all-purpose flour
½ cup sugar
¼ teaspoon salt
½ cup (1 stick) unsalted butter, chilled
1 egg, beaten with 1 teaspoon water

FOR THE FILLING

6 medium cooking apples (about 3 pounds)
2 egg yolks
1 cup sweetened condensed milk
¼ cup evaporated milk
Juice of 1 lime
Fresh Banana Ice Cream

In the bowl of a food processor, combine the flour, sugar, and salt. Process briefly to blend. Cut the butter into small pieces and add to the work bowl. With several quick, short pulses, blend in the butter until the mixture resembles the texture of coarse meal. With the motor running, pour in the egg mixture. Process just until the mixture forms a ball around the blades, about 15 seconds. Remove the dough to a floured work surface and knead lightly to form a smooth ball. Place in the center of a 10-inch pie plate. Working from the center out, extend the pastry to evenly line the plate. Crimp the edges decoratively. Refrigerate for at least 30 minutes, but no more than 2 hours.

Preheat the oven to 425° F. Peel and grate all but one of the apples. In a large mixing bowl, combine the grated apples with the egg yolks, the condensed and evaporated milk, and the lime juice. Stir to blend. Transfer to the lined pie pan. Peel and core the remaining apple, cut it in half, and slice it very thinly. Arrange the slices in a decorative pattern over the grated apple mixture.

Place the pie in the oven and immediately reduce the heat to 375° F. Bake until the pastry is golden around the edges and the apples are caramel colored, about 45 minutes.

Cool the pie completely before slicing. Serve with Fresh Banana Ice Cream (recipe follows).

SERVES 6 to 8.

FRESH BANANA ICE CREAM

3 cups heavy cream
8 ripe bananas
1 cup sugar

Pour 2 cups of the heavy cream into a shallow baking dish and freeze until solid. Break the frozen cream into chunks, transfer to a mixing bowl, and beat with an electric mixer until very fluffy.

Peel the bananas and cut them in half lengthwise. Remove the black seeds from the center.

In the bowl of a food processor, combine the bananas, the remaining cup of cream, and the sugar and process until smooth. Carefully fold this into the whipped cream. Immediately transfer to a chilled large serving bowl or chilled individual molds. Freeze until ready to serve.

SERVES 8.

ABOVE: *A bonfire, made from driftwood gathered on Las Alamandas's beach, is a spectacular form of entertainment.*

Robin Leach

◆ ◆ ◆ ◆ ◆ ◆ ◆ ◆ ◆ ◆

"In 1963, I cooked my first—and last—steak, and nearly burned the apartment house down in the process."

"My most reliable cooking method is simple: I always cook by smell. And I plan my menus with two things in mind—Friday night and Saturday night. On Friday, anything I cook must be made in one single pot. All the ingredients go into one giant covered pot, and after about an hour in the oven (at the proper temperature, may I add), Rich-and-Famous Chicken is completely ready to set before my guests, who are usually a few out-of-towners recovering from a week's work in the big city. Everyone helps set the table and we drink some Champagne and have a good laugh about everything that comes to mind. If it's Saturday night, the process is just about the same food-wise, except that a hefty bottle of really good Champagne—like Cristal—goes into the cooking pot to give a little extra richness to the dish, and we use the good napkins.

"I have a retreat on a lake in Connecticut that I don't get to nearly as often as I'd like. It's fully stocked with all kinds of toys—jet skis, a power boat, rafts for floating around the lake. I tell friends who are coming up to wear a bathing suit and a T-shirt, so I'm not about to start cooking or serving anything formal. The freezer is filled with sauces and stocks for pasta or salmon from the grill, and the Champagne is always chilling in the fridge.

"Now you know a bit about the way I live when I'm not having a heart-to-heart with a leading lady of the stage, or chatting with a major industrial mogul in his private plane, or conducting an interview with a deposed head of a recently renamed African country, or walking the halls of Hollywood's most sparkling stars' mansions. Most of my time, however, is taken up with planning another season of my shows, *Lifestyles of the Rich and Famous* and *Run Away with the Rich and Famous*. It's really a very exciting existence, which is why I keep my cooking efforts down to a minimum—I have to do all the work myself, because thus far, I haven't had time to hire a cook! If I ever do, you're all invited for dinner. Champagne, caviar, the works!"

THE MENU

◆ ◆ ◆ ◆ ◆ ◆ ◆

ASPARAGUS WITH HAZELNUT VINAIGRETTE

RIZ PILAF

ESSENCE OF SILVER AND GOLD

RICH-AND-FAMOUS CHICKEN

OPPOSITE: *Robin Leach lives for the weekends and a chance to relax on the deck of his lakeside home in Connecticut. Weather permitting, dinner is often served here.*

RIZ PILAF

1 cup long-grain rice
2 tablespoons (¼ stick) unsalted
  butter
1 large onion, coarsely chopped
½ teaspoon salt
¼ teaspoon freshly ground pepper
⅛ teaspoon ground cumin
2 cups Essence of Silver and Gold
  (page 154)

ASPARAGUS WITH HAZELNUT VINAIGRETTE

20 to 30 asparagus spears
¼ cup balsamic vinegar
¼ cup Champagne vinegar
1 cup light olive oil
½ teaspoon honey
½ teaspoon Dijon mustard
Salt and freshly ground pepper
¾ cup chopped, toasted hazelnuts

Fill a skillet with about an inch of water and fit with a steamer; bring to a boil.

Trim the asparagus, peeling the spears if they are fat, and put them in the steamer. Reduce the heat to moderate and steam 2 to 3 minutes if the spears are thin, 5 to 6 minutes if fat.

Remove the asparagus from the steamer and quickly run under cold water to stop the cooking process. Remove to drain on paper towels. Place the asparagus in a single layer on a serving platter.

Place the vinegars, olive oil, honey, mustard, and salt and pepper in a glass jar with a tight lid. Add half of the hazelnuts to the jar. Cover and shake to mix thoroughly.

Drizzle the vinaigrette over the asparagus and sprinkle with the remaining chopped nuts. Serve at room temperature.

SERVES 4 to 6.

Preheat the oven to 325° F. Rinse the rice under cold water. Over moderately high heat, melt the butter in a medium, flame-proof casserole with a tight-fitting lid. Add the onion and cook until softened, about 3 minutes. Add the salt, pepper, cumin, and rice. Reduce the heat to moderate and stir until the rice is coated and slightly transparent, 2 to 3 minutes.

Meanwhile, bring the Essence to a boil. Pour into the rice mixture and stir well. Cover the casserole and bake for 20 minutes. Remove from the oven, stir gently to separate the grains, then replace the lid and let sit for 5 more minutes. Season to taste with additional salt and pepper if necessary. Serve at once.

SERVES 4.

TOP: *Robin is an avid collector of pottery plates, especially those with colorful Caribbean themes.* ABOVE: *Once a year, Robin makes herb- and fruit-scented vinegars for holiday gifts and for cooking at home.* OPPOSITE: *"I redesigned my kitchen three years ago. Now everyone pulls up a stool and helps with the chopping."*

TOP: *"Rich-and-Famous Chicken is the easiest and tastiest one-hour dish on the face of the earth,"* says Robin of his favorite homemade meal.
ABOVE: *Depending on the season, the vegetables Robin serves vary. Asparagus, tiny French green beans called* haricots verts, *and broccoli are favorites.*

ESSENCE OF SILVER AND GOLD

2 1-pound pieces bottom round of veal, boned and tied
2 whole chicken breasts, about 1 pound each, bone in
4 pounds veal bones
2 leeks, trimmed, washed thoroughly, and coarsely chopped
2 celery stalks, thickly sliced
2 medium carrots, halved and thickly sliced
3 to 4 branches fresh thyme (2 teaspoons dried)
2 bay leaves
2 large onions, stuck with 2 whole cloves
2 teaspoons salt
20 whole black peppercorns
12 cups water
4 cups good-quality dry white wine★

Trim the veal and the chicken of any fat. Have the butcher saw the veal bones into 3 to 4 large pieces.

Combine all the ingredients in a large, nonreactive stockpot. Bring to a boil over moderately high heat, then reduce the heat to moderate and simmer, uncovered, 2 to 3 hours or until the liquid measures about 4 cups. Periodically skim off any residue that rises to the top.

Line a large sieve or colander with a double layer of cheesecloth or coarse muslin and set it inside a large bowl. Carefully ladle in the hot stock, discarding the solids. Let the stock cool to room temperature, then cover and refrigerate. Remove any fat that hardens on top.

MAKES ABOUT 4 CUPS.

★ Use your best wine for this sauce. Spare not and the results will pay off in praise.

◆ ◆ ◆ ◆ ◆ ◆ ◆

RICH-AND-FAMOUS CHICKEN

8 tablespoons (1 stick) unsalted butter
3 tablespoons all-purpose flour
2 cups Essence of Silver and Gold (see preceding recipe)
Salt and freshly ground pepper
2 large onions (about 1 pound), sliced
1 whole chicken (3½ to 5 pounds), cut into 8 pieces
1 cup Champagne
¼ cup fresh basil leaves, finely chopped (2 tablespoons dried)
2 tablespoons fresh oregano, finely chopped (1 tablespoon dried)
½ teaspoon dry mustard
1 tablespoon freshly squeezed lemon juice
2 teaspoons steak sauce
½ pound white mushrooms, trimmed, wiped clean, and thinly sliced
1 pound carrots, trimmed, peeled, halved, and cut into 1-inch pieces

1 cup green peas
4 medium potatoes (about 2
    pounds), peeled and cut into
    ½-inch cubes
1 cup heavy cream

NOTE: This recipe can be done in a "romertopf" (a clay pot designed for kitchen use), in a covered baking dish, or in a Dutch oven. If using a romertopf, consult a clay pot cookbook for cooking times and temperatures.

Preheat the oven to 425° F for a baking dish, 475° for a clay pot.

In a medium, heavy saucepan, melt 3 tablespoons of the butter over moderately high heat. Stir in the flour. Reduce the heat to moderate and cook slowly, whisking constantly, until well blended, about 3 to 5 minutes. Stir in the Essence of Silver and Gold and bring to a boil. Reduce the heat and simmer until the sauce is thickened and smooth, 7 to 10 minutes, stirring often. Season to taste with salt and pepper. Remove from the heat and keep warm.

Place the sliced onions in the bottom of a clay pot or baking dish. Cut 2½ tablespoons of the butter into thin slices and distribute evenly over the onions.

Rinse and pat the chicken dry. Season with salt and pepper. Place the chicken on top of the onions and sprinkle with 2 tablespoons of the Champagne. Add the basil, oregano, mus-

tard, lemon juice, and the steak sauce.

Arrange the mushrooms, carrots, and peas on top of the chicken. Top with thin slices of the remaining butter. Sprinkle with 2 more tablespoons of the Champagne.

Pour the sauce of Silver and Gold over the chicken and sprinkle with the remaining Champagne. Sink the potato cubes into the sauce, leaving them only slightly submerged. Cover the pot tightly and bake until the vegetables are soft and the chicken is done, about 45 to 50 minutes.

Remove the cover and cook until the protruding bits of potatoes are lightly browned, about 10 more minutes.

Arrange the chicken and vegetables on a serving platter. Cover to keep warm.

In a medium saucepan over high heat, boil the cream until it has reduced by half, 3 to 5 minutes. Add the reduced cream to the pan juices and boil for several minutes to reduce and thicken slightly. Pour over the chicken and serve immediately.

SERVES 4 to 6.

TOP: *Robin's Riz Pilaf is so flavorful, you might want to double the recipe. It goes fast!* ABOVE: *Dinner is served!*

Armen Petrossian

♦ ♦ ♦ ♦ ♦ ♦ ♦ ♦ ♦ ♦

"WHEN MY FATHER AND UNCLE THOUGHT
OF IMPORTING CAVIAR FROM RUSSIA TO
PARIS, IT WAS CONSIDERED A RADICAL PLAN.
WESTERN EUROPEANS KNEW ABOUT CAVIAR,
BUT IT SIMPLY WASN'T AVAILABLE."

Armen Petrossian's family were pioneers in importing caviar from Soviet Russia. Their biggest challenge was shipping the fragile sturgeon eggs without damaging them.

"Caviar must be kept cold to prevent spoilage, and there were no refrigerated transportation methods in the 1920s," Armen explained. "So my father and uncle had the caviar delicately packed in tins, placed in giant wooden barrels surrounded by ice inside and out. It was sent by various overland methods—including horse and wagon, truck, and train—all the way to Paris."

The Petrossians introduced caviar at a time when Parisians craved anything new and chic. *Haute couture* fashions, Champagne, stylish automobiles, art, jazz, new and exotic cuisines—especially caviar—were the rage. The mystique of caviar comes from its luxury status.

"Purists, like my uncle Christian Petrossian, would say caviar should be eaten alone, with per-

> ## THE RECIPES
>
> ♦ ♦ ♦ ♦ ♦ ♦
>
> BLINIS AND CAVIAR
> CAVIAR AND SCALLOP CEVICHE
> CAVIAR OMELETTE

OPPOSITE: *The blue tin bearing the Petrossian name has long been the symbol of the world's finest caviar. Armen Petrossian proudly displays his heritage.*

haps a piece of buttered toast. Discovering caviar, which should be eaten plain off a palette placed directly in the mouth, *is* a great sensation as the little eggs explode. However, caviar does combine well with certain very simple foods in cooking, as long as the caviar is the ingredient which adds a touch of unique flavor. Caviar is like truffles. You want only a pure taste.

"We eat caviar at home, of course. My children know how to eat caviar and they like it very much. At our frequent dinner parties, we always serve caviar as an appetizer. A *presentoire* of caviar is refilled again and again until everyone is satisfied.

"Besides caviar, one of the great pleasures of giving a dinner party at home is the look of the table —that is *my* first course. My wife makes very unique table settings, sometimes incorporating pieces from our collection of antique objects. The silver and the flowers are always very beautiful."

ABOVE, LEFT: *Delicious and tender, the Petrossian blini, served in the New York restaurant of the same name, is one of the best ways to serve caviar. Spread atop these blinis is pressed caviar, a very popular substitute for fresh, especially at a luncheon.* ABOVE, RIGHT: *Armen fills the* presentoires *with beluga, osetra, and sevruga caviar for a private tasting.*

BLINIS AND CAVIAR

2 cups milk
½ tablespoon active dry yeast
2 teaspoons sugar
3 cups flour
3 eggs, separated
5 tablespoons unsalted butter, melted
½ teaspoon salt
1 tin (125 grams or 4.4 ounces) beluga, osetra, or sevruga caviar

In a medium, heavy saucepan, scald the milk. Remove from the heat and cool to lukewarm. Add the yeast and blend until it has dissolved. Gradually blend in the sugar and half the flour. Cover the pan with a damp towel and set in a warm area until the batter has doubled in bulk, about 2 hours.

In a small bowl, beat the egg yolks, butter, and salt. Pour into the risen batter, add the remaining flour, and blend until smooth. Cover again and let rest in a warm place until doubled in bulk, about 2 more hours.

Beat the egg whites until stiff peaks form. Fold into the batter and set aside for 10 minutes.

Butter a small skillet and set over moderately high heat. When hot, spoon in 1½ tablespoons of batter per blini. Fry on both sides until golden brown.

Serve, topped with spoonfuls of caviar.

CAVIAR AND SCALLOP CEVICHE

8 small leaves Boston lettuce, washed, rinsed, and patted dry
2 teaspoons lemon juice
1½ ounces (50 grams) pressed caviar
10 to 12 large sea scallops, about ½ pound
1 tablespoon (1 ounce) salmon roe
2 tablespoons extra-virgin olive oil
¼ teaspoon freshly ground white pepper
Several sprigs fresh chervil

Place 4 4-inch ring molds on individual serving plates.

Stack the lettuce leaves on top of each other and, using a sharp knife, cut into long, thin strips. Toss with the lemon

MAKES 40.

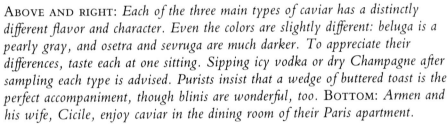

ABOVE AND RIGHT: *Each of the three main types of caviar has a distinctly different flavor and character. Even the colors are slightly different: beluga is a pearly gray, and osetra and sevruga are much darker. To appreciate their differences, taste each at one sitting. Sipping icy vodka or dry Champagne after sampling each type is advised. Purists insist that a wedge of buttered toast is the perfect accompaniment, though blinis are wonderful, too.* BOTTOM: *Armen and his wife, Cicile, enjoy caviar in the dining room of their Paris apartment.*

juice and arrange on the bottom of the ring molds. Sprinkle the caviar among the beds of lettuce.

Slice the scallops horizontally as thin as possible into "petals." Arrange the circles in the shape of a flower, edges overlapping, on top of the caviar. Place a small mound of salmon roe in the center of the scallops. Brush the scallops with olive oil, season with a tiny amount of white pepper, and garnish with the chervil sprigs. Remove the ring and serve at once.

SERVES 4.

CAVIAR OMELETTE

3 tablespoons clarified butter (see note)
1 large all-purpose potato, grated
Salt and freshly ground white pepper
5 asparagus, trimmed to 4-inch spears
1 heaping tablespoon pressed caviar, chopped
1 tablespoon vegetable oil
1 shiitake mushroom, trimmed, wiped clean, and thinly sliced
1 large oyster mushroom (pleurote), trimmed, wiped clean, and thinly sliced
½ tablespoon chopped fresh chives
1 tablespoon heavy cream
1 tablespoon unsalted butter
3 eggs
1 tablespoon crème fraîche

ABOVE: *At home, the Petrossian table is set lavishly.*

Preheat the oven to 350° F.

Place 2 tablespoons of the clarified butter in a small, ovenproof, non-stick sauté pan set over high heat. When it is very hot, add the potatoes, season with salt and pepper to taste, and then press down to form a small cake. Shaking the pan constantly, fry the potato cake on one side until lightly browned, 3 to 5 minutes, taking care it does not stick. Carefully turn out onto a large plate, browned side up. Gently slip the cake back into the sauté pan and brown the other side, about 3 more minutes, shaking the pan constantly to prevent sticking. (If needed, add additional clarified butter to the pan before returning the cake to brown on the second side.) Return the cake to the pie plate and place in the oven until ready to use. (This frees up the pan to make additional potato cakes as needed.)

Bring a large pot of salted water to a boil. Add the asparagus spears, bring back to a boil, and cook rapidly until the spears are barely tender, 1 to 2 minutes. Drain and rinse under cold water. Drain again and set aside.

Shape the pressed caviar into a small, compact cylinder about 2 inches long. Set aside.

Heat the vegetable oil in a small sauté pan set over moderate heat. Add the mushrooms and season with salt and pepper to taste. Add the chives. Sauté until the mushrooms are golden brown. Add the cream and increase the heat to high. Bring to a boil and stir constantly until mixture is reduced and glossy, about 2 minutes.

Cut the potato cake in half and slice each half horizontally. Spoon the mushroom filling evenly over the bottom halves of the potato cake and set the top halves on the filling.

Melt the remaining tablespoon of clarified butter in a small pan. Add the asparagus spears and toss until heated through.

Melt the unsalted butter in a small omelette pan set over

high heat. In a small bowl, beat the eggs with salt and pepper to taste. When the butter ceases to bubble, add the eggs and cook until barely set in the center. Place the caviar cylinder in the center, add the *crème fraîche*, and fold the edges to meet in the center. Turn the omelette onto a serving plate. Arrange the halves of the filled potato cake and asparagus spears slightly fanned. Serve at once.

SERVES 1.

NOTE: To clarify butter, melt unsalted butter in a heavy saucepan over very low heat. Remove from the heat and let stand until the milky residue settles on the bottom. Line a sieve with a dampened cheesecloth and set over a bowl. Carefully ladle the golden liquid into the sieve, avoiding the residue at the bottom.

ABOVE: *A* presentoire *is a special dish created just for presenting and serving delicate caviar, which must be kept cold at all times. The* presentoire *can be passed at the table, and also makes a beautiful centerpiece while the caviar course is in progress. The Petrossians have collected antique* presentoires *over the years from Paris flea markets and small antiques shops.* LEFT: *Even after a lifetime of firsthand experience with what is perhaps the world's most luxurious food, Armen Petrossian says he will never tire of the special qualities and tastes of caviar.*

Marylou Vanderbilt Whitney

◆ ◆ ◆ ◆ ◆ ◆ ◆ ◆ ◆

"WE MAKE A LOT OF MAGIC
IN THIS KITCHEN."

Lunch at Marylou Whitney's Saratoga home, Cady Hill, can be a magical event. She has more secret and stylish locales than anyone you'll ever meet: a gypsy wagon, a tree house, a gazebo, and an authentic, handmade tepee. Perhaps the location the Saratoga set knows best is the gleaming white, wicker-clad North Porch of Cady Hill's stately hundred-year-old house.

"This is the first lunch of the season," Marylou declared, "and every lunch and dinner for the next month we'll have people over, as well as houseguests."

No matter how informal a North Porch lunch may seem, a team of well-seasoned veterans work side by side in the kitchen to create the meals for which Cady Hill is so well known. Each phase of the menu, from creating a list of six complementary courses to choosing the exact serving platter, bowl, or basket, is determined long before chef Corky and kitchen staff director Eddie put on their white jackets. With as many as ten people sharing the same space, organization is crucial. When the meal is

---

THE MENU

◆ ◆ ◆ ◆ ◆ ◆ ◆

SOLID SOUP
PASTA WITH BASIL AND PROSCIUTTO
COBB SALAD
PECAN PUFFS

OPPOSITE: *Cady Hill offers guests turn-of-the-century hospitality: rooms are ready upon arrival, a nap in the afternoon is a must, there's always a glass of iced tea waiting, and everyone dresses for dinner.*

---

ready to be served, the staff swings into action, as they have season after season for Marylou's casual Saratoga lunches and formal dinners.

Saratoga has been synonymous with horse racing for almost a century, and, for the best part of that century, the Vanderbilts and Whitneys have been a part of the scene. To this day, the most coveted lunch and dinner invitations come from Marylou Vanderbilt Whitney. Though she looks as if she just stepped off the pages of *Vogue*, this inveterate party planner is no stranger to the kitchen. "Oh, I just love to cook. I'd rather be *in* the kitchen than doing all the planning and organizing, and there are so many recipes I love to make myself," she says in her half-Southern, half-sophisticated city accent.

A stay at Cady Hill recalls the turn-of-the-century hospitality of great hostesses. The dining room is a stage where conversation is sparkling, witty, and sophisticated. It's a trip back in time to gentler, more elegant days, and Marylou Whitney makes it look effortless.

PASTA WITH BASIL AND PROSCIUTTO

3 tablespoons olive oil
2 garlic cloves, minced
1 cup freshly grated Parmesan
   cheese
1 cup heavy cream
¼ cup chopped fresh basil
3 ripe tomatoes, peeled, seeded,
   and chopped
¼ pound prosciutto, diced
1 pound angel hair pasta

Heat the olive oil in a large saucepan over moderately high heat. Add the garlic and stir until softened, about 1 minute.

In a small bowl, whisk ¾ cup of the cheese with the cream. Add to the saucepan, lower the heat to moderate, and simmer until the mixture has thickened slightly, about 5 minutes. Add the basil, tomatoes, and prosciutto. Continue cooking over moderate heat until the tomatoes have softened, about 5 minutes.

Meanwhile, bring a large pot of salted water to a boil, and cook the pasta according to package directions. Drain and rinse the pasta under cool water, and return it to the pot. Add the sauce, and simmer until the pasta is heated through, 2 to 3 minutes. Arrange on serving plates and sprinkle with the remaining cheese. Serve at once.

SERVES 4 to 6.

TOP: *Cornelius "Sonny" and Marylou Vanderbilt Whitney divide their time between Kentucky and Saratoga Springs, involved in the world of horse racing and breeding—two great American traditions.*
ABOVE: *Cady Hill, a working farm, provides its own food, water, and power. It has been in Sonny's family since the 1850s.*

SOLID SOUP

1 8-ounce package cream cheese,
   softened
1 teaspoon curry powder
1 teaspoon freshly squeezed lemon
   juice
1 10½-ounce can beef consommé
Stuffed green olives, sliced
Several parsley sprigs

In a food processor or blender, process the cream cheese, curry powder, lemon juice, and half of the consommé until smooth. Pour the mixture into 6 demitasse cups and refrigerate until firm, about 3 hours. Divide the remaining consommé among the cups and chill until firm, about 2 hours. Garnish with a slice of olive and a bit of parsley.

SERVES 6.

COBB SALAD

6 cups shredded iceberg lettuce
3 cups cooked chicken, chopped
3 hard-boiled eggs, chopped
2 medium tomatoes, seeded and
    chopped
¾ cup blue cheese, crumbled
    (about 3 ounces)
6 slices crisp bacon, drained and
    crumbled
1 medium avocado, halved, pitted,
    peeled, and cut into wedges

On 6 salad plates, arrange beds
of lettuce. Arrange the chicken,
eggs, tomatoes, blue cheese,
and bacon in rows on top.
Garnish with avocado wedges
placed on the side. Serve with
Brown Derby French Dressing
(recipe follows) and crusty
garlic bread.

SERVES 6.

BROWN DERBY
FRENCH DRESSING

⅓ cup red wine vinegar
1 tablespoon freshly squeezed
    lemon juice
1 teaspoon Worcestershire sauce
½ teaspoon salt
½ teaspoon sugar
½ teaspoon dry mustard
½ teaspoon freshly ground black
    pepper
1 garlic clove, minced
½ cup olive oil

In a screw-top jar, combine the
vinegar, lemon juice, Worcestershire sauce, salt, sugar, mustard, pepper, and garlic. Cover
and shake well. Add the olive
oil and shake again. Chill thoroughly. Shake vigorously before serving.

MAKES 1 CUP.

◆ ◆ ◆ ◆ ◆ ◆ ◆

PECAN PUFFS

½ cup (1 stick) unsalted butter
2 tablespoons granulated sugar
1 cup pecans, finely ground
1 cup sifted cake flour
Confectioners' sugar

Preheat the oven to 300° F and
lightly butter a baking sheet. In
a mixing bowl, cream the butter and granulated sugar until
smooth. Stir in the pecans and
flour.
   Roll the dough into ¾-inch
balls. Place the balls on the
baking sheet. Bake until the
puffs are golden brown, about
30 minutes, checking often, as
they burn easily.
   Remove the puffs from the
oven and roll in confectioners'
sugar while hot, and again after
the puffs have cooled.
   Serve with lemon sherbet
and fresh raspberries.

MAKES ABOUT 4 DOZEN
1-INCH PUFFS.

TOP: *The creative kitchen staff
prepares fantasy hors d'oeuvres.*
CENTER: *After a day at the races,
houseguests Mary Ann Mobley and
Gary Collins grab a snack of
Marylou's famous chicken sandwiches.*
BOTTOM: *The first lunch of the
season is a great chance for Marylou
and Sonny to catch up on the latest
gossip.*

Jean LeClerc

◆ ◆ ◆ ◆ ◆ ◆ ◆ ◆ ◆

"EVERYONE ALWAYS TELLS ME I SHOULD OPEN A RESTAURANT."

"I started out cooking in the way most men do when they want to feed themselves. The first thing I did, an omelette. The next thing was spaghetti, and I was asking my mother for help on the phone as I cooked. 'Now I put in the bay leaf, what do I do next?' and she said, 'Stir it!' After I got started, it wasn't too difficult, and after traveling through France and Italy, sampling the true flavors in the regions best known for their cuisines, I began to refine my own cooking. For instance, I was interested in making lighter dishes ten years ago, so I would take a classic like vichyssoise and put in half potatoes and half sautéed cucumber, and what a difference. These kinds of changes—improvements—are very personal to my approach. Now that I know how to cook very well, I have some different concerns. I want to make sure my guests are fed well, and that the mood is always fantastic. And I love it when people laugh and make jokes and have a great evening. And eat!"

THE MENU

◆ ◆ ◆ ◆ ◆ ◆

COLD CUCUMBER SOUP

FRESH MUSHROOM SALAD

ROLLED VEAL ROAST

SALAD WITH PEPPER VINEGAR

BERRIES AND *CRÈME FRAÎCHE*

OPPOSITE: *Star of* All My Children, *films, and Broadway plays, Jean LeClerc takes a minute to relax in the garden of his Manhattan apartment with Kismet, one of his two identical longhair Himalayan cats.*

In Jean's distinctive French-Canadian accent, this star of *All My Children* boasts about his pride and joy—a farmhouse, which originally was a sawmill, near his hometown of Montreal. Inside, many interesting spaces have been created specifically for parties and other gatherings. Jean often asks his guests to choose the place they prefer: the formal dining room, the breakfast room, the patio by the pool, a picnic area around the outdoor fireplace—each with a mood all its own.

When questioned about how he intends to expand his passion for eating and entertaining, this lover of good Bordeaux said, "A wine cellar. I'm having one built right now at the farm.

"After you discover that herbs can also come from a garden, and not just from those little bottles, there is hope for you to be a good cook. The next thing is the love of entertaining and making people happy and comfortable, because there's nothing worse than eating alone."

COLD CUCUMBER SOUP

4 small, crisp cucumbers (about 1
   pound)
½ cup kosher salt
1 stick (½ cup) unsalted butter
1 small onion, chopped
1½ cups chicken stock, preferably
   homemade
3 large all-purpose potatoes (about
   1½ pounds), peeled and cut into
   ½-inch cubes
1 cup heavy cream
¼ cup chopped fresh chives

Peel, seed, and thinly slice the cucumbers. Place in a single layer on a large plate and cover with the salt. Set aside for about 30 minutes to remove bitterness. Rinse under cold water, then pat dry.

Melt the butter in a medium saucepan over moderately high heat. Add the onion, reduce the heat to moderate, and cook until softened but not browned, 3 to 5 minutes. Add the cucumbers and stir until they are thoroughly coated with butter and onion. Pour in the chicken stock and add the potatoes. In-

crease the heat to high and bring to a boil, then immediately reduce the heat to low and simmer until the potatoes are cooked through, about 20 minutes. Allow to cool slightly.

Transfer to the bowl of a food processor or blender and puree until very smooth. Refrigerate until thoroughly chilled, about 2 hours. Just before serving, stir in the cream. Garnish with the chives.

SERVES 4.

FRESH MUSHROOM SALAD

¼ cup freshly squeezed lemon juice
1 pound white mushrooms, wiped
   clean, trimmed, and thinly sliced
½ teaspoon seasoned salt
3 scallions, white part only, thinly
   sliced
2 tablespoons chopped fresh parsley
1 cup crème fraîche (see note)
Freshly ground pepper

In a medium mixing bowl, combine the lemon juice and the mushrooms. Gently toss or stir. Add the seasoned salt, the scallions, the parsley, and the crème fraîche. Gently fold the ingredients together until well blended. Add pepper to taste. Serve at room temperature or chilled.

SERVES 4.

NOTE: Crème fraîche is available in the dairy section of fine food stores. It can be made at home as well: In a glass jar, add 2 tablespoons cultured buttermilk to a cup of heavy cream. Cover and let stand in a warm spot until thickened, 12 or more hours. Stir, cover, and refrigerate until ready to use.

OPPOSITE: *A creative cook by nature, Jean revises many standard recipes with a light, low-calorie touch. His Cold Cucumber Soup is one such adaptation.* TOP AND ABOVE: *Weekends and holidays are spent at home on the farm near Montreal, where Jean was born. His is a working farm with a well and lots of animals.* LEFT: *Fresh Mushroom Salad.*

ROLLED VEAL ROAST

½ pound assorted wild mushrooms
  (shiitake, oyster, or chanterelles)
4 tablespoons (½ stick) unsalted
  butter
1 small veal breast, boned (about 2
  pounds)
1 to 2 tablespoons freshly squeezed
  lemon juice, to taste
2 tablespoons chopped fresh parsley
½ pound country pâté,★ cut
  lengthwise into ½-inch strips
¼ to ½ cup Dijon mustard
1 cup red wine, Calvados, or
  cognac
1 cup chicken or veal stock
8 to 12 small new potatoes (about
  2 pounds)
8 to 12 small white boiling onions
  (about 2 pounds)

Preheat the oven to 450° F.
Trim, clean, and chop the
mushrooms finely. In a small
sauté pan over high heat, melt
2 tablespoons of the butter.
Add the mushrooms and sauté
until slightly softened, about 2
minutes.

On a large work surface, lay
the veal flat. Sprinkle with the
lemon juice, parsley, and
mushrooms. Arrange the strips
of pâté down the center. Fold
the sides of the meat over to
cover the stuffing completely.
Tie securely with kitchen string
in 4 or 5 places. Brush with the
mustard to taste.

In a roasting pan set over
moderately high heat, melt the
remaining 2 tablespoons of the
butter. Add the roast and sauté
on all sides, turning frequently,
until browned, about 5 minutes. Carefully pour in the
wine, Calvados, or cognac and
the chicken or veal stock. Increase the heat to high and boil
vigorously until the liquid is
slightly reduced, about 5 minutes. Add the potatoes and the
onions, stirring to coat.

Place the pan in the pre-
heated oven. Immediately de-
crease the temperature to
350° F. Cook, uncovered, until
the roast is done but rare,
about 30 minutes; do not overcook. Let stand at room temperature for 5 to 10 minutes
before slicing. Serve on a platter surrounded by the potatoes
and the onions.

SERVES 4.

★ Country pâté is available in many specialty food stores. If unavailable, substitute
strips of boiled ham or cooked chicken
breasts.

ABOVE: *Follow these steps, along
with the recipe instructions, as Jean
demonstrates how to roll a veal
roast—it's simple!*

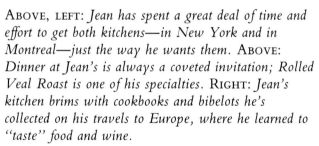

ABOVE, LEFT: *Jean has spent a great deal of time and effort to get both kitchens—in New York and in Montreal—just the way he wants them.* ABOVE: *Dinner at Jean's is always a coveted invitation; Rolled Veal Roast is one of his specialties.* RIGHT: *Jean's kitchen brims with cookbooks and bibelots he's collected on his travels to Europe, where he learned to "taste" food and wine.*

TOP: *According to Jean, any day the sun shines is the right day to serve outside in the garden.* ABOVE: *Jean tastes to make sure the* crème fraîche *is just right.*

SALAD WITH PEPPER VINEGAR

2 heads Boston lettuce
2 bunches arugula
¼ cup extra-virgin olive oil
2 tablespoons pepper vinegar (see note)
½ cup rose water (see note)
2 tablespoons whole red peppercorns

Wash the lettuce and arugula thoroughly in cold water. Dry and lay out on paper towels, then loosely roll and set aside for about 1 hour to absorb additional moisture. Gently place the leaves in airtight plastic bags. Refrigerate until crisp and chilled, about 2 hours.

In a large salad bowl, combine the olive oil, the vinegar, and the rose water. Place the prepared lettuce on top and sprinkle with the peppercorns. Toss just before serving.

SERVES 4.

NOTE: Pepper vinegar is available in many specialty food stores. It can also be made at home: Combine several small, hot peppers (such as jalapeño or cayenne) and 3 cups white wine vinegar in a 1-quart jar with a tight-fitting lid. Let sit at room temperature for 2 to 3 weeks to absorb flavors. If to be held for longer, transfer to sterilized jars. Process according to jar manufacturer's instructions.

Rose water is available in some specialty food stores and in many pharmacies.

◆ ◆ ◆ ◆ ◆ ◆ ◆

BERRIES AND CRÈME FRAÎCHE

2 cups crème fraîche *(see page 169)*
½ cup high-quality imported strawberry preserves
1 cup fresh strawberries, raspberries, or wild strawberries

Divide the *crème fraîche* among 4 elegant, stemmed serving goblets or dishes. Place 2 tablespoons preserves atop each serving. Chill until ready to serve.

Just before serving, hull, rinse, and pat dry the berries. Slice or leave whole, as desired, and use to garnish the *crème fraîche* and preserves. Serve at once.

SERVES 4.

◆ ◆ ◆ ◆ ◆ ◆ ◆

OPPOSITE: *Fresh berries and* crème fraîche—*so simple, so splendid with Champagne—are a perfect dessert.*

Dame Barbara Cartland

◆ ◆ ◆ ◆ ◆ ◆ ◆ ◆ ◆ ◆

"Anything to do with love makes me happy."

Does *Love in the Clouds* have a familiar ring? How about *Love at the Helm*? These are some of Dame Barbara Cartland's most memorable books, the latter written in collaboration with Lord Mountbatten. And though you might know her as the author of more than five hundred romance novels, the most prolific fiction writer in the world is an accomplished cookbook author as well. In fact, at her ninetieth-birthday party, many dishes served at the spectacular buffet came from her most popular cookbook, *The Romance of Food*.

On July 14, 1991, one hundred and fifty of Dame Barbara's best friends, from authors to British society's crème de la crème, gathered at her home in the English countryside to toast this celebrated lady.

Looking lovely in pink, Dame Barbara greeted her friends while a talented pianist from London played and sang any song requested. Champagne and Pimm's Punch, with an assortment of flavorful fruit in each glass, flowed freely. After speeches by

---

THE MENU

◆ ◆ ◆ ◆ ◆ ◆

Mini Pastry Shells with Shrimp

Salmon with Lemon-Dill Mayonnaise

Hard-Boiled Eggs with Caviar

Pimm's Punch

Lemon Shortcake

OPPOSITE: *Dame Barbara Cartland's ninetieth birthday was celebrated all over England. The BBC even made a film about her astounding career as a romance writer. She has also written extensively on health and longevity.*

---

her sons Ian and Glen and a toast in Barbara Cartland's honor, guests headed eagerly for the buffet table, which featured Nigel Gordon's poached Scottish salmon and other special creations. Nigel, Dame Barbara's chef of ten years, was also her partner in writing *The Romance of Food*, which, she said in the book's introduction, "will put a song in the heart of even the most jaded lover."

Later came desserts of every variety, including giant bowls of berry jelly, mousses, delicate cream-filled meringue cookies, lovely lemon shortbread tarts, and, of course, birthday cake, decked out in shocking pink. It seemed as if the guests were even more enthusiastic about the desserts than the buffet.

On such a divinely warm and sunny afternoon, sharing the day with her family and friends, this beloved author's birthday speech was quite fitting. Dame Barbara smiled and said, "You have to give love to get love, and I love you one and all." Everyone had a great time.

In a small mixing bowl, combine the mayonnaise, cream, Worcestershire sauce and ketchup, stirring well to blend. Fold in the shrimp.

Place the pastry shells on a serving platter and fill with the shrimp mixture. Garnish the platter with parsley sprigs and lemon wedges.

SERVES 10.

◆ ◆ ◆ ◆ ◆ ◆ ◆

SALMON WITH LEMON-DILL MAYONNAISE

2 cups mayonnaise
1 teaspoon grated lemon zest
1 tablespoon freshly squeezed lemon juice
2 tablespoons chopped fresh dill
Salt and freshly ground pepper
1 6-pound salmon, dressed, with head and tail removed
2 cups aspic (recipe follows)
1 medium cucumber
1 lemon
Several parsley sprigs

In a small mixing bowl, combine the mayonnaise with the lemon zest, lemon juice, and dill. Add salt and pepper to taste. Cover and refrigerate for at least 2 hours before serving.

Preheat the oven to 350° F. Lay the salmon on a large piece of aluminum foil. Place in a roasting pan large enough to

MINI PASTRY SHELLS WITH SHRIMP

20 frozen mini pastry shells, about 1½ inches in diameter
1 pound medium shrimp, shelled and deveined
¾ cup mayonnaise
2 tablespoons heavy cream
2 tablespoons Worcestershire sauce
3 tablespoons ketchup
Parsley sprigs and lemon wedges

Bake the pastry shells according to the instructions on the package. Cool completely.

Bring a large pot of water to a boil. Add the shrimp and bring back to a boil, cooking until firm and pink, about 3 minutes. Drain and cool.

hold the fish flat. Bake until the center reaches an internal temperature of 140° F, about 1¼ hours. Remove the salmon to a rack and cool. Carefully remove the skin from its top side.

Place the fish on a large serving platter, skinless side up. Cover the top with half of the aspic. Refrigerate until the aspic has set, about 1 hour.

Halve the cucumber and lemon lengthwise. Slice into very thin half-rounds. Arrange in alternating rows down the salmon to resemble scales. Cover with the remaining aspic and chill until set, about an hour. Garnish with several sprigs of fresh parsley, and serve with mayonnaise on the side.

SERVES 10.

ASPIC

1 envelope unflavored gelatin
¼ cup cold water
¼ cup boiling water
1½ cups fish stock or bottled clam juice
1 tablespoon freshly squeezed lemon juice
Pinch salt

In a medium bowl, sprinkle the gelatin over the cold water. Let sit for 5 minutes until the gelatin softens. Pour in the boiling water and stir until the gelatin

has dissolved completely.

In a mixing bowl set over ice water, combine the stock, lemon juice, and salt. Add the gelatin mixture and use a wooden spoon to stir. When the mixture reaches the consistency of a thick syrup, the aspic is ready to be used. If it starts to congeal, gently warm for 1 or 2 seconds over hot but not boiling water.

MAKES ABOUT 2 CUPS.

◆ ◆ ◆ ◆ ◆ ◆ ◆

ABOVE: *The kitchen was the site of all the party preparations.* RIGHT: *Nigel sees to last-minute details on the buffet.* BELOW: *Guests listen attentively as Ian and Glen give speeches about their famous mother.*

TOP: *Dame Barbara chats with one of her admirers, who was said to be a writer as well.* ABOVE: *Guests wish Dame Barbara well, and enjoy the unusually sunny day in the English countryside.* OPPOSITE, TOP LEFT: *Lemon Shortcake has a tart-sweet filling of lemon curd.* OPPOSITE, TOP RIGHT: *London society and guests from stately mansions arrived throughout the afternoon.* OPPOSITE, BELOW: *The cake was decked out in Cartland pink.*

HARD-BOILED EGGS WITH CAVIAR

10 hard-boiled eggs
1 to 1½ cups mayonnaise
1-ounce jar caviar
2 parsley sprigs, chopped

Peel the eggs and cut in half lengthwise. Arrange on a large serving platter, cut side up. Coat each half with mayonnaise, and top with a few caviar eggs and a sprinkling of parsley.

SERVES 10.

◆ ◆ ◆ ◆ ◆ ◆ ◆

PIMM'S PUNCH

1 fifth bottle Pimm's Number 1
1 32-ounce bottle ginger ale
2 quarts lemonade, preferably homemade
Assorted slices of fresh fruit (apples, oranges, lemons, pears, peaches), for garnish
½ medium cucumber, peeled, seeded, and thinly sliced
Several mint sprigs

In a large, nonreactive bowl, combine the Pimm's, ginger ale, lemonade, and fruit and cucumber slices. Stir to blend and add plenty of ice cubes. Serve in chilled glasses garnished with mint.

SERVES 15 to 20.

LEMON SHORTCAKE

FOR THE CAKE
1¾ cups all-purpose flour
5⅓ tablespoons (⅔ cup) unsalted butter, chilled and cut into small pieces
½ cup confectioners' sugar
2 egg yolks
1 teaspoon vanilla extract

FOR THE FILLING
1 cup heavy cream
1½ cups Lemon Curd (recipe follows)

FOR THE ICING
1¼ cups confectioners' sugar
2 tablespoons water
1 tablespoon freshly squeezed lemon juice

FOR THE GARNISH
2 lemons
2 strawberries, halved
2 tablespoons superfine sugar, sifted

First, prepare the cake. On a board or work surface, sift the flour into a mound. Make a well in the center, and add the butter, sugar, egg yolks, and vanilla. Incorporate the flour into the other ingredients, then knead together until the mixture forms a smooth paste. Gather into a ball, wrap in plastic, and refrigerate for 1 hour.

Preheat the oven to 350° F. and lightly butter three baking sheets. Divide the dough into thirds. Roll each out into an 8-inch round about ¼-inch

thick. Flute the edges with the back of a fork and prick all over with the tines. Transfer to the baking sheets and bake until lightly browned and a knife comes out clean when inserted in the center, about 10 minutes. Remove to wire racks and cool completely.

To prepare the filling, whip the cream until soft peaks form. Fold in the lemon curd. Keep chilled until ready to assemble the cake.

To prepare the icing, combine the sugar, water, and lemon juice in a large mixing bowl. Stir vigorously until smooth and fairly thick.

To assemble the cake, first remove the zest from one of the lemons, avoiding the bitter white pith, and julienne the zest. Cut the remaining lemon in half lengthwise and remove seeds. Slice into thin half-rounds.

Spread a layer of filling evenly on two rounds of short-cake and stack them. Spread the icing over the top layer, and decorate with the lemon zest, slices of lemon, strawberry halves, and superfine sugar.

SERVES 8 to 10.

LEMON CURD

2 large lemons
½ cup (1 stick) unsalted butter
1 cup sugar
3 egg yolks

Finely grate the zest of the lemons. Squeeze the juice, discarding seeds.

In a double boiler over simmering but not boiling water, melt the butter. Add the sugar, egg yolks, lemon zest, and lemon juice. Stir constantly until the mixture is the consistency of thick custard, about 10 minutes.

If it is not to be used right away, pour the lemon curd into sterilized jars and store in the refrigerator. Extra lemon curd can be used to fill cookies or cakes, or folded into whipped cream for a light dessert.

MAKES ABOUT 2 CUPS.

Relaxing
at Home
◆ ◆ ◆ ◆ ◆ ◆ ◆ ◆ ◆

Bruce and Kris Jenner

◆ ◆ ◆ ◆ ◆ ◆ ◆ ◆ ◆ ◆ ◆

"HOW DO YOU FEED EIGHT KIDS?
FREQUENTLY!"

"It's a party here every night," Kris Jenner said of the family dinner scene in her kitchen. "It's important to us to ask each of our kids what they did during the day—even though it takes time to go around the table."

"With our being away from home as much as we are, the family dinner has to be a priority," continued Bruce. "It's special when we're all together. To us, entertaining is just a matter of adding more pasta to the water and getting out a few more plates. Kris taught me how to make our favorite dishes. That's because if she decides to drink her wine before dinner, rather than with it, she'll get giggly and entertain everyone. Of course, the whole place is in stitches. "

"Christmas is my favorite holiday," interjected Kris. "I bring out the Spode Christmas plates and set the most magnificent table. With two sets of grandparents and many friends, along with the ten of us, the table goes on *forever!* I also love to create

> ## THE MENU
>
> ◆ ◆ ◆ ◆ ◆ ◆ ◆
>
> **SWORDFISH STEAKS**
> **PASTA PRIMAVERA**
> **GRILLED EGGPLANT**
> **CHEESE BREAD**
> **BROWNIES**

OPPOSITE: *Malibu Beach makes a perfect backdrop for the outdoor fêtes that Bruce and Kris love to throw for family and friends.*

an incredible flaming-red centerpiece to go with the holidays."

On the subject of entertaining, she summed it up simply: "My one tip is to buy all your dishes and table accessories at a store you really love. For years, I've shopped at Geary's, a store in Beverly Hills. So now, everything matches. And if anyone wants to give me a gift, they will know exactly where to shop."

Bruce and Kris are one couple who seem meant to be together. They were tricked into meeting by mutual friends who felt they were perfect for each other. They've been married since 1990 (each has four children from previous marriages), and it was love at first sight for both.

Bruce said, "The Olympics showed me what a great moment can be. I translated that into my daily life, which is incredibly full and varied. But, best of all, the kids and Kris keep life exciting and inspiring. It doesn't matter if it's a holiday or any day."

SWORDFISH STEAKS

*4 swordfish steaks, about 6 ounces
    each*
Salt and freshly ground pepper
*2 heaping tablespoons Dijon
    mustard*
2 garlic cloves, crushed
½ cup olive oil
Juice of 4 limes
¼ cup soy sauce
1 teaspoon freshly ground pepper
1 tablespoon chopped fresh dill
1 cup Salsa (recipe follows)

Trim the swordfish and season
on both sides with salt and
pepper to taste. Place in a glass
baking dish large enough to
hold the steaks in one layer.

In a small mixing bowl,
combine the mustard, garlic,
olive oil, lime juice, soy sauce,
pepper, and dill. Mix well and
pour over the fish. Cover with
plastic wrap and marinate in
the refrigerator for at least
2 hours, preferably overnight,
turning the steaks occasionally.

Preheat the broiler or light a
charcoal fire and let burn to a
gray ash. Broil or grill about
6 inches from the heat until
firm to the touch and done
through, about 4 minutes per
side. Serve with Salsa.

SERVES 4.

ABOVE: *Swordfish Steaks, hot off the
grill, with homemade salsa.* LEFT:
*Kris prides herself on creative table
settings. Her collection of brightly
colored pottery dishes comes from
Geary's of Beverly Hills, one of her
favorite shops.*

SALSA

2 large tomatoes, peeled, seeded,
  and chopped
1 medium onion, finely chopped
½ cup fresh chopped cilantro
1 teaspoon crushed red pepper
  flakes
1 teaspoon Tabasco
Juice of 2 limes
Salt
1 teaspoon Spike vegetable
  seasoning

In a large mixing bowl, combine the tomatoes, onion, cilantro, red pepper flakes, Tabasco, lime juice, salt to taste, and Spike. Stir well to blend. Cover and refrigerate for 2 hours before serving. Salsa will keep, refrigerated, for several days.

MAKES ABOUT 1 CUP.

LEFT: *Getting to know the peculiarities of the gas grill was paramount for this family. Of their most essential piece of cooking equipment, Bruce says, "It gets a workout several times a week."* BELOW, LEFT: *After marinating, swordfish goes on the fire.* BELOW, RIGHT: *The Jenners' lunch menu is perfect served at room temperature. Fresh flowers perk up the table. Behind, the pool beckons summertime guests to a pre-lunch dip. The Jenners entertain outdoors year-round, since the warm temperatures in California encourage al fresco meals.*

PASTA PRIMAVERA

¼ cup olive oil
1 garlic clove, minced
2 to 3 medium carrots, peeled and
*   cut into ½-inch dice*
2 cups broccoli flowerets
1 small zucchini, trimmed, halved,
*   and sliced ¼-inch thick*
1 red pepper, cored, seeded, and
*   julienned*
1 green pepper, cored, seeded, and
*   julienned*
1 yellow pepper, cored, seeded,
*   and julienned*
Salt and freshly ground pepper
1 pound bowtie pasta (farfalle)

In a large sauté pan, heat the
olive oil over moderately high
heat. Add the garlic and sauté
until softened, about 1 minute,
stirring often. Add the carrots
and cook until tender, 8 to 10
minutes. Stir and shake the pan
constantly to prevent sticking.
Add the broccoli and zucchini
and sauté for another 3 to 4
minutes, stirring frequently.
Add the pepper and cook for
2 more minutes, stirring and
shaking the pan constantly.
Season with salt and pepper to
taste.

Bring a large pot of lightly
salted water to a boil and cook
the pasta according to package
directions. Drain well and
transfer to a serving bowl.
Toss with the vegetables and
season with salt and pepper.

SERVES 4.

GRILLED EGGPLANT

2 medium eggplants, thickly sliced
Salt and freshly ground pepper
1 garlic clove, minced
2 scallions, trimmed and finely
   chopped
Olive oil (for brushing)

Pat the eggplant dry and place
in a glass baking dish. Season
with salt and pepper to taste.
Sprinkle with the garlic and
scallion, and drizzle with the
olive oil. Cover with plastic
wrap and marinate in the refrigerator for at least 2 hours,
turning once.

Preheat the broiler or prepare
a charcoal fire and let burn
down to a gray ash. Broil or
grill about 6 inches from the
heat until well done and dark,
about 2 minutes per side. Serve
at once.

SERVES 4.

OPPOSITE: *Pasta Primavera can be
eaten hot or at room temperature.*
CLOCKWISE FROM LOWER LEFT:
*Bruce's finest moment—winning the
Decathlon in the 1972 Olympics;
Kris helps make Pasta Primavera,
one of Bruce's favorite dishes; before
grilling, eggplant marinates with
garlic cloves in oil; Bruce's Gold
Medal sits with family photographs;
sauté fresh ingredients al dente—they
keep their beautiful color, and they
taste better.*

A family portrait: Bruce and Kris with Burt, Casey, Brandon, Brody, Kourtney, Kimberly, Khloe, and Robert.

CHEESE BREAD

4 large sourdough rolls
8 tablespoons (1 stick) unsalted
  butter, softened
3 garlic cloves, minced
½ cup freshly grated Parmesan
  cheese
1 cup freshly grated mozzarella
  cheese

Preheat the broiler.
  Slice the rolls in half. Spread each half with about 1 table-spoon of the butter. Sprinkle with the garlic, Parmesan, and mozzarella, divided equally among the halves. Broil until the cheeses are bubbling and the bread is toasted around the edges. Serve hot.

SERVES 4.

♦ ♦ ♦ ♦ ♦ ♦ ♦

BROWNIES

4 1-ounce squares unsweetened
  chocolate, coarsely chopped
2 tablespoons (¼ stick) unsalted
  butter
4 eggs
2 teaspoons vanilla extract
2 cups sugar
1 cup all-purpose flour
½ teaspoon baking powder
½ teaspoon salt
1 cup chopped walnuts
1 12-ounce package mini semisweet
  chocolate chips
Confectioners' sugar (optional)

Preheat the oven to 350° F. Butter a 9-by-13-inch baking pan. Combine the unsweetened chocolate and the butter in the top of a double boiler. Stir over hot but not boiling water until melted and smooth. Remove from heat and set aside.

In the bowl of a food processor, process the eggs, vanilla, sugar, flour, baking powder, and salt until smooth. Add the melted chocolate and process until smooth. Add the walnuts and chocolate chips and pulse briefly to mix. Pour the batter into the prepared pan and bake until a toothpick inserted in the center comes out clean, 25 to 30 minutes. Invert onto a rack and cool completely. Sprinkle with confectioners' sugar if desired. Cut into squares and serve with vanilla ice cream.

MAKES ABOUT 30 2-INCH
BROWNIES.

◆ ◆ ◆ ◆ ◆ ◆

ABOVE: *Bruce travels frequently, lecturing, making television appearances, and anchoring sports events like the Barcelona Olympics. He also represents a variety of sports-related products. Bruce and Kris take advantage of the times when they are home together by having friends and family over.* BELOW: *The Jenner family's favorite dessert: dense, rich, killer Brownies!*

Eva Gabor

◆ ◆ ◆ ◆ ◆ ◆ ◆ ◆ ◆ ◆

"MY GOULASH DOESN'T LOOK HUNGARIAN,
BUT, *DAHLING,* IT *IS* DELICIOUS."

Eva Gabor is seen in all the right places—from Hollywood's grandest charity events to Elizabeth Taylor's wedding —usually on the arm of Merv Griffin.

Eva recently admitted, "Lately, I have been so busy with my one-woman stage show, I haven't entertained at home much, but bringing out my antique Haviland dishes and Baccarat crystal glasses inspired me to have a dinner party. I always have ten for dinner, because my dining-room table seats ten. My style of entertaining is never a buffet with a plate on your lap. Everyone must have a proper place to sit. And because I want my guests to feel comfortable and stay a long time, I always invite interesting people with something to say. This makes the most satisfying party.

"I seat everyone next to a person they aren't best friends with, so the conversation is always lively, although Merv and I always sit next to each other. He makes me laugh so much, dahling. And that's the most important thing in the world.

"I like to have fun with my menu!" added Eva. "Everyone expects me to serve a Hungarian dinner,

---

THE MENU

◆ ◆ ◆ ◆ ◆ ◆

BOGRÁCSGULYÁS (HUNGARIAN
GOULASH)
CHICKEN *PAPRIKÁS*

OPPOSITE: *Eva Gabor, a gracious hostess, loves to pamper her guests with great food and good cheer. Her sparkling nature and witty conversation, overflowing with laughter, is always as delicious an experience as her menus.*

---

so I do. Usually I make goulash or chicken *paprikás,* and sometimes the most delicious cold cherry soup. For dessert, I always serve a nice Hungarian apple strudel. After that, the Alka-Seltzer, because, you know, Hungarian food is very hearty," Eva said with a laugh.

One would never believe the slim-and-trim Eva was raised on Hungarian cuisine. She exercises daily to keep her tiny, size-six figure. "I am very lucky that I never gain weight, because, *dahling,* I eat much more than anyone you know."

Eva admitted her specialty is decorating the table with an abundance of freshly cut flowers from her garden.

"I never call a florist, because I love natural arrangements. Just before my guests arrive, I do the flowers," she says. "My garden is truly my pride and joy. The orchids and roses are like my children. Some of the plants I've had for twenty years.

"And one of the flowers, the purple rose, is named after me," she shyly added. "Isn't that wonderful?"

BOGRÁCSGULYÁS (HUNGARIAN GOULASH)

2 tablespoons lard
2 medium onions, coarsely chopped
2½ pounds beef chuck or round,
* cut into ¾-inch cubes*
½ pound beef heart, cut into
* ¾-inch cubes*
1 garlic clove
¼ teaspoon caraway seeds
½ teaspoon salt
2 tablespoons imported sweet
* Hungarian paprika*
2½ quarts water
1 medium tomato, peeled and diced
2 green or Italian frying peppers,
* cored and sliced*
3 to 4 medium all-purpose
* potatoes, peeled and diced*
Salt
1 egg
3 tablespoons flour
Pinch salt

In a large covered casserole or
Dutch oven, melt the lard over
moderate heat. Add the onions
and cook until transparent,
about 5 minutes. Add the
meats and continue cooking
until all traces of pink have disappeared, about 10 minutes,
stirring often. Remove from
the heat and set aside.

   Using the flat side of a heavy
knife, crush the garlic. Transfer
to a mortar and pestle, and
grind with the caraway seeds
and salt until the mixure forms
a thick paste. Add to the meat
and stir in the paprika. Set the

pot over moderate heat, add the water, and bring to a simmer. Reduce the heat to moderately low and cook until the soup has thickened, about 1 hour.

Add the tomato, peppers, and potatoes to the meat mixture, season with salt to taste and continue cooking until the potatoes are tender, about 30 more minutes. Add water if necessary, to obtain the consistency of hearty soup.

To make the dumplings, combine the egg, flour, and salt in a small bowl. Mix with a fork until a soft dough forms. Just before serving, spoon the mixture into the boiling soup ¼ teaspoon at a time. Cook for 2 to 3 minutes, then ladle into warmed bowls. Serve immediately.

SERVES 8.

◆ ◆ ◆ ◆ ◆ ◆ ◆

OPPOSITE, TOP: *"Dahling, you can have anything you want in life. I am the living proof."* OPPOSITE, BELOW: *In front is Eva's tender Chicken* Paprikás, *and behind is her specialty—Hungarian Goulash, served with homemade dumplings.*

ABOVE: *Treasures from Eva's travels all over the world are displayed for everyone's enjoyment. Her love for animals—even porcelain pets—is obvious.*

CHICKEN *PAPRIKÁS*

FOR THE CHICKEN

2 tablespoons lard
2 medium onions, finely chopped
1 small chicken, about 3 pounds,
    cut into 8 pieces
1 large tomato, peeled and coarsley
    chopped
1 heaping tablespoon imported
    sweet Hungarian paprika
½ cup chicken stock (or water)
1 teaspoon salt
2 tablespoons sour cream
1 tablespoon flour
1 teaspoon cold water
1 medium green pepper, cored and
    thinly sliced
2 tablespoons heavy cream

FOR THE DUMPLINGS

1 egg
3 tablespoons lard
⅓ cup water
1 teaspoon salt
1½ cups flour
2 cups chicken stock

ABOVE: *"I never call a florist,
because I love natural arrangements.
Just before my guests arrive, I do the
flowers,"* Eva said. *"My garden is
truly my pride and joy. The orchids
are like my children—some of the
plants I've had for twenty years."*
LEFT: *Just imagine the fragrance!*

Melt the lard in a large, heavy
casserole or Dutch oven over
moderately high heat. Add the
onions and cook until softened,
about 5 minutes, stirring often.
Add the chicken and tomatoes,
cover, and cook for 10 minutes. Stir in the paprika,
chicken stock, salt. Bring to a
simmer, then reduce the heat to
low, cover again, and cook for
2 minutes. Remove the lid, increase the heat to moderately
high, and let the liquid evapo-
rate. Brown the chicken in the

residual fat, but do not let it burn. Remove the chicken pieces to a platter and keep warm.

Reduce the heat to moderately low and add the sour cream, flour, and cold water to the Dutch oven; stir until smooth. Add the green pepper, replace the chicken, and season with salt to taste. Reduce the heat to low, cover again, and cook for 5 to 10 more minutes. Stir in the cream just before serving.

To prepare the dumplings, combine the egg, lard, water, and salt in a large mixing bowl. Mix in the flour just enough to give the dough an even texture. Set aside and let rest for 10 minutes.

Bring the chicken stock to a boil in a medium saucepan. Drop the dumplings by large spoonfuls into the stock. Reduce the heat to moderate, cover, and cook until firm, about 15 minutes. Lift the dumplings out with a slotted spoon and serve with the chicken.

SERVES 4.

◆ ◆ ◆ ◆ ◆ ◆ ◆

ABOVE: *Hand-cut crystal decanters are some of Eva's favorite objects. Afternoon light spills into the dining room of her Beverly Hills home, highlighting her collection.* RIGHT: *Haviland china and Baccarat crystal combine to create Eva's deliciously feminine place settings.*

Jackie Zeman

♦ ♦ ♦ ♦ ♦ ♦ ♦ ♦ ♦ ♦

"I BELIEVE IN SECONDS, AND
LOTS OF DIFFERENT DISHES, SO I ALWAYS
COOK FOR AN ARMY."

Both Jackie Zeman, who has portrayed Bobbie on *General Hospital* for fourteen years, and her husband, real estate developer Glenn Gorden, are from meat-and-potatoes backgrounds; the newness and freshness of California cuisine was a great change for them both, and has influenced their cooking style. When they redesigned the kitchen in their Los Angeles hillside home, their first priority was to install a gas grill and lots of extra counter space.

"We love to eat," said Jackie. "Bread, desserts, seconds, and by candlelight every night, even with our little daughter, Cassidy.

"We really enjoy cooking. Glen is more of a flipper, a barbecue type. I like to experiment with the grill—that's how I came up with the grilled fruit with baked salmon. I suppose I had it in some restaurant, because everything grilled is very trendy now in L.A., and I figured if they could do it, so could I, but the fruit combination is really me. It's also low in calories, which is always a considera-

---

THE MENU

♦ ♦ ♦ ♦ ♦ ♦

BAKED SALMON WITH MUSTARD
BALSAMIC GRILLED VEGETABLES
GRILLED FRUIT
PINEAPPLE ICE
CHOCOLATE CARAMEL CHEWS

OPPOSITE: *Jackie Zeman is devoted to cooking and keeping up with all the activities connected with her home life. She loves to entertain California-style—simple and relaxed.*

tion," she added with a laugh. "I tend to cook more than I need, so the next day there's a lot left over for salads or salmon with bagels and cream cheese."

When it comes to giving a dinner party, which Jackie does frequently, she is very firm about the number of people invited to her table. "Eight is enough, never more. Otherwise, you get too many conversations going at one time. And after dinner, dessert is always served in the living room around the coffee table. That way, people can sit next to someone else for the last part of the meal.

"We're very relaxed about entertaining at home. Fifteen years ago, I thought everything had to be served on silver and bone china, because I didn't have confidence in myself as a hostess—I must have been trying to impress people. Now, everybody knows to come early and help out with the chopping. I just say to everyone, 'There's beer and wine in the fridge, and the glasses are over there, help yourself.'"

BAKED SALMON WITH MUSTARD

¼ cup Dijon mustard
¼ cup olive oil
2 tablespoons dry white wine
2 tablespoons chopped fresh dill
1 teaspoon freshly ground pepper
1 garlic clove, minced
1½ to 2 pounds salmon fillet with
   skin on, preferably cut from the
   center

Preheat the oven to 350° F.

In a small bowl, combine the mustard, olive oil, white wine, dill, pepper, and garlic. Mix well with a wire whisk.

Set the fish in the center of a large baking dish. Brush with half the marinade and bake until cooked through, about 30 minutes. Remove from the oven and brush with the remaining marinade just before serving.

NOTE: The salmon can be served cold, if desired: Cool to room temperature, cover with plastic wrap, and refrigerate (for up to two days) until ready to serve.

SERVES 4.

BALSAMIC GRILLED VEGETABLES

½ cup balsamic vinegar
¼ cup olive oil
¼ teaspoon salt
⅛ teaspoon freshly ground pepper
2 medium zucchini, cut into
   ¼-inch slices
2 medium yellow squash, cut into
   ¼-inch slices
1 small eggplant (about ½ pound),
   cut into ½-inch cubes
1 green pepper, seeded and cut into
   1-inch squares
2 small yellow onions, peeled and
   quartered

To prepare the balsamic vinaigrette, combine the vinegar, oil, salt, and pepper in a small bowl. Whisk well to blend.

In a large mixing bowl, combine the zucchini, yellow squash, eggplant, green pepper, and onion. Add the vinaigrette and toss to coat the vegetables. Leave to marinate at room temperature for 2 to 3 hours. Use a large spoon to reach deep into the bowl and stir from time to time to redistribute the sauce that settles in the bottom.

Prepare a charcoal grill. Allow the coals to become ash gray with no sign of flames, starting about 1 hour in advance.

Thread the marinated vegetables, alternating shapes and colors, through several 8-inch

TOP: *Jackie's favorite kitchen tool—the stovetop grill—gets a lot of use. Hot-off-the-grill vegetables,* CENTER, *are but one of her inspired creations.* BOTTOM: *Baked Salmon with Mustard is served surrounded by grilled fruit on a bed of saffron-flavored rice.*

or 10-inch skewers. When the coals are ready, grill about 4 inches away from the source of heat until the vegetables are browned but the onions and peppers are still crunchy, 5 to 7 minutes. Serve at once.

SERVES 4 to 6.

◆ ◆ ◆ ◆ ◆ ◆ ◆

GRILLED FRUIT

4 tablespoons (½ stick) unsalted
 butter, melted
2 tablespoons brown sugar, packed
½ teaspoon ground ginger
1 medium pineapple, peeled, cored,
 and cut into large chunks
2 unripe bananas, peeled and cut
 into 1-inch slices
3 to 4 ripe but firm peaches,
 quartered

In a small bowl, combine the butter, brown sugar, and ginger. Whisk to blend.

Thread the pineapple chunks, banana slices, and peach quarters on 8-inch or 10-inch skewers. Brush with the butter sauce and set aside.

Prepare a charcoal grill. Allow the coals to become ash gray with no sign of flames, starting about 1 hour in advance. When the coals are ready, grill the fruit skewers over low heat, 4 to 5 inches away from the source of heat, until lightly colored and

cooked through, 5 to 10 minutes. Turn often and baste frequently with the butter sauce. Serve warm with Pineapple Ice (recipe follows).

SERVES 4.

◆ ◆ ◆ ◆ ◆ ◆ ◆

PINEAPPLE ICE

⅓ cup cold water
⅔ cup sugar
1 medium pineapple, peeled, cored,
 and cut into 1-inch chunks
 (about 4 cups)

Combine the water and sugar in a small, heavy saucepan. Stir over low heat until the sugar has dissolved. Increase the heat to high and bring the liquid to a boil, washing down any crystals that form on the side of the pan with a wet brush. Boil vigorously, undisturbed, until thick and syrupy, about 5 minutes. Remove from heat and cool slightly.

In the bowl of a food processor, combine the pineapple chunks and the sugar syrup. Process until smooth, about 1 minute. Pour into a nonreactive, shallow baking dish and freeze for 6 to 10 hours, stirring about every half hour.

MAKES ABOUT 1½ PINTS.

ABOVE: *From the blender to the freezer to dessert glasses, Pineapple Ice is quick to make and serve. Jackie has one "dessert" rule: there must always be chocolate on the table! Chocolate Caramel Chews (page 200) are her favorites. When it comes to entertaining, Jackie says, "The only really important thing to know is the preference of your guests, especially vegetarians or those who will eat chicken or fish but not red meat. Otherwise, you might end up like me—in the kitchen, trying to stir up an asparagus-and-pasta dish for someone who couldn't eat the lasagna smothered in meat sauce that was getting cold on the table."*

TOP: *Fresh flowers and candlelight are the norm at Jackie's table, even for casual family meals with Glen and Cassidy.* ABOVE: *Cassidy loves to "help" in the kitchen.* OPPOSITE: *Married on Valentine's Day, Jackie and Glen indulge in a romantic moment whenever they can.*

CHOCOLATE CARAMEL CHEWS

FOR THE COOKIE BASE

4 ounces unsweetened chocolate, coarsely chopped
¾ cup (1½ sticks) unsalted butter
1¾ cups brown sugar, packed
½ teaspoon salt
2 teaspoons vanilla extract
2 eggs, lightly beaten
1½ cups all-purpose flour

FOR THE CARAMEL TOPPING

1⅓ cups brown sugar, packed
¾ cup heavy cream
¾ cup light corn syrup
⅓ cup (5⅓ tablespoons) unsalted butter
⅛ teaspoon salt
2 teaspoons vanilla extract
1½ cups chopped, toasted walnuts or pecans

FOR THE CHOCOLATE GLAZE

2 ounces semisweet chocolate, coarsely chopped
1 tablespoon heavy cream
1 teaspoon vanilla extract

Preheat the oven to 350° F. Butter a 9-by-13-inch baking pan.

To prepare the cookie base, in a heavy, medium saucepan over low heat, melt the chocolate and butter until smooth, stirring constantly. Remove from the heat. Beat in the brown sugar, salt, vanilla, and eggs with a wooden spoon until smooth. Add the flour, ½ cup at a time, blending well after each addition. Empty into the prepared baking pan and spread the dough out evenly. Bake until a toothpick inserted in the center comes out clean, 25 to 30 minutes. Remove to a wire rack and cool for 1 hour.

When the cookie base is almost cooled, prepare the caramel topping. Combine the brown sugar, cream, corn syrup, butter, and salt in a heavy, medium saucepan. Stirring occasionally over moderately high heat, cook the mixture until it forms a 2-inch thread when dropped from a spoon into ice water or until it reaches 230° F on a candy thermometer. Remove from the heat and stir in the vanilla and the nuts. Immediately spread the hot caramel evenly over the cookie base. (Do not allow the mixture to cool or the caramel will harden.) Let stand until cool.

To prepare the glaze, combine the chocolate and cream in a small saucepan. Stir constantly over low heat until the chocolate is melted and smooth. Remove from the heat and stir in the vanilla. Drizzle the chocolate glaze over the caramel topping in a lacy pattern.

Let the chocolate glaze set before cutting into 1-by-2-inch bars, or "chews." Store in an airtight container at room temperature for up to 10 days. The chews can be frozen, too, if desired.

MAKES 4½ DOZEN BARS.

Randy Travis

◆ ◆ ◆ ◆ ◆ ◆ ◆ ◆ ◆ ◆

"I COOK FOR FUN NOW, BUT THERE WAS A
TIME WHEN I HAD TO COOK TO KEEP A ROOF
OVER MY HEAD."

Country singing star Randy Travis is an intensely private person. When he's not on the road performing, he raises and trains horses on a ranch outside Nashville, Tennessee. One of his favorites is a palomino whose grandfather was none other than Roy Rogers's famed steed, Trigger.

Friends and family are always dropping by the ranch, and with true Southern hospitality, everyone stays for dinner.

"I really don't have a passion for *cooking* anymore—I had to do it professionally, as a restaurant chef, in the early years of my career. That was when there wasn't much success to fall back on, and times were kind of lean. When I do cook now, it's usually just for me and Lib, my wife. Thankfully, Lib is a great cook and does most of it with a little help from whoever we have over. But I do have a passion for *eating*! Ask anyone who

---

THE MENU

◆ ◆ ◆ ◆ ◆ ◆ ◆

FRIED CHICKEN

FIELD PEAS

SQUASH CASSEROLE

SOUTHERN CORN BREAD

OLD-FASHIONED BUTTERMILK PIE

OPPOSITE: *Randy Travis has spent almost a decade at the top of the charts, and helped usher in the burgeoning mainstream popularity of country music. He is popular in Europe and Japan, as well as points north all over the USA.*

---

knows me. I certainly help out in the kitchen and I'm big on barbecuing," Randy said. "Mainly, though, I'm interested in the eating aspects of it all."

Randy and Lib have cooked up more than a few traditional Southern-style meals in their kitchen. They've even put together a small book of the recipes they have gathered over the years—black-eyed peas, grits, and Southern-fried chicken—with some solid down-home advice on getting Southern cooking right. Tips on gravy-stirring and making coffee over an open fire are offered, and how long to keep a catfish in the frying pan. (Their book is sold only in Randy's gift shop on Demonbreun Street in Nashville.)

Randy admitted with a grin, "I really was the singing cook at the Nashville Palace near Opryland. And I toured in a bread truck, but that was a long time ago."

FRIED CHICKEN

1 small chicken, 2½ to 3 pounds,
  cut into 8 pieces
Vegetable shortening for frying
1 cup all-purpose flour
½ teaspoon salt
½ teaspoon freshly ground pepper

Pat the chicken pieces dry, place on a large plate or platter, cover with plastic wrap, and refrigerate overnight.

In an electric frying pan or skillet, add enough shortening to measure 1½ to 2 inches deep. Heat to 375° F.

In a brown paper bag, combine the flour, salt, and pepper. Close tightly and shake to mix. Add the chicken pieces, one at a time, and shake the bag to coat completely. Remove the chicken, shake off the excess flour, and drop into the hot fat. Cover and fry for about 5 minutes. Turn the chicken over, cover again, and cook for about 5 more minutes. Reduce the heat to 350° F and cook until the chicken is golden brown and cooked through, 20 to 25 minutes. Turn the chicken only once during this time. Drain on paper towels and keep warm until ready to serve.

SERVES 4.

◆ ◆ ◆ ◆ ◆ ◆ ◆

FIELD PEAS

3 slices bacon
1½ cups water
½ teaspoon salt
¼ teaspoon freshly ground pepper
2 cups shelled fresh field peas

In a small skillet, sauté the bacon until crisp. Drain on paper towels and set aside.

In a small saucepan, bring the water to a boil. Add the salt, pepper, and any bacon drippings. Add the peas, reduce the heat to moderately high, and cook until the peas are

BELOW: *Randy prides himself on his grilling skills. He says he can carry on a conversation or sing a tune while tending the steaks or barbecuing chicken.*

tender, about 30 minutes. Drain and transfer to a serving bowl. Crumple the cooked bacon over the peas just before serving.

SERVES 4.

♦ ♦ ♦ ♦ ♦ ♦ ♦

SQUASH CASSEROLE

3 to 4 medium yellow squash,
* trimmed and sliced ¼-inch thick*
1 small onion, thinly sliced
6 tablespoons (¾ stick) unsalted
* butter*
2 eggs
1 cup milk
1 teaspoon salt
½ teaspoon freshly ground pepper
1 cup freshly grated cheddar cheese
1 cup crushed cracker crumbs

Bring a large pot of salted water to a boil. Add the squash and cook until tender, about 3 minutes. Drain well and place in the bottom of a buttered 9-by-13-inch baking dish. Scatter the onions over the squash. Cut the butter into small pieces and distribute over the squash and onions.

Preheat the oven to 375° F. In a small bowl, beat the eggs, milk, salt, and pepper until well blended. Pour over the squash. Sprinkle the cheddar and cracker crumbs over the top. Reduce the heat to 350° F

and bake until the cheese is browned and bubbling, 30 to 40 minutes.

SERVES 4 TO 6.

♦ ♦ ♦ ♦ ♦ ♦ ♦

SOUTHERN CORN BREAD

2 tablespoons vegetable shortening
1 cup white or yellow cornmeal
1 cup all-purpose flour
1 tablespoon baking powder
3 tablespoons sugar
½ teaspoon salt
2 eggs
1½ cups milk

Preheat the oven to 350° F. Spread the shortening over the bottom of a heavy cast-iron skillet and place in the oven.

In a large mixing bowl, combine the cornmeal, flour, baking powder, sugar, and salt. Add the eggs and milk, stirring quickly to form a stiff batter. Do not overwork or the corn bread will be tough.

Pour the batter into the hot skillet. Bake until golden brown and a toothpick inserted in the center comes out clean, 30 to 45 minutes. Turn out onto a large work surface or cutting board. Cut into wedges and serve warm.

SERVES 4 TO 6.

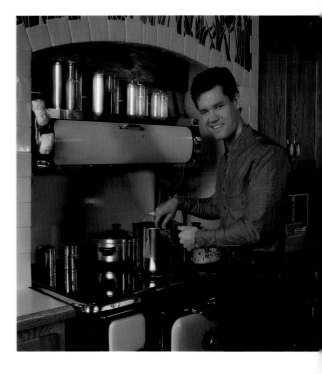

ABOVE: *Don't let Randy's dashing good looks and charismatic voice fool you. He's talented in many ways, including stirring up almost any Southern favorite you can name. Years as a professional chef taught him a few things about the kitchen before he hit the big time onstage.*

OLD-FASHIONED BUTTERMILK PIE

3 tablespoons unsalted butter
1¼ cups sugar
3 eggs
1 tablespoon flour
½ cup buttermilk
1 teaspoon vanilla extract
1 9-inch pie shell, unbaked

Preheat the oven to 300° F.

In a mixing bowl, cream the butter and sugar. Stir in the eggs, flour, buttermilk, and vanilla. Pour into the pie shell. Bake until the tip of a knife comes out clean when inserted in the center, about 45 minutes. Cool slightly before serving.

SERVES 8.

◆ ◆ ◆ ◆ ◆ ◆ ◆

When you sit down to supper with Randy, honest country fare—fried chicken, buttermilk biscuits, corn bread, and lots of vegetables—is sure to be on the table. This man really knows how to cook!

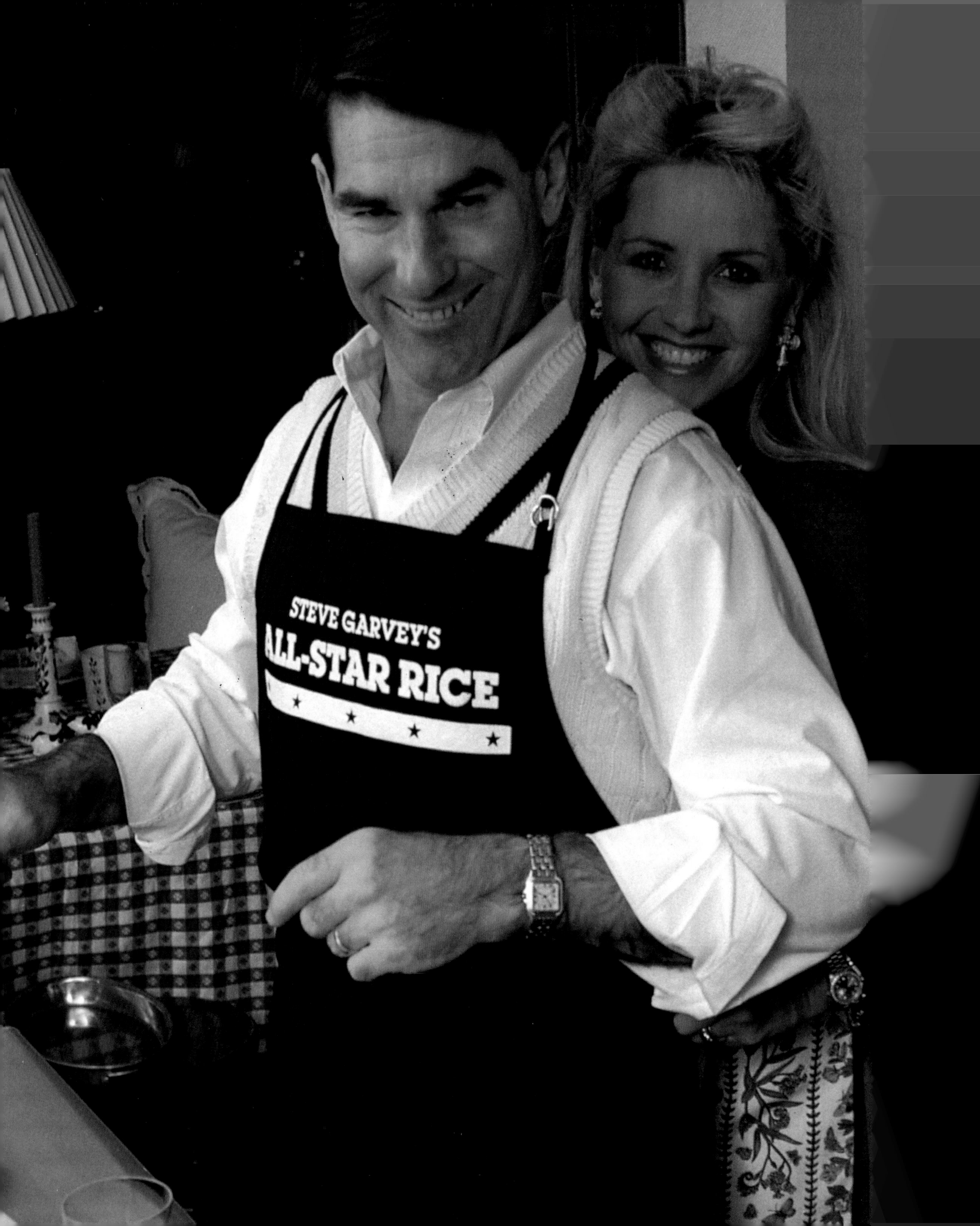
STEVE GARVEY'S
ALL-STAR RICE

Steve and Candace Garvey

◆ ◆ ◆ ◆ ◆ ◆ ◆ ◆ ◆ ◆ ◆

"STEVE DIDN'T MARRY ME FOR MY COOKING,
THAT'S FOR SURE. WHEN WE GOT MARRIED,
THE ONLY THING I COULD MAKE WAS A
RESTAURANT RESERVATION."

"Through much experimentation, and a few cooking classes, too, I learned to cook. Since I love sweets, I make great desserts—especially those that look beautiful on the table. I was an interior decorator for seven years, so I love to make everything look great, as well as taste delicious.

"Currently, we entertain by seating everyone in small, intimate groups. We first remove almost everything from the living room, then set up four or five small tables that seat four. We create a romantic mood by having a fire in the fireplace, candles on the tables, and music. As the courses are served and cleared away, the tables are reset, and everyone switches tables to sit with a different group. That way, there are new conversations at each table, and our guests get to know each other. As far as I am concerned, dessert is always the best part of the meal—especially if it has lemon in it," Candace emphasized.

> ## THE MENU
> ◆ ◆ ◆ ◆ ◆ ◆ ◆
> FILLET OF SALMON
> GREEN SALAD WITH TRUFFLE DRESSING
> LEMON TARTS

OPPOSITE: *While in Alaska filming a television special on fishing, the Garveys cooked fresh-caught salmon over an open fire. They brought some back to prepare in a more civilized environment—their California kitchen.*

"I have many decorating tricks for my parties, but I think a good florist—one who knows when to stop—is always essential. I like low arrangements with a variety of fresh and fragrant flowers. That's sort of my trademark," said Candace, referring to a special dinner she created in the backyard. "There's a perfect spot in the corner of the yard where I like to set a table with my best china and Champagne. It's very romantic. Steve is so appreciative of the extra time I put into setting the mood as well as preparing the food. Sometimes *he* does the cooking, and he's not a bad cook, either.

"We've also started a few family traditions in the kitchen. Once a week the girls, Shaunna and Taylor, cook dinner for us. I take them to the market and help them shop, but they do everything else. I want them to have confidence in this area long before they get married. They love to serve us and watch our reactions to the first bite."

FILLET OF SALMON

TOP: *Fillet of Salmon.* ABOVE: *Steve now writes and produces sports-oriented television shows—even one with a cooking twist—with Candace, and is able to spend more time with his family.*

1 cup pecan pieces
1 cup honey
¾ cup unsalted butter (1½ sticks)
¼ cup vegetable oil
4 salmon fillets, 4 to 6 ounces each
Salt and freshly ground pepper

Preheat the oven to 350° F. Spread the pecans in a single layer on a small baking sheet. Bake until darkened and crisp, about 5 minutes, stirring 2 or 3 times to toast the pecans uniformly. Cool to room temperature, then coarsely chop.

To prepare the glaze, combine the honey, half the butter, and the pecans in a small saucepan. Over moderately high heat, cook until the pecans are coated in a glossy glaze, 7 to 10 minutes. Remove from the heat and keep warm.

In a large sauté pan, melt the remaining butter with the oil over high heat. Season the fish with salt and pepper to taste. Sauté until the fillets are firm to the touch, about 4 minutes per side. Transfer to serving plates and spoon with the glaze.

SERVES 4.

◆ ◆ ◆ ◆ ◆ ◆ ◆

GREEN SALAD WITH TRUFFLE DRESSING

½ tablespoon Dijon mustard
¼ teaspoon salt
⅛ teaspoon freshly ground pepper
¼ cup red wine vinegar
¼ cup water
¼ cup olive oil
¼ cup truffle juice (see note)
6 to 8 cups washed and dried salad
   greens, loosely packed

In the bottom of a salad bowl,
stir the mustard, salt, pepper,
and vinegar together until well
blended. Whisk in the water,
oil, and truffle juice. Pile the
salad greens on top and bring
to the table. Toss just before
serving.

SERVES 4.

NOTE: Canned truffle juice is
available in specialty food stores
or by mail order.

ABOVE: *Candace keeps all the right accoutrements on hand for imaginative table settings, and brings them out often, especially for romantic dinners with Steve,* LEFT.

Top: *Candace loves to entertain, and desserts are her specialty.* Above: *Candace's collection of pill boxes, many of Limoges porcelain, are her favorite treasures; Steve always knows to buy another for special gifts. Candace also uses the smallest ones for salt and pepper cellars.*

LEMON TARTS

FOR THE PASTRY

1¼ cups all-purpose flour
¼ teaspoon salt
2 tablespoons sugar
3 tablespoons unsalted butter,
    chilled and cut into small pieces
3 tablespoons vegetable shortening,
    chilled
2 tablespoons ice water
½ teaspoon freshly squeezed lemon
    juice.

FOR THE FILLING

½ cup freshly squeezed lemon juice
¼ cup sugar
3 eggs
3 egg yolks

FOR THE MERINGUE

5 egg whites
¾ cup sugar

To make the pastry, combine the flour, salt, and sugar in the work bowl of a food processor; pulse briefly to mix. Cut in the butter and the shortening with several quick pulses. Do not overmix. With the motor running, gradually pour in the ice water and the lemon juice and process just until the dough forms a mass around the blade. Turn the dough out onto a floured work surface and knead briefly. Gather the dough into a small ball, wrap in plastic, and refrigerate for at least 2 hours or up to 2 days.

To prepare the filling, combine the lemon juice, sugar, eggs, and egg yolks in a double boiler set over hot but not boiling water. Whisk to blend, then stir constantly with a wooden spoon until the mixture is the consistency of thick custard, about 12 minutes. Pour into a shallow dish and let cool completely, then cover with plastic wrap and refrigerate until firm, about 2 hours.

When ready to make the tarts, cut the dough into 4 equal pieces and roll each one into a circle 6 inches by ⅛-inch thick. Line each of 4 tartelet molds 4½ inches wide with a circle. Refrigerate the pastry for at least 20 to 30 minutes before baking.

Preheat the oven to 425° F. Prick the bottoms of lined pastry shells with a fork. Line the shells with foil and fill with pastry weights or dried beans

to prevent the dough from puff-
ing up. Bake until the edges are
browned and the dough is set,
about 15 minutes. Remove the
foil and weights and continue
baking until the shell is uniformly brown, 3 to 5 minutes
more; do not let the pastry
scorch. Remove to a wire rack,
unmold, and cool completely.

To make the meringue, beat
the egg whites with the remaining ¾ cup sugar until the
whites are stiff and shiny. Reduce the oven temperature to
350° F. Fill the shells with the
lemon custard and place on a
baking sheet. Divide the meringue among the 4 and use a
knife to spread over the filling.
Bake until the meringue is
lightly browned on top, about
15 minutes. Let cool slightly
before serving.

MAKES 4 4½-INCH TARTS.

ABOVE: *Desserts are frequently served
with coffee and cognac in front of the
fire.*

LEFT: *Now that he is retired from two
decades on the baseball diamond,
Steve's mementos are tucked away on
the top shelf, but in plain view for
those who wish to catch a glimpse of
his astounding career as one of
baseball's greats.*

Barbara Taylor Bradford

♦ ♦ ♦ ♦ ♦ ♦ ♦ ♦ ♦ ♦

"I ENTERTAIN IN TWO DIFFERENT WAYS.
EITHER I WILL HIRE A CHEF TO COME IN AND
COOK WITH ME, OR I'LL DO IT ALL MYSELF,
BUT ONLY FOR VERY, VERY CLOSE FRIENDS."

"When friends are coming over, my first consideration is personal," said this best-selling author. "If I am working on a book, or when I'm entertaining on a large scale, I hire a cook to come in. When *I* cook, I make a simple one-dish meal and serve everyone right from a terrine on the table. I always think of the simplest dishes if I'm preparing the dinner, starting with a wonderful pâté from a gourmet shop, or smoked salmon, for the perfect appetizer, so I can spend more time with my guests.

"For one recent party for twelve, I prepared a big Irish stew with carrots, onions, potatoes, peas, steamed vegetables, and lovely pancakes. When it's cold outside, I especially like to serve pot roast. It's also a favorite holiday meal of mine. My husband, who loves good wines, always selects the right wines to accompany the dinner.

"I love to set a fancy table. I collect antique dishes

THE RECIPES

♦ ♦ ♦ ♦ ♦ ♦ ♦

ENGLISH COTTAGE PIE
VEAL CASSEROLE
CHICKEN IN THE POT
SUMMER PUDDING

OPPOSITE: *Barbara Taylor Bradford's dog, Jemma, loves to sit beneath her desk as she writes. Jemma has been with the family since Barbara's first book,* A Woman of Substance, *was published in 1984.*

---

and soup bowls, which I match together and use frequently. I used to write on antique collecting and decorating, which are still my hobbies. I might typically have a flower arrangement or an antique bowl on the table. I love to light the candles, no matter who is coming over for dinner.

"Probably my favorite party ever was not even in my home," Barbara reminisced. "We celebrated our twenty-fifth wedding anniversary in the private L'Orangerie dining room at New York's Le Cirque restaurant with about forty people. It was a truly romantic evening.

"When my husband and I want to spend some special time together, dining alone, we usually go to the South of France. We've got to be careful with all the wonderful food so we don't gain weight. Our favorite food is French, and we *love* Paris. And that's why I have a lot of the city throughout my books."

ENGLISH COTTAGE PIE

8 medium all-purpose potatoes,
  peeled and quartered
Salt and freshly ground pepper
2 tablespoons unsalted butter
2 medium onions, coarsely chopped
2 pounds ground beef
½ cup beef stock

Place the potatoes in a large soup kettle or stockpot. Cover with cold water, add a pinch of salt, and bring to a boil over high heat. Reduce the heat to moderately high and cook until tender, 20 to 25 minutes. Drain and, while still hot, press them through a coarse sieve to form a puree. Season with salt and pepper to taste. Set aside and keep warm.

Over moderately high heat, melt the butter in a large sauté pan. Add the onions and sauté until golden brown, 5 to 7 minutes. Add the beef and stir until the meat is crumbled and has lost all traces of pink, about 5 minutes. Stir in the beef stock. Transfer to a shallow 2-quart buttered ovenproof dish or casserole.

Preheat the oven to 350° F. Spread the pureed potatoes evenly over the meat. Press the tines of a fork around the outer edge to make a decorative border. Bake for 25 minutes, then increase the oven temperature to 500° F for the final few minutes to brown the potato crust.

SERVES 6 TO 8.

◆ ◆ ◆ ◆ ◆ ◆ ◆

VEAL CASSEROLE

2 tablespoons (¼ stick) unsalted
  butter
1 3-pound veal roast (shoulder or
  rump), boned and tied
Salt and freshly ground pepper
1 cup tomato juice
1 cup chicken stock
2 medium onions, finely chopped
2 celery stalks, finely chopped
6 medium carrots, coarsely chopped
4 sprigs fresh parsley
1 bay leaf
1 teaspoon fresh thyme
  (½ teaspoon dried)
2 sprigs fresh rosemary
  (½ teaspoon dried)
6 medium parsnips, trimmed and
  thickly sliced
3 cups mushrooms, about
  1½ pounds, trimmed and
  quartered
6 large tomatoes, cored and
  quartered

Preheat the oven to 325° F. In a covered casserole or Dutch oven over high heat, melt the butter. Add the veal and brown on all sides. Drain off the butter and season the veal with salt and pepper to taste. Add the tomato juice, chicken stock, onions, celery, and carrots.

Place the parsley, bay leaf, thyme, and rosemary in a small piece of moistened cheesecloth. Bring up the corners and tie with kitchen string. Add to the casserole. Cover and place in the oven. Cook until juices from the veal run clear, about 1½ hours, basting from time to time with the juices that accumulate in the bottom of the pan. After 1 hour, add the parsnips and mushrooms. Cover and return to the oven. Add the tomatoes for the last 15 minutes of cooking time.

Transfer the veal to a large serving platter and surround with the vegetables. Discard the cheesecloth containing the herbs. Set the casserole over moderately high heat and bring the liquid to a boil, stirring to scrape the cooking juices from the bottom and sides. Boil until the gravy is reduced and slightly thickened, about 5 minutes. Serve with the veal and vegetables.

SERVES 6.

◆ ◆ ◆ ◆ ◆ ◆ ◆

When she's not working on a book, Barbara makes a point of having friends over for brunches and dinners. A gracious hostess, Barbara loves to have lively conversation dominate the mood at her dinner table.

CHICKEN IN THE POT

6 chicken legs
6 boneless chicken breasts
8 to 10 cups homemade chicken
  stock
6 bay leaves
Several small sprigs fresh thyme,
  or 1 teaspoon dried thyme
Freshly ground pepper
Small pinch grated nutmeg
2 tablespoons finely chopped fresh
  parsley or 2 tablespoons dried
6 large carrots, cut into 1-inch
  pieces
6 parsnips, cut into 1-inch pieces
1 small onion, finely chopped
12 large mushrooms (about
  ¾ pounds), cleaned and halved
12 small red new potatoes, peeled
  and halved
4 fresh, peeled tomatoes or 1
  16-ounce can peeled tomatoes
1 cup fresh green peas or 1
  10-ounce package frozen green
  peas

Place the chicken pieces in a
large soup kettle and add
enough chicken broth to cover
generously. Add the bay
leaves, thyme, pepper, nutmeg,
parsley, carrots, parsnips, and
onions to the pot. Bring to a
boil over high heat, reduce the
heat to medium and simmer,
uncovered, for 30 minutes,
stirring occasionally.

Add the mushrooms, pota-
toe, tomatoes, and peas. Cook
for an additional 30 minutes. If
necessary, add small amounts
of the remaining broth to keep

ingredients covered at all times.

Divide the chicken, vegetables and liquid among 6 large soup bowls and serve at once.

SERVES 6.

♦ ♦ ♦ ♦ ♦ ♦ ♦

SUMMER PUDDING

6 to 8 thin slices white bread,
  preferably 2 days old
4 cups raspberries, rinsed well
4 cups red currants, rinsed well
  (see note)
1 tablespoon water
1 cup sugar
1 cup heavy cream

Remove the crusts from the bread. Reserve 1 or 2 slices to cover the top of the pudding. In a 2-quart glass bowl, arrange the remaining slices to cover the entire inside.

In a heavy, nonreactive saucepan over moderate heat, combine the raspberries, currants, water, and sugar. Bring to a simmer and cook just until the berries begin to give off juice, about 2 minutes. Immediately transfer to a mixing bowl and let cool completely.

When they have cooled, pour the berries and the juice into the bread-lined mold. Cover with the reserved bread slices. Place a plate on top and weight down with heavy cans, a paperweight, a brick, or any similar object. Refrigerate overnight.

When ready to serve, whip the cream until stiff. Invert the pudding onto a serving plate. Cut into wedges and add a dollop of whipped cream to each serving.

SERVES 6 to 8.

NOTE: If fresh red currants are unavailable, substitute very ripe strawberries. Halve or quarter strawberries so they are about the same size as the raspberries.

OPPOSITE, TOP: *Chicken in the Pot is best served from a tureen on the table. That way, seconds are easier to pass.* OPPOSITE, BOTTOM: *Before she began writing novels, Barbara wrote articles about antique collecting. When she found this set of mid-1800s English stoneware soup plates in perfect condition, she had a bottom plate custom-made to match.* ABOVE: *Barbara's dining room provides a spectacular view of Manhattan's Upper East Side and the glittering skyline beyond.*

Dina Merrill

◆ ◆ ◆ ◆ ◆ ◆ ◆ ◆ ◆ ◆ ◆

"I TYPICALLY COOK WITH A SAUTÉ PAN,
A FEW CHERRY TOMATOES, OLIVE OIL, FRESH
GARLIC, AND PASTA, BECAUSE I'M REALLY
A 'SHORT-CUT' COOK."

Dina Merrill and her husband, movie producer Ted Hartley, have devised a recipe for successful parties at their home in the Hamptons: guests play tennis with Dina and Ted all afternoon, then relax while Dina, Ted, and their cook, Effrem, create a simple yet elegant buffet dinner. Dina's "short-cut" cooking style focuses on good taste and beautiful presentation as much as on healthful, low-calorie cooking; she puts together the most unusual combinations of vegetables and serves them with marinated fish or chicken. For dessert there's usually a fresh berry sorbet with wafer-thin ginger cookies.

Though Dina now knows her way around a kitchen with ease and confidence, this was not always the case. The daughter of E. F. Hutton and General Foods heiress Marjorie Merriwether Post, she grew up in Mar-a-Lago, the biggest house in Palm Beach. "I remember feeling guilty if I went

---

THE MENU

◆ ◆ ◆ ◆ ◆ ◆

CHILLED CURRIED ZUCCHINI SOUP
TARRAGON CHICKEN BREASTS
MIXED GREEN SALAD
MINTED ORANGE ICED TEA

OPPOSITE: *Whether Dina Merrill and her husband, Ted Hartley, entertain for business or pleasure, the theme is always casual, especially when Dina is doing the honors in the kitchen.*

---

in the kitchen and took some little thing to eat. This was not my domain, and the cooks let me know it," Dina remembers. Years later, when she developed her own informal style of cooking and entertaining, "simple" and "easy" were her watchwords after her formal childhood.

With its relaxed atmosphere and floor-to-ceiling windows, the Hamptons house is an indoor-outdoor experience where guests are encouraged to find a place on one of the couches and prop their plates on the huge, hand-carved coffee table.

Dina concentrates on vegetables in her everyday cuisine as well. Leftover vegetables never go to waste, because she always has a "second-time-around" vegetable soup in the works. "I serve this anytime, whether the occasion is fancy or family, New York or Palm Beach," she adds. This *is* the work of a true short-cut gourmet.

CHILLED CURRIED ZUCCHINI SOUP

3 tablespoons unsalted butter
3 medium scallions, white part only, thinly sliced
1 large celery stalk, thinly sliced
1 teaspoon curry powder (or more to taste)
6 medium zucchini (2½ to 3 pounds), seeded and cut into 1½-inch chunks
4 cups chicken broth
3 tablespoons chopped fresh Italian (flat-leaf) parsley
Juice of ½ lemon
Salt and freshly ground pepper
1 cup buttermilk

In a large stockpot or saucepan, melt the butter. Add the scallions and celery. Cook over moderately low heat until softened, about 5 minutes, stirring often. Add the curry powder and continue stirring for 2 to 3 minutes.

Add the zucchini to the pot and cook until it begins to soften, about 5 minutes.

Pour in the chicken broth. Bring to a boil, then lower the heat and simmer until the zucchini is very soft, about 15 minutes. Stir in the parsley, lemon juice, salt, and pepper.

Working in batches, puree the soup in a food processor. Transfer the puree to a large bowl and allow it to cool to room temperature. Stir in the buttermilk, cover with plastic

wrap, and chill for at least 4 hours or overnight. If you prefer thinner soup, add more buttermilk. Taste for seasoning just before serving, adding salt and pepper to taste.

SERVES 4 to 6.

TOP: *Unlike those in many chilled soups, the ingredients in Dina's Chilled Curried Zucchini Soup are sautéed to blend the delicate flavors.* ABOVE, LEFT: *Dina and Ted, married since 1991, agree that a buffet featuring an array of low-calorie selections is their favorite way to serve a daytime meal.* ABOVE, RIGHT: *Cabbage porcelain dinnerware.*

TARRAGON CHICKEN BREASTS

8 skinless, boneless chicken breasts, about 4 ounces each

4 tablespoons olive oil

2 teaspoons seasoned salt

¼ teaspoon freshly ground black pepper

3 tablespoons unsalted butter

1 cup chicken stock

1 cup dry vermouth or dry white wine

3 tablespoons fresh tarragon, chopped, or 1 tablespoon dried, crumbled

Brush the chicken breasts with 1 tablespoon of the olive oil. Season with seasoned salt and pepper. Cover with plastic wrap and let stand at room temperature for 30 minutes.

In a large skillet over medium-high heat, melt the butter and the remaining olive oil. Brown the breasts until they are golden brown, about 1 minute on each side. Pour off the fat. Add the stock, the wine, and the tarragon. Cover and cook over low heat until the chicken is firm to the touch and all traces of pink have disappeared, about 10 minutes.

Remove to a platter and keep warm.

Bring the pan juices to a boil. Cook rapidly until thick and syrupy, 2 to 3 minutes. Pour over the breasts just before serving. Serve warm or at room temperature.

SERVES 4 to 6.

◆ ◆ ◆ ◆ ◆ ◆ ◆

ABOVE: *Just beyond the back door of her kitchen is Dina's flower garden, which provides all the arrangements throughout the house. Dina tends her cutting garden with a passion whenever she and Ted spend time in the Hamptons.*

MINTED ORANGE ICED TEA

1 quart water
Several sprigs fresh mint
4 tea bags (preferably English Breakfast tea)
1 cup freshly squeezed orange juice

In a large, nonreactive saucepan, boil the water with the mint sprigs. Add the tea bags and steep until strong but not acrid, about 5 minutes. Remove the bags, pour into a pitcher, and cool to room temperature.

In the bottoms of four tall glasses, place a fresh sprig of mint. Bruise the mint, using a long-handled iced-tea spoon. Fill the glasses with ice cubes, pour in the iced tea, and stir one-fourth cup of orange juice in each glass. Garnish with additional mint leaves.

SERVES 4.

◆ ◆ ◆ ◆ ◆ ◆ ◆

ABOVE: *In all their homes, Dina and Ted always make a place for family mementos and photographs. On the piano in the Hamptons, photos of their wedding day are displayed.*
OPPOSITE: *Special occasions require a special table setting, like these colorful porcelain dishes shaped like cabbages, created by West Palm Beach artist Dodi Theyer. These are some of Dina's favorite things, and she purchases a few place settings and accessory pieces on her annual Thanksgiving visit to Palm Beach.*

MIXED GREEN SALAD

10 cups salad greens, loosely packed (see note)
¼ cup freshly squeezed lemon juice
½ cup soy oil
2 teaspoons vegetable seasoning (such as Spike)
2 teaspoons sugar (or more to taste)

Rinse the salad greens in cold water. Dry them thoroughly, then roll in damp kitchen towels. Refrigerate until ready to assemble the salad.

Chill the salad plates and forks.

In a glass jar with a tight-fitting lid, combine the lemon juice, soy oil, vegetable seasoning, and sugar. Cover and shake vigorously to blend.

When ready to serve, tear the greens into small pieces and place in a large salad bowl. Shake the jar of dressing again and drizzle enough over the leaves to lightly coat them. Gently toss and serve the salad immediately on the chilled plates, before the lettuce starts to lose it crispness.

NOTE: Use a combination of the following: Belgian endive, leaf lettuce, oak leaf lettuce, watercress, and Bibb lettuce, or use your favorite salad greens.

SERVES 4 to 6.

Ruth and Skitch Henderson

♦ ♦ ♦ ♦ ♦ ♦ ♦ ♦ ♦ ♦

"WHEN FRIENDS COME UP FROM THE CITY,
WE WANT THEM TO HAVE FOOD THAT REFLECTS
OUR FARM—COUNTRY CUISINE—RELAXED
AND SIMPLE."

For twenty sparkling, fun-filled years, the Hendersons lived right in the center of the action in New York City. Skitch, then musical director for *The Tonight Show* and the New York Pops, and Ruth were famous for the lavish parties they threw for a star-studded list of people from the worlds of music, film, theater, politics, and fashion. Though she was busy raising their two children, Ruth found time to sharpen her culinary skills and to develop a repertoire of recipes that would place her in a spotlight of her own.

In 1973, the Hendersons abandoned city life for a 300-acre working farm in Litchfield, Connecticut. After successfully farming their land, raising a variety of animals, and converting two barns into warm, inviting living and entertaining spaces, they also created their cooking school, The Silo.

Over the years, these two talented cooking en-

THE MENU

♦ ♦ ♦ ♦ ♦ ♦ ♦

HOT PEPPER JELLY CHEESE PUFFS
WHOLE MEAL SALAD
ROSEMARY GRILLED CHICKEN
LOBSTER LENTIL SALAD
MIXED BERRY POT PIE
PLACE CARD COOKIES

OPPOSITE: If you're in the neighborhood, stop by the Hendersons' farm. Their widely acclaimed cooking school, The Silo, and their cookware shop and art gallery offer hours of browsing.

---

thusiasts have devised a relaxed and simple entertaining style they call country cuisine. Ruth's menus are created to please everyone, including herself. Her informal meals are typically served at midday, and the recipes can easily be increased to accommodate extra guests. Most of the ingredients are grown or raised right on Hunt Hill Farm. "This makes our menus seasonal; changes follow the growing season," Ruth explains. "We owned and ran four successful restaurants in the same way—no unnecessary fussing, just good healthy food, and lots of it!"

Around this philosophy, the Hendersons developed their current country favorites, which center on Skitch's barbecuing and grilling skills. When Skitch fires up the coals, Henry and Nancy Kissinger and Bill Blass are among the friends and neighbors who come over to "break bread."

TOP: *Jacques Pépin, Julie Sahni, Giuliano Bugialli, Sheila Lukins and Julee Rosso of the Silver Palate, and Martha Stewart are just some of the cooking professionals who have shared culinary tricks, tips, and genius at The Silo over the years.* ABOVE: *The Hendersons love to "eat out" from May to October.* OPPOSITE: *Skitch even conducts a class on grilling at The Silo.*

HOT PEPPER JELLY CHEESE PUFFS

½ pound sharp cheddar cheese, grated
6 tablespoons (¾ stick) unsalted butter, chilled and cut into small pieces
1 cup all-purpose flour
½ cup hot pepper jelly

In the bowl of a food processor, combine the cheese, butter, and flour. In several 1-second pulses, blend until the mixture resembles coarse meal, then let the food processor run for 5 to 6 seconds until the dough forms into a ball around the blade. Do not overwork the dough. Remove from the bowl, wrap in plastic, and refrigerate for 30 minutes.

Preheat the oven to 400° F.

Roll the dough into 1-inch balls, working quickly (dampen your hands if the dough sticks), and place the balls one inch apart on a large, ungreased baking sheet.

Bake the cheese puffs until the bottoms are lightly colored but not browned, about 5 minutes. Remove the baking sheet from the oven and form a small depression in the top of each puff with the back of a teaspoon. Fill each with about ¼ teaspoon hot pepper jelly. Immediately return to the oven and continue cooking until golden brown, about 5 more minutes. Cool slightly before serving.

MAKES 36.

♦ ♦ ♦ ♦ ♦ ♦ ♦

WHOLE MEAL SALAD

1 pound dried red beans
2 bay leaves
½ teaspoon Tabasco
5 pounds small new potatoes, scrubbed but not peeled
2½ pounds sugar snap peas, trimmed and rinsed
2 heads romaine lettuce
1 head red leaf lettuce
2 bunches scallions
1½ pounds mushrooms
4 bunches radishes with leaves intact, tied
1 large red onion
1 cup pitted and chopped oil-cured French olives
Salt and freshly ground pepper
2½ cups Mustard Vinaigrette (recipe follows)

Fill a large stockpot with water and soak the beans overnight. Drain and rinse the beans well under cold running water. Place them back in the pot with the bay leaves, Tabasco, and enough cold water to cover. Over moderately high heat, bring to a boil. Reduce the heat and simmer until tender, about 30 minutes.

Drain and rinse in cold water to stop the cooking process.

Place the potatoes in a large pot and cover with lightly salted cold water. Bring to a boil, reduce the heat, and cook until tender, about 20 minutes. Drain and cool to room temperature. Set aside until ready to assemble the salad.

Meanwhile, steam the peas over boiling water until tender, about 3 minutes. Do not overcook. Immediately immerse them in ice-cold water to set the bright green color and to stop the cooking process. Drain on paper towels and set aside.

Wash and trim the romaine and red lettuce leaves. Dry them in a salad spinner, wrap securely in plastic bags, and refrigerate until ready to assemble the salad.

Wash and peel the scallions, trimming them to include 1 inch of the green tops. Clean and quarter the mushrooms. Wash the radishes, leaving them tied together. Chop the onion coarsely. (See note.)

Just before serving, cut the potatoes in half. Line a large serving bowl or container with the lettuce leaves. In a separate large bowl, combine the beans, potatoes, peas, mushrooms, chopped onion, and olives. Gently mix together with half of the dressing, adding more dressing if necessary. Season to taste with salt and pepper. Spoon into the lettuce-lined bowl, and garnish with the

scallions and radish bunches. Serve at room temperature, and pass the remaining salad dressing.

SERVES 10.

NOTE: Everything can be done in advance up to this point. Keep the vegetables well covered in a cool spot or in the refrigerator. Sprinkle the mushrooms with a little lemon juice to prevent them from turning brown. A word of caution: the potatoes can turn dark when exposed to air. If they are done in advance, keep whole and cut in half at the last minute. If the vegetables have been refrigerated, remove them from the refrigerator and leave at room temperature for about ½ hour before assembling the salad.

MUSTARD VINAIGRETTE

½ cup Dijon mustard
½ cup balsamic vinegar
¾ cup olive oil
½ cup mayonnaise
2 tablespoons sugar
¼ teaspoon freshly ground pepper

In a small bowl, combine the mustard and vinegar. Slowly whisk in the oil until thoroughly blended. Whisk in the mayonnaise, sugar, and pepper. Set aside until ready to dress the salad.

MAKES ABOUT 2½ CUPS.

ROSEMARY GRILLED CHICKEN

½ tablespoon salt
½ tablespoon freshly ground
 pepper
2 large garlic cloves, crushed
½ tablespoon dried marjoram
2 to 3 whole chickens (3½ to 5
 pounds each), quartered
2 to 3 tablespoons fresh rosemary,
 minced (plus several bunches for
 grilling)
4 cups buttermilk

In a small bowl, blend the salt, pepper, garlic, and marjoram by mashing with a fork. Sprinkle over the chicken on both sides. Cover and refrigerate for one hour.

Stir the rosemary into the buttermilk. In a large shallow glass pan, place the chicken in one layer, then cover with the buttermilk. Turn to coat on all sides. (Add additional buttermilk, if necessary, to completely cover the chicken.) Cover with plastic wrap and refrigerate overnight.

Prepare a charcoal fire. After the fire has subsided, place several branches of rosemary on the coals; this imparts a wonderful smell and flavor to the chicken as it cooks.

When the coals are glowing with a layer of white ash, grill the chicken pieces about 4 to 6 inches away from the coals until the skin is golden and the meat is cooked through, basting frequently with the marinade. Check white meat for doneness after 30 to 35 min-

utes; dark meat usually takes 5 to 7 minutes longer. Serve immediately.

SERVES 10.

◆ ◆ ◆ ◆ ◆ ◆

LOBSTER LENTIL SALAD

5 lobsters (about 1¼ pounds each)
2½ pounds dried lentils (½ red
 and ½ brown)
2 bay leaves
2 garlic cloves
1 teaspoon salt
¾ cup Lemon Pepper Dressing
 (recipe follows)
1 small red pepper, seeded and
 chopped
1 small green pepper, seeded and
 chopped
2 bunches fresh lovage or parsley
5 lemons, halved

Over high heat, bring a very large pot of lightly salted water to a boil. Drop in the lobsters, bring back to the boil, reduce the heat, and simmer for about 12 minutes or until the lobsters are bright red. Drain, cool, and cut in half lengthwise. Refrigerate until completely chilled, for at least 2 hours but no more than 24.

Place the lentils in a large stockpot and add water to cover. Add the bay leaves, garlic, and salt. Bring to a boil, then lower the heat and simmer just until the lentils are tender, 5 to 6 minutes, taking care not to overcook. Drain and rinse under cold water to stop the cooking process. Drain well again and transfer to a large bowl. Stir in the Lemon Pepper Dressing, cover with plastic wrap, and let marinate for at least 3 hours at room temperature, or up to 24 hours in the refrigerator.

Just before assembling the salad, remove the bay leaves and the garlic cloves from the lentil mixture, and stir in the chopped peppers. Line a platter or a large shallow serving bowl with the lovage or parsley. Fill with the lentil mixture and arrange the lobster halves over the top in a sundial pattern. Garnish with the lemon halves around the sides.

SERVES 10.

LEMON PEPPER DRESSING

½ cup freshly squeezed lemon juice
¼ cup white wine vinegar
2 tablespoons sugar
Salt and freshly ground pepper

In a small bowl, combine the lemon juice, vinegar, and sugar. Whisk together to blend. Season with salt and pepper to taste.

MAKES ABOUT ¾ CUP.

OPPOSITE: *Ruth's favorite serving tray is a turn-of-the-century hand-carved trough she picked up in a local antiques store.* ABOVE: *Ruth always serves good, healthful food—and lots of it! Lobster Lentil Salad is especially popular, since the vegetables can be cooked and refrigerated the night before the salad is assembled,* LEFT.

MIXED BERRY POT PIE

FOR THE CRUST
2½ cups all-purpose flour
½ teaspoon salt
½ cup (1 stick) unsalted butter, cut
    into small pieces and chilled
½ cup solid vegetable shortening,
    chilled
1 teaspoon grated lemon zest
¼ cup cold *freshly squeezed*
    lemon juice

FOR THE FILLING
4 cups strawberries, washed and
    stemmed
2 cups blueberries, washed and
    stemmed
3 tablespoons instant tapioca
½ cup or more red currant
    preserves

FOR THE EGG WASH
1 egg
1 tablespoon water

First, make the crust. Sift the flour and salt into a large bowl. Cut in the butter and shortening with two knives or a pastry blender until the mixture is the size of peas. Cut in the lemon zest and mix well. Add the lemon juice a little at a time and toss just until mixture forms a soft dough. Do *not* overwork the dough. Form the dough into a ball, wrap it in wax paper, and refrigerate for at least 1 hour. (The dough can be made a day in advance.

Cover it tightly with plastic wrap and keep refrigerated until ready to use.)

Preheat the oven to 475° F.

When ready to assemble the pie, layer the strawberries, then blueberries, tapioca, and currant preserves in a 2-quart glass or crockery baking dish. Roll out the dough into a large round about ¼-inch thick. Center on top of the fruit and flute the edges. Cut any extra pieces of dough into attractive shapes and decorate the top. Using the tip of a sharp knife, make ¼-inch slits to allow the steam to escape. Mix egg and water together and lightly apply a thin layer of the egg wash with a pastry brush.

Place the pie in the upper third of the oven and bake for 15 minutes. Reduce the heat to 375° F and continue baking until the crust is golden brown and the filling is bubbling, about 15 minutes more. Remove to a wire rack and cool for at least 10 minutes before serving. Top each serving with a dollop of vanilla *crème fraîche* (recipe follows).

SERVES 10.

VANILLA *CRÈME FRAÎCHE*

4 cups heavy cream
3 tablespoons buttermilk
1 vanilla bean

Mix the cream and buttermilk in a large bowl. Pour into a glass jar with a tight-fitting lid, cover, and let stand in a warm place for at least 12 hours or until it has thickened.

Chop the vanilla bean into small pieces and add to the cream. Refrigerate overnight.

Just before serving, lightly whip the *crème fraîche* with a whisk or an electric mixer set on the slowest speed.

Crème fraîche will keep in the refrigerator for up to 10 days.

MAKES ABOUT 1 QUART.

❖ ❖ ❖ ❖ ❖ ❖ ❖

PLACE CARD COOKIES

FOR THE COOKIES
1½ cups (3 sticks) unsalted butter, softened
2 cups granulated sugar
2 eggs
2 teaspoons vanilla extract
3 cups all-purpose flour
1 teaspoon baking powder
1 teaspoon salt

FOR THE ICING
3 cups confectioners' sugar
4 tablespoons (½ stick) unsalted butter, softened
4 tablespoons milk
Pinch salt
1 teaspoon vanilla extract

To make the dough, in a large mixing bowl cream the butter and sugar until light and fluffy. Beat in the eggs and vanilla.

In a separate bowl, sift together the flour, baking powder, and salt. Add to the creamed mixture all at once and combine to form a soft dough; do not work the dough too much. Cover with plastic wrap and refrigerate overnight.

Preheat the oven to 375° F. On a lightly floured board, roll out the dough to ¼-inch thick. Cut into shapes with cookie cutters. Place on an unbuttered baking sheet, and bake until lightly browned, about 12 to 15 minutes. Remove the cookies to a rack and let them cool completely before icing.

To make the icing, blend the sugar and butter in a large bowl. Add the milk, salt, and vanilla, and beat at a moderate speed until thick and creamy. If necessary, add more sugar to thicken or more milk to thin to form a thick, spreadable icing.

Fill a pastry bag fitted with a plain tip and decorate the cookies with guest's names or with other designs.

MAKES ABOUT 10 7-INCH COOKIES.

OPPOSITE, TOP: *A mix of fresh-picked berries in a pot pie is a delightful finish to the meal.*
OPPOSITE, BOTTOM: *The Hendersons recently published* Seasons in the Country, *a collection of family recipes and entertaining tips for setting out a country-style spread. Their holiday cookbook is on the way.*
ABOVE: *Edible place cards are one of Ruth's trademarks. Guests go wild over them, and they're so easy to make.*

Favorite
Recipes

◆ ◆ ◆ ◆ ◆ ◆ ◆ ◆ ◆ ◆

Princess Yasmin Aga Khan

◆ ◆ ◆ ◆ ◆ ◆ ◆ ◆ ◆ ◆

"WHEN I PLAN A MENU, THE FIRST THING I
THINK ABOUT IS WHETHER THE PLATE WILL
GRAB MY GUESTS' ATTENTION. A PLATE
SHOULD ALWAYS HAVE LIVELY, COLORFUL
COMBINATIONS OF FOOD."

Princess Yasmin is the daughter of the late screen legend Rita Hayworth and Prince Aga Khan. She lives a fast-paced life in New York City with her real-estate executive husband, Christopher Jefferies.

"A few years ago, we would have thrown a dinner party in a chic restaurant," Yasmin said. "Today, we much prefer to give intimate dinners at home. Seating eight or ten people at a round table is perfect. It's casual.

"I like to serve eye-catching and colorful dishes. Usually, I plan an array of vegetables, served with chicken or my favorite, veal piccata. Chris and I actually prefer to entertain in the summer at our house in Westhampton, where it's quieter—more relaxed. My menus there are much lighter, and always include lots of colorful vegetables and fruits, like my dietetic invention, Grapefruit Soup—it's simply grapefruit sections served in strained, fresh grapefruit juice. Pastas are high on my list, too, since they can be served year-round, hot or cold. Sometimes, though, I like to end a meal with two desserts: a light fruit salad, and also a fattening dessert."

She continued, "For the past eight years, I have been on the planning committee for the Rita Hayworth Gala, a fund-raising evening for the National Alzheimer's Association. As a committee, we have selected some very interesting and delicious menus for our galas. After we narrow down our choices, the Tavern on the Green Restaurant, where we hold the gala, prepares a tasting lunch for the committee members so we can decide on the final menu. We want the guests to remember the lovely decorations, seeing their friends all dressed up, but, most of all, a delicious dinner."

Chicken with Pasta

2 tablespoons (¼ stick) unsalted
  butter
2 tablespoons vegetable oil
8 medium shiitaki and white
  mushrooms, about ½ pound
  total, quartered
Salt and freshly ground pepper
1 pound boneless, skinless chicken
  breasts, cut into 1½-inch pieces
¼ cup Cognac
2 cups chicken stock
1 cup heavy cream
1 pound pasta
1 small black truffle, peeled and
  finely chopped (optional)

In a large sauté pan, melt the butter and oil over moderately high heat. Add the mushrooms, season with salt and pepper to taste, and sauté until lightly browned, about 2 minutes. Remove with a slotted spoon and set aside. Add the chicken and sauté until lightly colored, about 2 minutes, adding more butter and oil if needed to prevent sticking. Remove the chicken and set aside.

Reduce the heat to moderate. Carefully add the Cognac to the pan. (Shield your face, as the Cognac could ignite.) Increase the heat to high and whisk, picking up any bits from the bottom of the pan. Boil until the Cognac is reduced to 2 tablespoons. Pour in the chicken stock and bring to a boil; continue boiling rapidly until it is reduced to ½ cup, about 10 minutes. Add the cream, bring back to a boil, and cook until reduced to ¾ cup, about 5 minutes. Reduce the heat to low, stir in the chicken and mushrooms, and cover. Cook gently until chicken is done through, about 5 minutes. Season with salt and pepper to taste.

Bring a large pot of salted water to a boil. Add the pasta and cook according to package directions. Drain and pour into a large serving bowl. Top with chicken and mushroom sauce. Sprinkle with truffles, if desired, and toss just before serving.

SERVES 4 TO 6.

OPPOSITE: *Princess Yasmin Aga Khan relaxes at home.* TOP: *Dinner in the formal dining room doesn't mean the food has to be fussy.* ABOVE: *Yasmin's affectionate cat, Veni.*

Joan Collins

◆ ◆ ◆ ◆ ◆ ◆ ◆ ◆ ◆ ◆

"WHEN YOU'VE GOT A GOOD THING, WHY CHANGE IT?"

To her fans, Joan Collins is *Dynasty*'s Alexis Carrington, the embodiment of romance and femininity at their beautiful best. To her friends, she's a hardworking actress, businesswoman, and mother. She's also involved in a very private relationship with the man of her dreams, and with the recent publication of *Love and Desire and Hate*, she's a successful novelist. Since there's not much time left in her life for cooking, Joan relies on a few standby recipes—old favorites—that are both delicious and easy to prepare.

For more intimate occasions, she might be found putting together an elegant tray of smoked Scottish salmon and melon, but for just about everything else, she makes her signature dish: Spaghetti Bolognese. Whether she's

ABOVE: *Joan prepares her favorite dish in the kitchen of her Hollywood hideaway.* OPPOSITE: *Always glamorous, Joan even serves spaghetti on dishes accented with 24-karat gold!*

at her London flat, her French Riviera hideaway, or her Los Angeles hillside house, the menu will almost invariably be the same.

"Spaghetti Bolognese has gotten me through the most unbelievable situations. I've served it to a prince and princess, the head of Warner Brothers, and absolutely all my friends, a thousand times. Even my sister, Jackie, approves!" Joan said.

Joan's recipe is so hearty that it needs only a salad to be a complete meal; she tosses together everything in the vegetable bin to make a superb salad. "Extravagance is the only way when it comes to buying beautiful dresses and to making salads," Joan stated emphatically, "especially when it's followed by Spaghetti Bolognese."

SPAGHETTI BOLOGNESE

½ cup olive oil
3 large onions, finely chopped
2 medium carrots, peeled and
  finely chopped
1 celery stalk, thinly sliced
2 pounds ground beef
2 pounds ground veal
2 pounds ground pork
1 pound button mushrooms,
  trimmed, wiped clean, and
  thinly sliced
1 28-ounce can tomatoes, drained
1 28-ounce can tomato sauce
¼ teaspoon salt
1 teaspoon sugar
2 tablespoons Worcestershire sauce
3 bay leaves
1 garlic clove, minced
2 cups hearty red wine
5 pounds spaghetti
Grated Parmesan cheese

In a very large soup kettle or stockpot, heat the olive oil over moderately high heat. Add the onions and stir quickly to coat, then add the carrots and celery. Reduce the heat to moderate and cook, stirring frequently, until the vegetables have softened, about 5 minutes.

Break the meat into the pan. Increase the heat to moderately high and stir until the meat is cooked through, 5 to 7 minutes.

Add the mushrooms, tomatoes, tomato sauce, salt, sugar, Worcestershire sauce, bay leaves, garlic, and wine. Bring

to a boil, then reduce the heat to very low and cook at a slow simmer, uncovered, until all but a few tablespoons of liquid remain and the sauce is thick, about 5 to 6 hours. Stir frequently to avoid scorching.

Just before serving, cook the spaghetti according to package directions. Drain in colanders.

In large serving bowls, toss the pasta with half of the sauce.

Serve with the remaining sauce and plenty of Parmesan on the side.

SERVES 20.

NOTE: If serving fewer than 20, freeze the remaining sauce and reduce the amount of spaghetti accordingly.

Chris Evert

◆ ◆ ◆ ◆ ◆ ◆ ◆ ◆ ◆ ◆

"ONE THING YOU'LL NEVER FIND ON MY
GROCERY SHOPPING LIST IS A CANDY BAR."

When you're as busy as Chris Evert is, a collection of super-healthful recipes is a must. Married since 1988 to world-class ski champion Andy Mill and since the fall of 1991 the mother of Alex Mill, Chris no longer competes on the tennis court professionally. Instead, she is the hub of a successful company in Boca Raton, Florida, that carries her name.

"Here in Florida, everyone loves to eat outside. We live a very casual life in Boca Raton."

Chris continued, "To know me is to know my favorite holiday: Thanksgiving! I love the whole meal, and all the wonderful accompaniments and trimmings for the turkey. Andy picks the wines whenever we have a nice dinner in the dining room, and on holidays we always do. I make a point of being home in Florida for Thanksgiving. It's such a *family* time of year. Plus, everybody likes to bring stuff they've made at home. I can hardly wait until the next Thanksgiving—it'll be little Alex's first, though I doubt he'll be into turkey yet. Not enough teeth!"

Perhaps Chris's second-favorite meal of the year is the one served at her Pro-Celebrity Benefit to fight drug abuse. This yearly fund-raising gala has attracted such major stars as Olivia Newton-John and Whitney Houston, whose performances have contributed to the worthy cause.

"This is one meal I leave to the planning committee—of which I am a part. When it comes time to sample the meal before the gala, I'm there to make sure it meets with my approval. I'm such a 'vegetable' person, though, that I would be satisfied with steamed veggies and a salad —which is why I need a committee to help create the dinner. I guess it comes from spending over half my life on a tennis court instead of in the kitchen."

CHICKEN SALAD

4 cups cooked chicken, cubed

1 cup fresh pineapple chunks

1 celery stalk, thinly sliced

2 scallions, trimmed and thinly
   sliced

¼ cup unsalted peanuts, coarsely
   chopped

½ teaspoon salt

2 tablespoons Major Grey's
   chutney

Juice of ½ lemon (about 2
   tablespoons)

½ teaspoon grated lemon zest

½ teaspoon curry powder

⅔ cup mayonnaise

4 pineapple leaves

1 tablespoon freshly chopped
   parsley

In a large mixing bowl, combine the chicken, pineapple
chunks, celery, scallions, peanuts, salt, chutney, lemon
juice, lemon zest, curry powder, and mayonnaise. Gently
stir with a wooden spoon until
well blended. Cover with plastic wrap and chill.

Serve on whole wheat or pita
bread or on a bed of lettuce.
Garnish with pineapple leaves
and chopped parsley.

SERVES 4.

OPPOSITE: *Chris Evert and Andy
Mill in their spacious modern dining
room.* ABOVE: *Chris serves Chicken
Salad for lunch or dinner.*

Florence Griffith Joyner

◆ ◆ ◆ ◆ ◆ ◆ ◆ ◆ ◆ ◆

"I CAN'T IMAGINE MYSELF MARRIED TO A
MAN WHO COULDN'T COOK."

"My father is a great cook. As far as I was concerned, no man could outdo him in the kitchen—until Al came along! On our first "big" date, he cooked a barbecued steak for me on Catalina Island—I can still remember the flavor, and the aroma is emblazoned in my memory forever! You can be sure it influenced me to say yes to his marriage proposal a lot faster. At that time, I was thinking more about my schedule than my appetite. But now, with Mary Ruth as a part of our family, my schedule has only gotten busier. I knew what qualities in a man were right for me and my incredibly busy life, and that's why I married Al.

"Cooking and entertaining is more fun when you serve an unexpected dish. However, first-time guests always get my favorite dinner: salad, bread, homemade soup, then the best part of the meal— shrimp Creole.

"Al and I have traveled all over the world competing in the various Olympics, international track and field, and athletic events. During our visits to foreign countries, we have always tried to experience the different cuisines. When our daughter, Mary Ruth, gets a little older, we're hoping to take her with us so she can experience the world at a young age.

"Besides cooking and bringing up my daughter, I'm coaching my husband, who is training for the Olympics, and I am actively involved in retaining my status in the world of track and field. I may not be the 'World's Fastest Woman' forever, but competitive racing keeps me in top physical shape. We have a very athletic point of view around our house, which is probably why few people can tell how much we love to cook and eat."

SPICY SHRIMP CREOLE

3 tablespoons unsalted butter
1 small onion, minced
1 stalk celery, minced
½ green pepper, cored, seeded, and
    minced
1 garlic clove, minced
2 medium tomatoes, peeled, seeded,
    and chopped
1 teaspoon salt
½ teaspoon cayenne pepper
1 teaspoon filé powder
2 cups water
1 cup long-grain rice
1 pound medium shrimp, peeled
    and deveined
Salt and freshly ground black
    pepper

In a medium skillet, melt 2 tablespoons of the butter over moderately low heat. Add the onions, celery, green pepper, and garlic. Cook until the vegetables are softened but not browned, about 3 minutes. Stir in the tomatoes and add ½ teaspoon of the salt, the cayenne pepper, and the filé powder. Increase the heat to high and boil until the sauce has thickened slightly, 5 to 10 minutes. Set aside.

Bring the water to a boil. In a small saucepan with a cover, melt the remaining tablespoon of butter over moderately high heat. Add the rice and stir until translucent, about 2 minutes, then pour the water over the rice. Bring back to a boil, then immediately reduce heat to low. Add the remaining ½ teaspoon salt, cover, and cook the rice for 20 minutes. Remove the rice from the heat, stir gently with a fork, recover, and let sit off the heat for 5 minutes.

Just before serving, add the shrimp to the tomato mixture. Bring the sauce to a boil and stir until the shrimp turn pink and are firm to the touch, about 5 minutes. Season the mixture to taste with additional salt and pepper, if desired.

Arrange the rice on a serving platter. Spoon the shrimp Creole over the rice and serve at once.

SERVES 4 TO 6.

OPPOSITE: *Florence, Al, and their daughter, Mary Ruth.* TOP: *Spicy Shrimp Creole is one of Florence's favorites.* CENTER: *Florence and Al share a romantic moment over dinner. Now that she is his coach, they spend almost all their time together.* BOTTOM: *Florence has designed and created a line of running and sports clothing that reflects her extremely athletic yet very feminine personality.*

Jerry Lewis

◆ ◆ ◆ ◆ ◆ ◆ ◆ ◆ ◆ ◆ ◆

"When I need a food fix, I go to France."

King of comedy Jerry Lewis and his wife, Sandee, have made it a lifelong mission to seek out the best food and wine that France has to offer. When it's time to relax and take a break from Jerry's hectic schedule of performances, the happy couple heads directly for their favorite region—the sunny South of France—and Jean-Jacques Jouteux's restaurant, Provence. From its terrace, suspended out over the sea,

ABOVE: *Jerry, Sandee, and Chef Jouteux have fun on the patio of the chef's restaurant, Provence.*

the restaurant offers a great view of the Mediterranean. Chef Jean-Jacques planned and cooked an unforgettable lunch for France's beloved funny man.

Jerry commented, "I love France; I feel quite at home here. The love affair that France and I have had with one another has been going on for about thirty-five years. I don't do jokes, I don't *talk* to the French, everything I do is mime, visual. And when I do speak to them, I speak in a frac-

tured French they love."

Knowing Jerry's reputation for amusing and wonderful antics, chef Jean-Jacques stayed by Jerry's side to experience the famed actor close up; he was not disappointed! Jerry turned the lunch into his own personal stage.

Jerry had many opportunities to put his passion for fine French food to the test all over the country. Whether he's visiting the poshest of Parisian eateries or enjoying a relaxed al fresco meal beside the azure waters at Saint Jean du Cap Ferrat, there's always a table waiting for him in France. But when he travels to the magical principality of Monaco—just a few miles south, the tables are turned. Jerry frequently stars on stage at Monte Carlo's famed night spot, the Sporting Club. He gets laughs out of adoring fans who gather to pay homage to the man they affectionately call "Doctor."

Roasted Snapper

4 red snapper fillets, 4 to 6 ounces
    each, skin attached
Salt and freshly ground pepper
1 large orange
½ cup cold-pressed, extra-virgin
    olive oil
4 large fig leaves (see note)
½ pound beef marrow, cut into
    thin rounds
4 whole fresh figs
Juice of 2 lemons
1 tablespoon coarse salt
1 tablespoon cracked white
    peppercorns

Season the fillets with salt and pepper to taste. Refrigerate until ready to proceed.

Preheat the oven to 475° F. With a vegetable peeler, peel the zest from the orange in long, thin strips, as though it were an apple. Avoid the bitter white pith. Place the orange strips on a small, unbuttered baking sheet and bake until lightly colored and shriveled around the edges, about 4 to 5 minutes. Remove and set aside. Leave the oven temperature set at 475° F.

In a large, non-stick sauté pan, heat 2 tablespoons of the olive oil. Add the fish fillets, skin side down, and cook over high heat without turning until the flesh is firm and the skin crisp, 3 to 5 minutes. Drain and place 1 fillet directly onto each fig leaf. Top the fillet with slices of marrow and strips of orange. Fold up the sides of the leaves to form a small bundle. Secure the ends with toothpicks. Place the bundles and the fresh figs on a large buttered baking sheet, and bake until the leaves are lightly browned, about 6 minutes. Transfer the bundles and figs to 4 individual serving plates. Remove the toothpicks and peel back the leaves to expose the fish partially. Drizzle the remaining olive oil and the lemon juice over the bundles, and sprinkle with the coarse salt and cracked peppercorns. Serve at once.

SERVES 4.

NOTE: Fig leaves are sometimes available in produce markets where fresh figs are sold. They are also bottled in ethnic markets. If bottled leaves are used, remove from brine, rinse, pat dry, and proceed as above. Substitute grape leaves if fig leaves cannot be found.

BELOW: *Roasted Snapper, fresh from the oven, is one of Jerry's favorites.*

Elle Macpherson

♦ ♦ ♦ ♦ ♦ ♦ ♦ ♦ ♦ ♦ ♦

"I THINK YOU EAT BETTER AT HOME, AND
HAVE THE PLEASURE OF PREPARING THE MEAL
YOURSELF."

One might never guess this six-foot-tall Australian model is a great cook, but Elle indulges in her passion for cooking whenever she can. She frequently puts her improvisational nature to work on the contents of her fridge, which is how her unique Smoked Salmon Bruschetta came about.

"I learned about taste and the elements of combining flavors while living in the French countryside," Elle said. "I lived in the Sologne region of France, which is known for its incred-

ible wild mushrooms and cheeses. Everything was so fresh there. The local country markets, fields, and streams provided everything we needed to create incredible feasts."

In her eighteenth-century French farmhouse, Elle and her friends cooked tantalizing dishes with veal, pheasant, and lamb. Her kitchen was equipped with two stoves, including one whose only source of heat

was wood—perfect for roasting wild game.

"I had guests from Australia all the time. If we weren't cooking, we were eating or planning our next meal. If we weren't planning, we were at the marketplace, out in the vegetable patch, or hunting and fishing. We really lived for mealtime."

Now, in her Upper East Side apartment in Manhattan, Elle combines all the techniques of good taste she learned while cooking in France with a few new ones, to make a lighter-style cuisine. Informal dinner parties at home might include simple pastas, broiled sea bass, crêpes filled with salmon and caviar—often served with her favorite rich, red Margaux wine.

Elle has very distinct rules for cooking and entertaining: "Lots of Champagne, no salt, and a maximum of eight guests for dinner—because that's how many fit at my table."

SMOKED SALMON BRUSCHETTA

3 tablespoons toasted pine nuts
2 medium tomatoes, peeled, seeded, and finely chopped
4 ounces fresh unsalted mozzarella cheese, cut into ¼-inch dice
4 ounces smoked salmon, finely chopped
2 tablespoons olive oil
Freshly ground white pepper
4 large slices French country bread
1 garlic clove, halved
8 fresh basil leaves, cut into thin strips

Preheat the broiler. In a small bowl, combine the pine nuts, tomatoes, mozzarella, salmon, and olive oil. Season with pepper to taste.

Toast the bread slices under the broiler until lightly browned. Remove toast from the broiler, and while it is still warm, rub one side of the toast with garlic. Spread with the tomato mixture, sprinkle with basil strips, and serve immediately.

SERVES 4.

OPPOSITE: *Elle Macpherson shops at one of New York's most revered gourmet markets, Balducci's, in Greenwich Village, for the freshest ingredients.* ABOVE: *Smoked Salmon Bruschetta is a flavorful replacement for brunch standards like bagels and cream cheese—with fewer calories, too.*

Peter Max

◆ ◆ ◆ ◆ ◆ ◆ ◆ ◆ ◆ ◆ ◆

"THE OTHER DAY, MY FRIEND SHEP GORDON
CALLED TO TELL ME HE WAS BRINGING
OVER HIS SPECIAL MAUI ONION SOUP. SO I
QUICKLY GOT OUT THE BOWLS AND SPOONS."

The culinary tastes of this world-famous artist are much simpler than the wildly colorful palette he paints from.

"Macrobiotic dishes are my first choice. Especially rice, which I can cook blindfolded. When I go out, I frequently eat salmon. Not much variety but that's what I like," he said, laughing.

"When Shep called, I knew the soup would be something fantastic. Shep, super manager and movie producer, had been studying cooking with master-chef Roger Vergé in the South of France—so I didn't eat my rice. I figured I'd eat a lot of soup, and maybe Shep would teach me how to make it. Then I'd have two recipes—rice and soup. Almost enough for a dinner. I'm really getting into cooking now."

While serving the artist a large bowl of his highly acclaimed concoction, Shep Gordon said, "The key to making Maui Onion Soup is the onion itself.

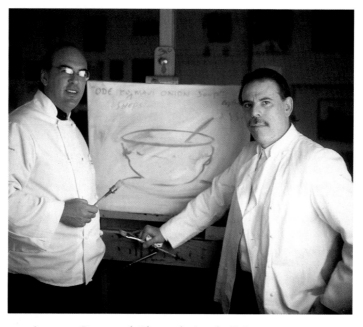

ABOVE: *Peter and Shep admire the Max masterpiece, created in honor of his favorite soup.*

Most people think regular onions are all right, but at the end of the three-hour cooking time, you get a very pungent, almost bitter, broth. Only Maui onions, or in a pinch, Walla Walla sweet onions or Vidalias from Georgia have the lightness and sweetness that hold up over the cooking time," he explained to Peter, for any future soup-making pursuits.

Peter, who has made an art of his macrobiotic diet, also entertains on a grand scale. When Jane Fonda and Ted Turner asked him to throw a party in his New York art studio to introduce Turner's Environmental Campaign, Peter wanted an extraordinary menu with lots of vegetarian dishes made from ingredients low on the food chain. Manhattan's Mood Food Caterers—known for creating some dazzling vegetarian meals—gave him exactly what he wanted. "I wanted an artistic yet 'environmentally kind' menu."

MAUI ONION SOUP

8 tablespoons (1 stick) unsalted
  butter
12 Maui onions, peeled and thinly
  sliced
1 4-inch piece fresh ginger root,
  peeled and grated
10 cups chicken stock
1 750-milliliter bottle dry white
  wine
10 sprigs fresh thyme or
  1 tablespoon dried
2 cups half-and-half
Salt and freshly ground pepper

In a large stockpot or soup kettle, melt the butter over moderately high heat. Add the
onions and ginger. Reduce the
heat to moderately low and
cook until the onions are transparent, stirring often, about
15 minutes. Do not allow the
onions to brown or the soup
will be bitter. Add the chicken
stock, wine, and thyme. Increase the heat to moderately
high and bring to a boil. Reduce the heat to moderate and
cook, slightly covered, for
about 3 hours.

Working in several batches,
puree the soup in a food processor or a food mill. Return
the puree to the pot and add
the half-and-half. Bring to a
boil over moderate heat. Season with salt and pepper to
taste. Ladle into warmed bowls
and serve at once.

SERVES 14 TO 16.

NOTE: The soup can be served
cold, too. Bring to room temperature, cover, and refrigerate for
several hours before serving in
chilled bowls. Add a dollop of
sour cream to the cold soup, if
desired.

◆ ◆ ◆ ◆ ◆ ◆ ◆

ABOVE: *The beautifully designed
plates are part of Peter's many new,
experimental works of art.* RIGHT: *In
1991, Peter created this poster for
Ted Turner's TBS Environmental
Campaign. Peter is the official artist
for the project.*

Roger Moore

◆ ◆ ◆ ◆ ◆ ◆ ◆ ◆ ◆ ◆

"Let me know if this is the best recipe
you have ever come across," wrote
Roger Moore, culinary genius.

After portraying "007" in countless James Bond movies, Roger Moore sometimes seems to have become the character of his most famous role—his looks and charm, of course, help to confuse the issue. Now just over sixty, but still tall, trim, and tan, Roger seems glad his role as 007 is long behind him. He says he can play parts closer to his age and without all the jumping around required of the famous James Bond character. This man with a dry martini manner is the son of a London policeman. Moore lives in Los Angeles and near Gstaad, Switzerland, where he spends time away from the camera schussing downhill at dangerous speeds on his racing skis—when he's not in the kitchen.

Of his egg-making pursuits, Roger, with unflappable charisma and one raised eyebrow, said,

ABOVE: *Roger enjoys relaxing in the backyard of his Los Angeles home.*

"For this divine concoction you require . . . four eggs, a nice medium-sized ripe tomato, some spring onions, or, as they say in the colonies, scallions, about four ounces of strong cheddar cheese, salt and pepper, and a sauté pan.

"So, put the tomato under boiling water and remove the skin. Put it in the pan and turn on the heat. Add the chopped-up onion. Add this cooked mixture to the cheese that has been grated and liquefied in the other saucepan that I forgot to mention. Add seasoning to taste, then stir the eggs (having first removed them from their shells) into this mess of tomato, cheese, and onion. Cook slowly over a medium flame and serve on toast. If you do not like it, then I suggest you look in the Yellow Pages for a caterer," concluded Roger with an impish laugh.

ENGLISH EGGS

2 tablespoons (¼ stick) unsalted
   butter
1 medium tomato, peeled, seeded,
   and chopped
2 scallions, trimmed and thinly
   sliced
4 eggs
Salt and freshly ground pepper
¼ pound (about ¾ cup) freshly
   grated sharp cheddar cheese

In a small sauté pan, melt
1 tablespoon of the butter over
high heat. Add the tomatoes
and scallions and cook until the
scallions have softened, about

3 minutes. Transfer to a bowl.
Melt the remaining tablespoon
of butter in the pan.

Meanwhile, beat the eggs
until well blended in a small
mixing bowl. Add salt and
pepper to taste. Pour the eggs
into the sauté pan, reduce the
heat to moderate, and scramble
by folding gently—not stirring
—until the eggs have set, about
3 minutes. Gently fold in the
scallion-tomato mixture.
Transfer to a serving platter
and sprinkle with the cheddar.
Serve immediately.

SERVES 2.

ABOVE: *Roger's version of scrambled
eggs, with a variety of "goodies" all
mixed in, is a perfect recipe for a
relaxed weekend breakfast.*

Regis and Kathie Lee

♦ ♦ ♦ ♦ ♦ ♦ ♦ ♦ ♦ ♦

"MADONNA ASKED TO BE A GUEST ON THEIR SHOW. ARSENIO HALL SAYS, 'YOU AIN'T HIP UNLESS YOU WATCH THEM.' EIGHTEEN MILLION VIEWERS A WEEK JUST CAN'T LIVE WITHOUT THEM. IT MUST BE SOME KIND OF CHEMISTRY!"

Co-hosting America's fastest-growing national talk show is a full-time job for both Kathie Lee Gifford and Regis Philbin. When not attending White House dinners and charity galas, or taping their popular daytime show out of town, they go home to separate lives after their workday is done. He to Joy, his wife, and two teenage daughters; she to a toddler named Cody, and husband Frank Gifford; and both to a raft of friends and relatives.

Cooking and entertaining are high on the list of activities of these two celebrities. They've even compiled all the recipes they've cooked on camera for the past few years in a book—*Cooking with Regis and Kathie Lee*—which should hit the stores sometime in 1993.

Kathie Lee frequently thanks her mother, Joan Epstein, on the show for being her "food guru." "Everything I love to eat is what my mother made,

---

THE RECIPES

♦ ♦ ♦ ♦ ♦ ♦ ♦

KATHIE LEE'S TURKEY AND STUFFING
JOY'S PASTA À LA PASSION FOR REGIS

OPPOSITE: *Joy joins Kathie Lee and Regis in the kitchen on the set of* Live . . . , *at ABC-TV studios in New York.*

---

and that's the way I love to cook." According to Kathie Lee, many of the delightful and down-home recipes she's cooked before national TV audiences have been lifted right from her mother's recipe files. Included in this collection is her stick-to-the-ribs turkey stuffing that has become a holiday standard in the Gifford household.

Regis, on the other hand, has no recipes at all. He does, however, have Joy to provide him with a delectable repertoire of recipes. "Joy knows exactly what I like . . . at least, that's what she always tells me." One of his favorites is Joy's Pasta à la Passion for Regis. "It's really the only pasta recipe you need," Joy said. "It's one of those versatile dishes that can be dressed up for fancy dinners or made simply any day of the week. To taste it is to love it. Just ask Regis—or, better yet, try it yourself!"

KATHIE LEE'S TURKEY AND STUFFING

1 large turkey (about 20 pounds)
Salt and freshly ground pepper
½ pound (2 sticks) unsalted butter,
 melted
1 large onion, minced
8 celery stalks, minced
2 pounds ground pork sausage
4 cups croutons or stuffing crumbs
2 to 3 tablespoons chopped fresh
 sage

Preheat the oven to 325° F. Pat the turkey dry and place it, breast side up, in a large roasting pan. Season with salt and pepper to taste.

Pour half the butter into a large skillet. Set over moderately high heat. Add the onions and celery, and sauté until softened, about 5 minutes. Meanwhile, in a separate skillet brown the sausage over moderately high heat until no traces of pink remain, about 5 minutes. Drain off the fat and transfer the cooked sausage to a large mixing bowl. Add the onion and celery, the croutons or stuffing crumbs, and the sage. Season with salt and pepper to taste and mix well with your hands. Add small amounts of water to reach a moist but not wet consistency.

Loosely fill the cavity of the turkey with the stuffing. (Place any excess stuffing in a buttered casserole dish, add to the oven during the last hour of roasting, and serve on the side.) Roast the turkey about 20 minutes per pound, or until the skin is golden brown and the thickest part of the drumstick feels soft when pressed between the fingers; a meat thermometer inserted in the thickest part of the drumstick should register 180° F. Let the turkey rest for about 30 minutes before carving.

SERVES 15 TO 20.

◆ ◆ ◆ ◆ ◆ ◆ ◆

JOY'S PASTA À LA PASSION FOR REGIS

1 pound farfalle (bow-tie) pasta
2 tablespoons plus ¼ cup olive oil
2 garlic cloves, minced
2 boneless, skinless chicken breasts,
 about ½ pound each, julienned
2 cups broccoli flowerets
1 cup oil-packed sun-dried
 tomatoes, drained and sliced
2 tablespoons chopped fresh basil
Pinch red pepper flakes
¼ cup dry white wine
¾ cup chicken stock
Salt and freshly ground pepper
1 tablespoon unsalted butter
Freshly grated Parmesan cheese

Cook the pasta according to package directions. Drain well and place in a large mixing bowl. Pour 2 tablespoons of the olive oil over the pasta and stir to coat and separate. Set the pasta aside.

Pour the remaining olive oil into a large skillet or saucepan set over moderately high heat. Add the garlic and cook until slightly softened, about 1 minute. Add the chicken and cook thoroughly, about 5 minutes, turning occasionally. Remove the chicken to a plate, cover with foil to keep warm, and set aside. Reduce the heat to low and add the broccoli to the pan. Stir and toss until the broccoli is tender, about 10 minutes. Return the chicken to the pan and add the tomatoes, basil, red pepper flakes, wine, and chicken stock. Season to taste with salt and pepper. Add the butter, cover, and simmer over low heat for 5 minutes.

Add the chicken and broccoli mixture to the bowl of cooked pasta. Stir to blend and serve at once with lots of Parmesan cheese on the side.

SERVES 4.

OPPOSITE: *Kathie Lee's stuffing is so good, she frequently makes it to serve as a side dish.* ABOVE: *Colorful and delicious, Joy's Pasta à la Passion for Regis is a fresh interpretation of pasta primavera. One of Joy's best easy recipes, it is absolutely perfect party fare.*

Valentino

◆ ◆ ◆ ◆ ◆ ◆ ◆ ◆ ◆ ◆ ◆

"I AM A PERFECTIONIST. I DO NOT ACCEPT FAILURE—EVEN IN THE KITCHEN!"

With homes in Gstaad, London, Capri, New York, and, of course, with a palazzo in Rome, this master of the magnificent doesn't stop at the runway in his quest to design the best, the most beautiful, the freshest, and the most sublimely chic. When Valentino directs the creation of the cuisine in his homes, he insists on refined renditions of the Italian classics. In his private kitchens, chefs devise such slimming dishes as this risotto, and have created a variety of unique low-calorie but high-flavor tomato sauces for pasta, fish, and chicken.

In terms of essentials, Valentino's kitchen always has the best flour, pasta (preferably homemade, but De Cecco brand will also do), fresh fish (rarely chicken and never red meat), fresh parsley, tarragon, and basil (the most popular herb in the house), olive oil (from Valentino's partner Giancarlo Giammetti's villa in Cetona), onions (but for sauces only— Valentino doesn't like to "see" them, just taste them), and lots of fresh vegetables.

A designer of such extraordinary accomplishments in dressing the human form also knows exactly what he wants his table to look like for any occasion. Whether it's a buffet for twenty at Gstaad or a private dinner in his London town house, with his forty different sets of dishes and sixty different tablecloths in Switzerland alone, one can only imagine the level of creativity he puts to work to dress up the table at a Valentino soiree.

ABOVE: *The great designer, at home in Rome.*
OPPOSITE: *Risotto—especially Valentino's Risotto Verde, redolent of fresh herbs—is a delectable alternative to pasta.*

RISOTTO VERDE

4¼ cups chicken stock

½ cup fresh parsley leaves, loosely packed

1 cup fresh basil leaves, loosely packed

½ cup cooked spinach, excess moisture squeezed out

¼ cup fresh chives, finely chopped

2 tablespoons fresh tarragon, loosely packed

¼ cup fresh chervil, loosely packed

2 tablespoons unsalted butter

2 cups Arborio rice

½ cup heavy cream

½ cup freshly grated Parmesan cheese

Salt and freshly ground pepper

In the bowl of a food processor, combine 1 cup of the chicken stock with the parsley, basil, spinach, chives, tarragon, and chervil. Use several short pulses to blend well. Set aside.

In a medium saucepan over high heat, bring the remaining 3¼ cups of the stock to a boil.

Meanwhile, melt the butter in a large saucepan set over moderate heat. Add the rice and stir until warmed through, about 1 minute, then increase heat slightly to moderately high. Add the boiling stock in ½-cup increments, stirring constantly, until the rice has absorbed all the liquid (add the next ½ cup of boiling stock only when all the previous liquid has been absorbed). The rice should have cooked approximately 18 minutes when all the liquid has been added and absorbed.

Pulse the herbed chicken stock once again to blend, then add to the rice in ½-cup increments and cook until the liquid is absorbed. Stir in the cream, then remove from the heat. Stir in the cheese and season to taste with salt and pepper. Serve immediately.

SERVES 4 to 6.

Hollywood Stars Dine Out

◆ ◆ ◆ ◆ ◆ ◆ ◆ ◆ ◆

"GUESS WHO'S COMING TO DINNER?"

The dining room of this landmark on Sunset Boulevard in Beverly Hills is one of Los Angeles's best restaurants. Here, dinner should be ordered with a display of loyalty for your favorite film actor. Their favorite recipes are on the menu, and if proximity to your favorite star will make the meal taste better, then the table located just beneath the photograph of Liz or Frank or Liza or Sophia can be requested. If you're really lucky, one of those stars—Charlton Heston, for example—might even show up in person! It happens all the time in this culinary haven when Hollywood gets hungry.

Round about seven in the morning in the Polo Lounge, any day of the week, film producers start arriving for breakfast. In the evening the room is transformed into a dazzling cocktail lounge filled with Hollywood well-knowns as well as a fair share of Hollywood hopefuls. One-third of all the movies made in the past fifty years were negotiated over breakfast in the green velvet booths of the Polo Lounge, and Jackie Collins claims to use it as a place to gather gossip for her Hollywood-tell-all novels.

Another star-studded stop at the Beverly Hills Hotel is the Cabana Club and Pool, where umbrella-covered tables provide shade for the lunch crowd nibbling on salads while beautiful bodies splash in the crystal-clear water of the Olympic-sized pool.

The Beverly Hills Hotel and Bungalows have been providing accommodations to the rich and famous for over seventy years. So make your reservations early for dinner at eight in the dining room, because supper with a roomful of Academy Award winners is part of the experience of visiting the famed Pink Palace.

THE RECIPES

◆ ◆ ◆ ◆ ◆ ◆ ◆

LIZA'S SALADE DE PROVENCE

SALAD DIONNE

ELIZABETH TAYLOR'S CHILI

GREGORY PECK'S SPAGHETTINI WITH SEAFOOD

JIMMY STEWART'S SAND DABS

JOHNNY CARSON'S WHITEFISH

SOPHIA LOREN'S VITELLO TONNATO

STRAWBERRIES HESTON

OPPOSITE: *Over the years, the Beverly Hills Hotel and Bungalows have been a home away from home for the likes of Prince Rainier and Grace Kelly, Lauren Bacall and Humphrey Bogart, Marilyn Monroe, Dominick Dunne, and countless other Hollywood legends.*

LIZA'S SALADE DE PROVENCE

*4 to 5 ears of yellow corn, or
   2 cups frozen corn
1 medium pink grapefruit
1 cup hearts of palm (canned or
   frozen)
½ pound fresh mushrooms
1 teaspoon Dijon mustard
½ teaspoon salt
¼ teaspoon freshly ground pepper
2 tablespoons red wine vinegar
⅓ cup safflower oil*

Remove enough kernels from the cobs to measure 2 cups. In a small saucepan, combine the corn with a tablespoon of water. (If using frozen corn, thaw to room temperature.) Over moderate heat, cook until the corn is tender, about 2 minutes. Drain and set aside.

Peel and remove the white pith from the grapefruit. Separate the sections, cut each section in half, and pat dry with paper towels.

Cut the hearts of palm into thin slices. Wipe the mushrooms clean. Trim the ends and slice very thinly.

◆ ◆ ◆ ◆ ◆ ◆ ◆

LEFT, TOP: *Chef Michel Saragueta seeks the approval of Liza Minnelli, who frequently stays at the hotel.* BELOW: *Classic California palms surround the Beverly Hills Hotel.* OPPOSITE: *Portraits of Elizabeth Taylor,* TOP, *and Jimmy Stewart, Elizabeth Taylor, and Johnny Carson,* CENTER, *adorn the walls of the dining room.* OPPOSITE, BOTTOM: *Dionne Warwick and Chef Michel Saragueta.*

In a large salad bowl, combine the mustard, salt, pepper, and vinegar, stirring until everything has dissolved. Slowly pour in the oil, whisking constantly until smooth. Attractively arrange the grapefruit and vegetables in the bowl. Bring to the table and toss just before serving.

SERVES 2 to 4.

◆ ◆ ◆ ◆ ◆ ◆ ◆

SALAD DIONNE

*1 pound ziti
1 pound broccoli
1 teaspoon Dijon mustard
½ teaspoon salt
¼ teaspoon freshly ground pepper
2 tablespoons red wine vinegar
⅓ cup olive oil
¼ cup freshly grated Parmesan
   cheese
2 to 3 medium tomatoes*

In a large pot of salted, boiling water, cook the pasta according to package directions. Drain and rinse under cold water. Drain again and set aside.

Bring a large pot of salted water to a boil. Separate the broccoli into small flowerets, discarding the stems. Add the broccoli to the pot, bring back to a boil, and cook rapidly until soft, 2 to 3 minutes. Drain and refresh under cold running water. Drain again and spread out on paper towels to dry.

In a large bowl, stir the mustard, salt, pepper, and vinegar until everything has dissolved. Slowly add the olive oil, whisking until smooth. Add the pasta, broccoli, and cheese, but do not toss. Cover and refrigerate.

Just before serving, gently toss until the pasta, broccoli, and cheese are coated with the sauce. Core the tomatoes, cut into wedges, and use to garnish the salad.

SERVES 4 to 6.

◆ ◆ ◆ ◆ ◆ ◆ ◆

ELIZABETH TAYLOR'S CHILI

1 pound blade or chuck roast
2 or 3 tablespoons olive oil
1 small onion, chopped
½ pound ground sirloin
½ pound ground pork
3 to 4 medium tomatoes
1 to 2 tablespoons chili powder
1 cup red wine
3 cups cooked kidney beans
½ pound Cheddar cheese, grated
Salt and freshly ground pepper
Pinch cayenne pepper

Preheat the oven to 425° F.

Place the blade or chuck roast in a small roasting pan and roast until well done, 30 to 40 minutes. Remove from the oven and let cool. Cut the meat into chunks.

In a large saucepan or stock-

pot, heat the olive oil over moderately high heat. Add the onions and cook until soft, about 5 minutes, then add the ground sirloin and the ground pork. Sauté until all traces of pink have disappeared, about 5 minutes. Add the beef chunks and heat through.

Peel, seed, and chop the tomatoes. Add to the pot, along with the chili powder and the wine. Bring to a boil over moderately high heat, then reduce the heat to moderate and simmer until the flavors are blended, about 15 minutes. Stir in the beans, cheese, salt, black pepper, and cayenne pepper. Reduce the heat to low and simmer, covered, until the chili is thick and rich, at least 2 hours. Stir frequently to prevent scorching. Taste and adjust the seasoning as needed. Serve hot.

SERVES 6 to 8.

GREGORY PECK'S SPAGHETTINI WITH SEAFOOD

2 tablespoons olive oil
2 tablespoons (¼ stick) unsalted
   butter
2 garlic cloves, minced
4 shallots, minced
6 large tomatoes, peeled and
   coarsely chopped
¼ cup dry white wine
1 teaspoon green peppercorns
Salt and freshly ground black
   pepper
1 pound medium shrimp, peeled
   and deveined
1 pound sea scallops, cut into
   equal-sized pieces
1 tablespoon heavy cream
1 tablespoon capers
1 pound spaghettini

In a large sauté pan or skillet, melt the olive oil and butter over moderately high heat. Add the garlic and shallots and cook until softened but not burned, about 3 minutes, stirring frequently. Add the tomatoes, wine, peppercorns, salt, and ground pepper. Over moderate heat, cook, uncovered, until the sauce has thickened, about 20 minutes. Add the shrimp and scallops. Reduce the heat to moderately low and simmer until the seafood is opaque and firm, about 15 minutes. Stir in the cream, add the capers, and increase the heat to high. Bring to a boil, then remove from the heat and keep warm.

Meanwhile, in a large pot of boiling, salted water, cook the spaghettini according to package directions. Drain and turn out into a serving bowl. Add the sauce, toss gently, and serve at once.

SERVES 4.

♦ ♦ ♦ ♦ ♦ ♦

LEFT: *Gregory Peck's portrait hangs above his table.* OPPOSITE: *Gregory Peck's wonderful recipe for Spaghettini with Seafood is a popular item on the menu.*

JIMMY STEWART'S SAND DABS

2 tablespoons (¼ stick) unsalted
   butter
1 tablespoon olive oil
4 8-ounce sand dab fillets
Salt and freshly ground pepper
Hot Garlic Herb Butter

In a sauté pan large enough to
hold the fish in one flat layer,
melt the butter and the oil over
moderately high heat. When
bubbles have subsided, add the
fillets. Season with salt and
pepper to taste. Cook until
browned and firm to the touch,
2 to 3 minutes per side. Remove to a serving platter and
dot with Hot Garlic Herb Butter to taste (recipe follows).

SERVES 4.

HOT GARLIC HERB BUTTER

4 tablespoons (½ stick) unsalted
   butter
2 small garlic cloves, minced
1 tablespoon chopped fresh parsley
1 teaspoon fresh thyme leaves
   (½ teaspoon dried)
¼ cup shredded fresh basil, loosely
   packed
1 teaspoon grated lemon zest
¼ teaspoon red pepper flakes
Salt and freshly ground pepper

In the bowl of a food processor, combine the butter, garlic,
parsley, thyme, basil, lemon
zest, and pepper flakes. Blend
in several short, quick pulses
until the mixture is smooth.
Taste for seasoning, adding salt
and pepper as desired.

MAKES ABOUT ½ CUP.

♦ ♦ ♦ ♦ ♦ ♦ ♦

JOHNNY CARSON'S WHITEFISH

1 medium zucchini, cut into
   ½-inch cubes
1 carrot, cut into ½-inch dice
¼ pound green beans, trimmed and
   cut into 1-inch pieces
4 8-ounce whitefish fillets
¼ teaspoon salt
⅛ teaspoon freshly ground pepper
¼ to ½ teaspoon filé powder
Pinch cayenne pepper
1 pound dried angel hair pasta
1 ripe tomato, peeled, seeded, and
   diced
2 tablespoons extra-virgin olive oil
½ cup shredded fresh basil, loosely
   packed

In a large pot of boiling, salted
water, cook the zucchini until
tender, about 1 minute. Remove with a slotted spoon and
set aside. Add the carrots and
cook in the still-boiling water
until tender, 2 to 3 minutes.
Remove with a slotted spoon

and set aside. Finally, add the
green beans and cook until
tender, 2 to 3 minutes. Remove
as above. Keep the water at a
full boil until ready to cook the
pasta.

Preheat the broiler and broiling pan. Season the fish with
salt, black pepper, filé powder,
and cayenne pepper to taste.
Broil 4 to 5 inches away from
the source of heat until the fish
is lightly browned, firm to the
touch, and opaque, 7 to 10
minutes. Transfer to a platter,
remove the skin, and keep
warm.

Add the pasta to the pot of
boiling water and cook until al
dente, according to the package
instructions. Drain well. Return the drained pasta to the
pot, set over moderately high
heat. Add the cooked vegetables, chopped tomato, olive oil,
and the basil, then toss until
blended and heated through.
Transfer to a large serving platter. Gently place the fish on
top. Serve at once.

SERVES 4.

♦ ♦ ♦ ♦ ♦ ♦ ♦

OPPOSITE, CLOCKWISE FROM TOP
LEFT: *Charlton Heston's recipe for
Strawberries Heston; Liza Minnelli's
Salade de Provence; Johnny Carson's
Whitefish; and Sophia Loren's
Vitello Tonnato.*

SOPHIA LOREN'S VITELLO TONNATO

2-pound bottom round of veal
1½ to 2 cups dry white wine
1 large onion, coarsely chopped
1 medium carrot, coarsely chopped
2 garlic cloves, crushed
½ teaspoon salt
¼ teaspoon freshly ground pepper
½ cup canned tuna, packed in oil
3 to 4 anchovy fillets, rinsed,
  patted dry, and mashed
2 hard-cooked egg yolks
Juice of 1 lemon
2 tablespoons olive oil
1 tablespoon red wine vinegar
Pinch sugar
Capers (optional)

Place the veal in a small, deep, nonreactive bowl. Pour in enough wine to barely cover. Refrigerate overnight, covered tightly with plastic wrap.

In a large saucepan or stockpot, combine the veal with the wine marinade, onion, carrot, garlic, salt, and pepper. Bring to a boil over moderately high heat. Reduce the heat to moderately low and simmer, partially covered, until the veal is tender, about 1 hour. Remove the pot from the heat but leave the veal in the liquid to cool. Remove the veal to a cutting board, cover loosely with foil, and set aside.

Strain the cooking liquid through a sieve into a small bowl (you should have about 1

ABOVE: *When she is in the dining room, Sophia Loren often orders Vitello Tonnato. Her portrait graces the wall above her private table.*
RIGHT: *The famous pool, where having yourself paged is an effective way of getting attention—especially since some of Hollywood's biggest agents and producers might also be taking in the sun.*

cup). Discard the vegetables. Add the tuna, anchovies, egg yolks, lemon juice, olive oil, vinegar, and sugar to the sieve, and force this mixture through with the back of a large spoon. Mix the resulting sauce until it is well blended and smooth.

Cut the veal into thin slices. Arrange, overlapping, on a large serving platter. Spread the sauce over the veal. Garnish with capers, if desired.

SERVES 4 to 6.

◆ ◆ ◆ ◆ ◆ ◆ ◆

STRAWBERRIES HESTON

1 cup plain yogurt
2 tablespoons honey
⅛ teaspoon freshly grated nutmeg
Pinch cinnamon
1 pint fresh strawberries
Fresh mint sprigs (optional)

In a small bowl, whisk together the yogurt, honey, nutmeg, and cinnamon. Cover and refrigerate for 1 to 2 hours.

Hull the strawberries and rinse under cold water. Drain in a colander, then pat dry with paper towels. Divide between 2 serving bowls.

When ready to serve, pour the yogurt sauce over the berries. Garnish with sprigs of fresh mint, if desired.

SERVES 2.

ABOVE: *Chef to the stars Michel Saragueta was chef to New York society when he headed up the restaurant "21" before taking over the Beverly Hills Hotel's Dining Room.*

Acknowledgments

◆ ◆ ◆ ◆ ◆ ◆ ◆ ◆ ◆ ◆

While we were crossing continents and oceans researching this book, air travel was made possible thanks to our dear friends at **American Airlines** A▾A *Something special in the air.*

Many hotels graciously opened their doors to us as well. A special thanks to the following for taking such good care of us; we'll always remember you as a home away from home: The Draycott Residential Club, London, England; The Royal Monceau, Paris, France; Hôtel de Paris, Monte Carlo, Monaco; The Hotel Bel-Air, Los Angeles, California; The Beverly Hills Hotel, Beverly Hills, California; The Mansion on Turtle Creek, Dallas, Texas; Hotel Bel-Air Cap-Ferrat, Côte d'Azure, France; Hotel Hassler, Rome, Italy; Relais & Chateaux, Worldwide; Peabody Hotel, Orlando, Florida; Windsor Court Hotel, New Orleans, Louisiana; Chateau Marmont, Hollywood, California; and Checkers Hotel Kimpinski, Los Angeles, California.

To look at the jacket of this book, one would never guess it took almost a dozen people to assemble the beautiful array of food and tableware. Early one morning, we gathered at Renny Reynolds's townhouse and flower shop in Manhattan, bearing trays and containers of sumptuous food or laden with big boxes of dishes, silver, crystal, and linens. While the florists created arrangements from flowers they had just picked at the market, a table stylist set the most elegant yet welcoming table, and amid all the commotion, the photographer set up his lighting—all before the sun came up.

A special thanks to everyone involved in the creation of the magnificent jacket photograph:

Renny Reynolds of Design for Entertaining—Thank you for providing the location and gorgeous floral arrangements.

Mood Food Caterer of New York City—Thank you so very, very much for the food, the people who stayed up late the night before preparing the ingredients, and the talented catering chefs and helpers who began their work at 4:00 the day of the shoot.

Greg Lanza, party designer at Design for Entertaining—Thank you for coordinating the location and flowers. Your special talent for picking the perfect flower arrangement is most appreciated.

Jane French—Our special thanks for making the items on the table and through the room available to us, and for helping to set up the tables.

Thanks to the following companies: Puiforcat, for supplying the silver, flatware, and porcelain; Lalique, for the crystal; and Porthault, for the table linens.

Anita Bourne-Gottehrer, stylist/coordinator—Thanks for adding so much care and perfect taste in selecting, gathering, coordinating, and setting up the items seen on the table and throughout the room on the jacket.

Bruce Sobol, Caviarteria—A warm-hearted thanks for making our "caviar dreams" a reality by providing some of your finest for the photo shoot.

We would like to extend a very special thanks to all the companies who were involved in the creation of this book:

Van Rex Gourmet Foods, Inc., Culver City, California

Classic Party Rentals, Culver City, California

OHM Designs, Leo Montegut, designer/owner, New Orleans, Louisiana

Duggal Color Projects—New York, New York

Very special thanks to everyone at Duggal Color Lab, where we had our film developed and prints and duplicate slides made. The service was super-speedy and always superior in every way. Thanks especially to Robin George in the Corporate Department who watched over our account from day one, making sure we didn't lose one precious slide or photograph, and always coming through for us.

THE PEOPLE WHO HELPED US ALONG THE WAY

During the year it took to gather and coordinate the material, write, edit, design, and produce this book, many devoted people were involved, some on an almost day-to-day basis, others when the need arose. These people are precious to the book, and to Robin Leach and Diane Rozas, in a variety of ways and for a variety of different reasons. Without their efforts, there simply would not have been a book.

Charles Pierce—Thank you for doing such an outstanding job writing, re-creating, and testing all the recipes in this book.

Elaine Griffin—Thanks for coordinating dates, times, tickets, people, appointments, and much, much more.

The Staff at "Lifestyles of the Rich and Famous"—Thanks for all your support and help.

Anita Bourne-Gottehrer—Thanks for cooking, styling, and coordinating uncountable details throughout the process of this book's creation.

Michael Garth and Manhattan Transfer Travel Agency—Thanks so very much for hunting down travel bargains in your computer, and for your ever-cheery point of view.

Martha Crow—Thank you for staying late at your word processor for so many nights to complete the typing of the manuscript.

Vicky King, Bel-Air Hotel Company, Vicky King Public Relations

Linda Zimmerman, stylist

Meg McCombs, stylist

Margaret Ferrazzi, stylist

Nadia LaCoste, director of public relations, Société de Bain de Mer, Monaco

Mr. Della Antonio, general manager, Hôtel de Paris, Monaco

Sheila O'Brien and Tanya Beaver, Beverly Hills Hotel

Craig Claiborne, whose carrot soup recipe influenced Katie Couric's;

George Greiff—For your Roasted Red Pepper Soup recipe

Susan Gregory, Manager, Draycott Residential Hotel, London

Gearoid Cronin, Blakes Hotel, London

Roberto Wirth, Hotel Hassler, Rome

Peter Wirth, Waldorf Towers, New York City

Michael French, general manager, Peabody Hotel, Orlando

Renee Copeland, Tova 9

Simone Rothle-Enelow, Windsor Court Hotel, New Orleans

Yanou Collart, public relations, Paris

Daniel Boulud, executive chef, Le Cirque, New York City

Kerry Simon, executive chef, Edwardian Room, Plaza Hotel, New York City

The work of so many fine and talented photographers can be seen within this book. Working with them on the shoots was a lesson in technique and artistry. Their imaginations are endless, and that is proven over and over again by the beautiful photographs that appear in these pages.

In most cases, individual photographers hold the copyrights; photographers are listed alphabetically.

Allen Berliner—114 (bottom), 121 (top);

Charles Bush—188;

J. P. Calvet—244, 245;

Amy Cantrell—117;

Lans Christensen—226–33;

Philippe Costes—5, 68–75, 124–31, 158 (right);

Geoffrey Croft/Outline—73;

Maureen Donaldson—vii, 8 (right), 9, 10, 114–15 (across top), 118 (top), 180–89, 196–201, 242, 243;

John Dugdale—11, 248, 249;

Mark Ferri—132, 136;

Carol Ford—vi, 56–67, 100, 102–9, 166–73, 236, 237;

Peter Freed—vi, vii, 10 (top left), 12, 48–55, 158 (left), 214–19;

Charlie Freeman—40–47;

Steve Friedman—252;

Michael Geiger—135, 137;

Jackson Goff—204–7;

Phil Haggerty—162–65;

Paul Harris—114 (center);

Gregory Heisler—246;

Michael Jacobs—112 (bottom left and top right);

Armen Kachaturian—150–55;

Jeff Katz—202;

Claudia Kunin—vii, 8 (bottom left), 26–31, 84–91, 123, 190–95, 234, 239, 241, 247, 251, 254, 255, 257–67;

Lazaroff Personal Archives—115 (center and bottom), 116, 119 (top), 120 (bottom), 121 (bottom), 123 (bottom);

Marcel Loli—2 (right), 3 (left), 14, 16–23;

Dominick Marsden—ii, 3 (right), 10 (right), 92–99;

Michael Montfort—113 (bottom left), 119 (center);

Daniel Ray—208–13;

Stanley Rumbaugh—220–25;

Eddie Sanderson—238;

Roman Salicki—250;

Mark Sennet/*People*—113, 240;

Jerry Simpson—82;

Ann Summa—2, 6, 138–49;

Tony Thorinbert—256;

Eugenie Uhl—76–81, 83;

Pierre-Giles Vidoli—113 (bottom right), 121 (center);

Visages—24;

Kevin Winter—112 (top left);

Penny Wolin/Lazaroff—118 (center and bottom), 119 (bottom), 120 (top), 122;

Elizabeth Zeschin—4 (top right), 32–39, 134, 174–79.

Index